Collins

REIMAGINE
KEY STAGE 3 ENGLISH

Knowledge-rich projects to
build skills for GCSE (9–1)

Series editor: **Jo Heathcote**

Authors: **Caroline Davis**, **Jo Heathcote**,
Emma Slater and **Nicola Williams**

Published by Collins
An imprint of HarperCollins*Publishers*
The News Building
1 London Bridge Street
London SE1 9GF

HarperCollins*Publishers*
1st Floor, Watermarque Building,
Ringsend Road
Dublin 4,
Ireland

Browse the complete Collins catalogue at
www.collinseducation.com

© HarperCollins*Publishers* Limited 2020

10 9 8 7 6 5 4 3 2

ISBN 978-0-00-840050-7

British Library Cataloguing-in-Publication Data
A catalogue record for this publication is available from the British Library.

Series editor: Jo Heathcote
Authors: Caroline Davis, Jo Heathcote, Emma Slater and Nicola Williams
Publisher: Katie Sergeant
Product manager: Catherine Martin
Development editor: Caroline Low
Copyeditor: Caroline Low
Proofreader: Sonya Newland
Cover designer: Amparo Barrera, Kneath Associates
Internal designer and typesetter: Hugh Hillyard-Parker
Production controller: Katharine Willard
Printed and bound in Great Britain by Ashford Colour Press Ltd.

Contents

Introduction

Welcome to the Reimagine Key Stage 3 English Teacher Resource. We hope it will support and enrich your Key Stage 3 curriculum and help to ensure meaningful progression for students into Key Stage 4.

Jo Heathcote, *Series Editor*

The vision for these projects came following my return to Key Stage 3 teaching after being involved in the development of the new GCSE English Language specifications at Key Stage 4 for a leading awarding body, and several years teaching Key Stage 4 and Key Stage 5 in a large sixth-form college.

Within my own classroom, I sought to find ways to embed all the required skills from the more challenging work at Key Stage 4, without slipping into teaching GCSE from Year 7. In short, I began to reimagine Key Stage 3.

Within the nine *Reimagine* projects, you will find extracts from 19th-century fiction, classic poetry, and non-fiction from the 19th century and the present day. These mirror the kinds of texts students will meet at Key Stage 4. The extracts step up in word count and complexity across the three years of Key Stage 3 to gradually build reading stamina.

The text-based work also steps up in terms of skills to introduce and embed clear methods for comprehension work (AO1 at GCSE) and clear approaches for analysing language and structure (AO2 at GCSE). Subject terminology is introduced and reinforced, in context, throughout.

As well as being skills-rich, the projects are also knowledge-rich. The lessons encourage students to think critically and make meaningful links between texts, and to compare present-day experiences to those in the past, via thoughtful questioning and opportunities for exploration. In this way, students are learning to see contexts more subtly than simply as bolt-on historical fact.

Lessons are organised into six-week projects around a theme (for example, child labour or how we treat others) chosen to illuminate different contexts for GCSE. The projects follow a clear structure with a suggested two weeks' work on fiction and poetry complemented by a week of creative writing, then two weeks exploring non-fiction texts complemented by a week of discursive writing. Each suggested 'week' consists of two lessons comprising extracts, PowerPoints, worksheets and detailed lesson plans with suggested answers to tasks.

- Projects 7.1, 8.1 and 9.1 are all about 'Introducing…' skills in a supportive way.
- Projects 7.2, 8.2 and 9.2 have a focus on 'Developing…' learning with activities to thoroughly embed these skills.
- Projects 7.3, 8.3 and 9.3 are labelled 'Securing' and offer extra variety and practice of the skills, with a clear stepping stone in the final project, 9.3, to GCSE skills such as synthesis and comparison.

These projects can be used very flexibly across Key Stage 3. For example, you could:

- use each project to embed key skills at the start of each term, in sequence, before moving on to the study of a class reader or play on similar themes
- use each project *alongside* a class reader or play each term to complement its themes and ideas
- use the different projects with different sets or classes to teach the core skills in a differentiated way (e.g. Projects 7.1, 8.1 and 9.1 for those in need of more support; Projects 7.2, 8.2 and 9.2 for those on a pathway to GCSE Grades 5 to 7; Projects 7.3, 8.3 and 9.3 for those looking to extend their skills)
- use the projects as self-contained, meaningful units of work where you have split teaching across a class
- use the projects as a way of providing meaningful cover where a non-specialist may be teaching a group over a number of weeks.

Finally, I hope that these projects create some fun and memorable lessons for students, enabling them to grow in confidence and skill, and to feel empowered both as reader and writers.

Year 7, Project 1: The Natural World

- Builds contextual understanding for the following GCSE set texts: Romantic poetry

Week	Skill focus	Text	Learning objectives
1	Introducing older texts	*The Wizard of Oz* (1900) by L. Frank Baum	• To understand some of the key ideas in an extract from *The Wizard of Oz* • To begin to present ideas and support them with reference to the text • To explore some of the key ideas in an extract from *The Wizard of Oz* • To learn to present and support those ideas clearly using textual references
2	Introducing 19th-century poetry	'I wander'd lonely as a cloud' (1804) by William Wordsworth	• To develop confidence in exploring 19th-century poetry • To explore imagery, structure and mood in 'I wander'd lonely as a cloud' by William Wordsworth
3	Introducing creative writing: Creating your own landscape		• To plan a descriptive piece with a focus on setting and character • To plan and write the opening of a narrative • To hook your reader into your setting and character through carefully selected language
4	Introducing 19th-century non-fiction	'Making a Fossil Hunter', *All the Year Round* (1865) by Anon	• To read and understand key information in a 19th-century non-fiction extract • To begin to understand how the writer may present their views
5	Introducing connected modern non-fiction: Exploring connections and themes	'Sir David Attenborough and a macabre murder mystery in Lyme Regis' by Sarah Marshall, *The Telegraph*, 7 January 2018	• To use the theme of the environment to understand a modern text • To begin to explore how language is used to present thoughts or feelings • To explore how the writer shows feelings about nature • To introduce the IEC method (identify, exemplify, comment)
6	Introducing discursive writing: Planning a formal letter		• To introduce the elements of discursive writing • To use some of these elements in a speech • To plan a persuasive letter • To consider the elements of discursive writing and introduce the concept of formality and informality

Year 7, Project 2: Child Labour

- Builds contextual understanding for the following GCSE set texts: *A Christmas Carol*, *Great Expectations*, Romantic poetry

Week	Skill focus	Text	Learning objectives
1	Developing comprehension skills with the 19th-century novel	*The Water Babies* (1863) by Charles Kingsley	• To understand some of the key ideas in an extract from *The Water Babies* • To present and support those ideas clearly • To draw inferences from some of the key ideas in an extract from *The Water Babies* • To present those inferences clearly
2	Developing readings of 18th-century poetry	'The Chimney Sweeper', from *Songs of Innocence* (1789) by William Blake	• To understand the key ideas in a poem through exploring structure • To understand the key ideas in a poem through exploring imagery • To develop skills of making inferences and supporting ideas • To show developing understanding of key ideas and the writer's intention
3	Developing creative writing: Planning creative writing from a picture		• To gather ideas from a picture • To understand how to present the thoughts and feelings of a character • To plan a piece of creative writing • To write from a character's perspective or point of view
4	Developing ideas from 19th-century non-fiction	'Transcript of the Examination of Thomas Priestley' (1806)	• To understand the ideas in an extract of 19th-century non-fiction • To present and support those ideas clearly • To begin to comment on the experiences of others in the past
5	Developing connections with modern non-fiction	'Child labour "rampant" in Bangladesh factories' by Michael Safi, *The Guardian*, 7 December 2016	• To understand and make connections between child labour in the 19th century and today • To use developing comprehension skills to understand key ideas in a broadsheet article • To understand key aspects of language in a news article • To think about the effects of language in a non-fiction text
6	Developing persuasive writing skills: Planning a short speech		• To understand more key techniques for persuasion • To plan for an effective speech presenting a point of view • To write and present an effective speech presenting a point of view

Year 7, Project 3: Journeys and Explorations

- Builds contextual understanding for the following GCSE texts: *The Sign of Four, Jane Eyre*

Week	Skill focus	Text	Learning objectives
1	Securing supported comprehension of the 19th-century novel	*Around the World in 80 Days* (1872) by Jules Verne	• To be able to retrieve basic ideas/information from a prose text and make statements • To be able to support statements with embedded quotations • To make secure inferences from reading • To use the SQI method (statement + quotation + inference) confidently
2	Securing the understanding of key ideas in 19th-century poetry	'From a Railway Carriage' (1885) by R. L. Stevenson	• To explore how the poet uses key images to present ideas • To explore the use of comparative techniques to create imagery and their effect • To explore how writers use structure to present key ideas • To present analytical points using the IEC method
3	Securing creative writing: Writing a narrative with descriptive features		• To explore narrative voice and descriptive features • To plan and write a three-paragraph narrative using similes, adjectives and a distinctive narrative voice
4	Securing the exploration of ideas in 19th-century non-fiction	*Travels in West Africa* (1897) by Mary Kingsley	• To use inference to interpret 19th-century non-fiction • To show secure understanding of the SQI method • To be able to make secure inferences from reading about a writer's thoughts and feelings • To understand and empathise with different viewpoints through role play • To present those viewpoints using a persona
5	Securing connections with modern non-fiction	*Mud, Sweat and Tears* (2011) by Bear Grylls	• To begin to present key ideas with quotations and to see connections between texts from the 19th and 21st centuries • To be able to identify some of the key techniques used to convey these ideas • To make connections between writers' thoughts, feelings and experiences • To present those connections with secure comprehension skills
6	Securing discursive writing: Writing a travel article		• To understand the main features of travel writing • To plan and write a travel article for an audience of peers

Year 8, Project 1: Beyond our World

- Builds contextual understanding for the following GCSE texts: *The War of the Worlds*

Week	Skill focus	Text	Learning objectives
1	Introducing more skills with 19th-century fiction: Reading between the lines	*The Time Machine* (1895) by H.G. Wells	• To understand some of the key ideas in a 19th-century fiction text • To start to read between the lines of a 19th-century fiction text • To be able to explain your thoughts by referencing the text
2	Introducing more skills with 19th-century poetry: Language features	'The Starlight Night' (1877) by Gerard Manley Hopkins	• To explore imagery in poetry, prose and paintings • To introduce language features • To begin to explore the effect of language features
3	Introducing more skills with creative writing: Planning a narrative		• To introduce a narrative structure • To explore narrative structure using a well-known text • To plan your own narrative
4	Introducing more skills with understanding older non-fiction: Considering point of view	'How will the world end?' by Herbert C. Fyfe, *Pearson's Magazine*, 1900	• Reading and comprehending older non-fiction • To consider point of view in a older non-fiction text
5	Introducing more skills with linked modern non-fiction: Considering point of view	Tim Peake interview: 'I orbited the earth 2,720 times' by Joanne O'Connor, *The Guardian*, 25 November 2017	• To explore tone and point of view in an interview • To explore and compare point of view in different texts
6	Introducing more skills with discursive writing: Presenting a point of view		• To plan a piece of writing including a balanced point of view • To draft and review ideas ahead of writing

Year 8, Project 2: How We Treat Others

- Builds contextual understanding for the following GCSE texts: *A Christmas Carol*, *Great Expectations*, *Jane Eyre*, *Frankenstein*, *Silas Marner*, Romantic poetry

Week	Skill focus	Text	Learning objectives
1	Developing inferential reading with the 19th-century novel	*Jane Eyre* (1847) by Charlotte Brontë	• To develop skills of inference with a 19th-century novel • To build an interpretation of characters and their actions
2	Developing an understanding of an 18th-century poem: Exemplifying features	'A Poison Tree', from *Songs of Experience* (1794) by William Blake	• To develop an understanding of the structure and sequence of a poem • To develop an understanding of how a writer's choices create meaning • To develop an understanding of the ideas in a poem • To develop an understanding of the writer's intention
3	Developing more skills with creative writing: Imagining the 'red-room'	*Jane Eyre* (1847) by Charlotte Brontë	• To develop skills in creative writing by considering atmosphere, imagery, thoughts and feelings • To plan and write an effective first-person narrative
4	Developing understanding of 19th-century non-fiction: How points of view are presented	*The Bitter Cry of Outcast London* (1883) by Andrew Mearns and William C. Preston	• To select, retrieve and make inferences from a 19th-century non-fiction text • To write more developed comprehension answers about 19th-century non-fiction • To develop empathy and understanding of the issues in a 19th-century non-fiction text
5	Developing skills with connected modern non-fiction: Exploring how points of view are presented	'I've spent time in Britain's food banks – the destitution these people are facing is appalling' by Professor Green, *The Independent*, 9 November 2019	• To understand the key ideas in an issue-based article • To make inferences as to the writer's viewpoint • To develop an understanding of persuasive language techniques • To consider the effects of persuasive techniques
6	Developing more skills with discursive writing: Developing a debate speech		• To reflect and use the issues raised through the project to complete the writing of a speech • To show competent use of the persuasive techniques studied in your own writing

Year 8, Project 3: Growing Up

* Builds contextual understanding for the following GCSE set texts: *Great Expectations*, *A Christmas Carol*, *Jane Eyre*, *Frankenstein*, Romantic poetry

Week	Skill focus	Text	Learning objectives
1	Securing skills with the 19th-century novel: The SQI method	*What Katy Did* (1872) by Susan Coolidge	• To secure comprehension of a 19th-century fiction text • To use inference and deduction to explore character and meanings • To consider how language choices add to characterisation and meaning
2	Securing understanding of 19th-century poetry	'I Remember I Remember' (1827) by Thomas Hood	• To understand more language features • To explore how a poet uses language features to express a speaker's feelings • To understand more structural features • To secure use of the IEC method when exploring how a poet uses structure to enhance meaning
3	Securing creative writing: Presenting memories in real and fictional autobiographical writing		• To recognise features of first-person and autobiographical writing • To use those features in my own writing to engage my reader
4	Securing skills with understanding of 19th-century non-fiction: Comprehension task	'A Fearful State of Things in South Lambeth: Roughs Rule the Roost', *Illustrated Police News*, 30 July 1898	• To explore and discuss ideas about anti-social behaviour in the 19th century • To secure comprehension of a 19th-century non-fiction text • To understand how a writer can use language techniques to sensationalise their writing and express a viewpoint
5	Securing skills with connected modern non-fiction: Reporting on writer's point of view	'You did not act in time': a speech to the Houses of Parliament by Greta Thunberg, 23 April 2019	• To understand the writer's key ideas • To explore and comment on the writer's point of view • To understand how point of view is presented • To comment on the techniques of a persuasive speech
6	Securing discursive writing: Writing to argue both sides of a topic		• To write an op-ed for a magazine, arguing both sides of a topic • To include connectives and an informed opinion

Year 9, Project 1: The Unexplained

- Builds contextual understanding for the following GCSE texts: *Frankenstein, Dr Jekyll and Mr Hyde*

Week	Skill focus	Text	Learning objectives
1	Introducing ways to explore the 19th-century novel: Gathering ideas for a longer response	*Dracula* (1897) by Bram Stoker	• To explore the language in an extract from *Dracula* • To learn how to explain the effects of language
2	Introducing ways to explore 19th-century poetry: Commenting on the effect of choices of language and imagery	'The Laboratory' (1844) by Robert Browning	• To develop skills in reading and exploring language in 19th-century poetry • To explore the presentation of character in poetry • To comment on the effect of choices of language and imagery
3	Introducing ways to enhance creative writing: Creating a mysterious character		• To understand how the structure of a text is effective • To structure your work for effect • To develop your ideas and engage your reader
4	Introducing ways to comment on 19th-century non-fiction	'"Spring-Heeled Jack" in Darlington', *Daily Gazette for Middlesbrough*, 28 January 1884	• To make inferences from the text • To select relevant evidence to support viewpoint • To work towards a longer SQI response • To attempt critical evaluation and weighing up evidence
5	Introducing ways to comment on connected modern non-fiction	'Seeing is believing' by Merrily Harpur, *The Guardian*, 22 March 2006	• To develop inference skills using a 21st-century text • To make a link between 19th-century and 21st-century non-fiction texts • To introduce a comparative response
6	Introducing ways to improve discursive writing: Presenting a point of view		• To understand register and purpose in relation to a writing task • To complete part of a longer writing task

Year 9, Project 2: The Country and the City

- Builds contextual understanding for the following GCSE texts: *Dr Jekyll and Mr Hyde*, *The Sign of Four*, Romantic poetry

Week	Skill focus	Text	Learning objectives
1	Developing responses to the 19th-century novel: Planning an essay task	*Mary Barton* (1848) by Elizabeth Gaskell	• To understand key contrasts in images of the city and the countryside • To consider more developed inferences linked to contextual ideas • To understand the presentation of the countryside and consider the writer's intentions • To develop a mini essay-style response using familiar methods
2	Developing responses to 18th- and 19th-century poetry: Structure and imagery of two contrasting poems	'Composed upon Westminster Bridge' (1802) by William Wordsworth 'London', from *Songs of Experience* (1794) by William Blake	• To understand the viewpoint of a poet in presenting London compared to other forms • To consider the imagery of a 19th-century poem compared to other forms • To explore a contrasting view of London • To explore the language, imagery and structure of two poems about London • To write a comparative response to two classic poems
3	Developing skills in creative writing: Contrasting views of life in the city		• To develop an understanding of how contrasting images can be used in creative writing • To plan and write a creative piece using contrasting vocabulary, images and structural techniques
4	Developing an understanding of 19th-century non-fiction	*Passages in the Life of a Radical* by Samuel Bamford	• To understand key ideas and events in an eyewitness account • To draw inferences from those ideas and interpret with increased empathy • To explore the effect of the language choices in an eyewitness account • To consider the effect of the structure of the account
5	Developing skills with connected modern non-fiction: Exploring writer's point of view	'Cotton production linked to images of the dried up Aral Sea basin' by Tansy Hoskins, *The Guardian*, 1 October 2014	• To explore ideas around fast fashion • To understand the issues raised in a broadsheet newspaper article about cotton production • To develop empathy and understanding with the ideas and issues raised in the newspaper article • To present a more detailed inferential response to those ideas and issues
6	Developing discursive writing: Writing a persuasive blog post		• To develop an understanding of the connected ideas and issues of the project • To develop skills in planning a blog post on a key related issue • To write a blog post and evaluate those of your peers

Year 9, Project 3: Crime and Punishment

- Builds contextual understanding for the following GCSE texts: *Great Expectations*, *The Sign of Four*, *Dr Jekyll and Mr Hyde*

Week	Skill focus	Text	Learning objectives
1	Securing understanding of the 19th-century novel: Step-by-step essay task	*Oliver Twist* (1838) by Charles Dickens	• To read and understand 19th-century fiction • To explore how a writer presents a character's thoughts and feelings • To read and explore a 19th-century text • To develop critical evaluation of a text using familiar methods
2	Securing ways to explore 19th-century poetry: Building a convincing response	'The Ballad of Reading Gaol', Part 1 (1898) by Oscar Wilde	• To secure skills in understanding 19th-century poetry • To secure use of the IEC method when exploring the poet's use of structure • To explore and evaluate how a poet presents their point of view • To identify and analyse language and structure
3	Securing creative writing: Crime fiction		• To understand the conventions of crime and detective fiction • To structure, plan and write a piece of crime fiction using those conventions
4	Securing understanding of 19th-century non-fiction: Exploring more than one text	'The Murderer Hanged on the Sussex Downs', *Daily Telegraph*, 30 November 1881 From the diary of Francis Place describing 'the pillory', 1829	• To secure exploration of ideas and attitudes in 19th-century non-fiction texts • To consider how those ideas and attitudes are presented • To secure exploration of ideas in 19th-century non-fiction texts • To secure comprehension skills by synthesising those ideas
5	Securing skills with connected modern non-fiction: Comparing viewpoints from two texts	'Secret Teacher: teaching in prisons is where I can make a real difference', *The Guardian*, 3 May 2014 'The murderer hanged on the Sussex Downs', *Daily Telegraph*, 30 November 1881	• To understand a writer's viewpoint and methods in a piece of journalism • To present and support a response analysing viewpoint and method • To make comparisons between 19th-century and modern viewpoints and how they are presented • To write a comparative response
6	Securing persuasive writing: Presenting different sides to an argument		• To secure the conventions of arguing a case • To present speeches for the prosecution and the defence in a mock trial

Student progress trackers

Year 7, Project 1: The Natural World

Lesson focus	Key Skills Indicators *After completing these lessons I can:*	How well do I understand this skill? ☺ ☺ ☹	Comment and reflection
7.1.1 *The Wizard of Oz* **Older fiction** Date completed:	Read and understand an extract of non-fiction from 1900 Explore some of the key ideas in the text Present my ideas and reference the text		
7.1.2 **'I wander'd lonely as a cloud'** **19th-century poetry** Date completed:	Explore a poem and talk about what it makes me think, feel or imagine Consider the mood of a poem and how it might change		
7.1.3 **Creative writing** Date completed:	Plan the opening of a narrative, including: • character • setting • mood		
7.1.4 **'Making a Fossil Hunter'** **19th-century non-fiction** Date completed:	Read and interpret a non-fiction text from the 1800s Work out a writer's point of view Begin to understand the SQI method		
7.1.5 **David Attenborough interview** **Modern non-fiction** Date completed:	Read and interpret a non-fiction text from the 21st century Use the SQI method to respond to a question		
7.1.6 **Discursive writing** Date completed:	Plan a persuasive speech and letter using: • formal language, • facts and opinions • repetition • emotive language • statistics		

Year 7, Project 2: Child Labour

Lesson focus	Key Skills Indicators *After completing these lessons I can:*	How well do I understand this skill? ☺ ☺ ☹	Comment and reflection
7.2.1 *The Water Babies* **19th-century fiction** Date completed:	Use statement sentences to present my ideas Use supporting quotations Begin to write inferences		
7.2.2 **'The Chimney Sweeper'** **18th-century poetry** Date completed:	Understand and comment on what is meant by: • stanza • rhyme scheme • imagery		
7.2.3 **Creative writing** Date completed:	Create a character Plan a narrative Use adjectives and similes in my work		
7.2.4 **Life at Styal Mill** **19th-century non-fiction** Date completed:	Read and understand an extract of non-fiction from the 1800s Use more developed inferences to show my understanding		
7.2.5 **Child labour today** **Modern non-fiction** Date completed:	Read and understand a broadsheet news article Identify and understand why non-fiction writers use: • factual information • shocking statistics • quotations from real people		
7.2.6 **Discursive writing** Date completed:	Plan and write a speech using: • commands • direct address • repetition • solutions		

Year 7, Project 3: Journeys and Explorations

Lesson focus	Key Skills Indicators *After completing these lessons I can:*	How well do I understand this skill? ☺ ☺ ☹	Comment and reflection
7.3.1 *Around the World in 80 Days* **19th-century fiction** Date completed:	Retrieve basic ideas from an older text: • making inferences • using the SQI method • beginning to use embedded quotations		
7.3.2 **'From a Railway Carriage'** **19th-century poetry** Date completed:	Read and understand an older poem Begin to identify and comment on techniques a writer uses to create imagery, such as metaphor and simile Begin to use the IEC method		
7.3.3 **Creative writing** Date completed:	Identify a narrative voice and use in my own writing Use descriptive techniques such as adjectives, simile and metaphor		
7.3.4 *Travels in West Africa* **19th-century non-fiction** Date completed:	Read and understand older travel writing, making secure inferences about a writer's thoughts and feelings Use role play to identify with and relate to different viewpoints		
7.3.5 *Mud, Sweat and Tears* **Modern non-fiction** Date completed:	Read and understand modern non-fiction Make connections between modern and older texts Use the SQI method confidently		
7.3.6 **Discursive writing** Date completed:	Plan and use appropriate techniques to write a travel article such as: • facts and opinions • first-person viewpoint • anecdotes • humour • comparisons		

Year 8, Project 1: Beyond our World

Lesson focus	Key Skills Indicators *After completing these lessons I can:*	How well do I understand this skill? ☺ ☺ ☹	Comment and reflection
8.1.1 *The Time Machine* **19th-century fiction** Date completed:	Interpret and explain a 19th-century text Take ideas from a text and develop them in my own writing		
8.1.2 **'The Starlight Night'** **19th-century poetry** Date completed:	Explore how an idea or image is interpreted in a poem, prose or painting Understand the parts that make up an IEC paragraph		
8.1.3 **Creative writing** Date completed:	Recognise the parts of a narrative using 'The Three Little Pigs' Plan a narrative using a narrative arc		
8.1.4 **'How will the world end?'** **Older non-fiction** Date completed:	Interpret and explain a non-fiction text from 1900 Recognise and explore: • the key ideas • tone • writer's point of view		
8.1.5 **'I orbited the earth 2,720 times'** **Modern non-fiction** Date completed:	Explore the 'bigger questions' in a text and develop my point of view Explain similarities and differences between texts from different centuries		
8.1.6 **Discursive writing** Date completed:	Plan and write a piece of discursive writing that: • offers a balanced point of view • uses tone creatively		

Year 8, Project 2: How We Treat Others

Lesson focus	Key Skills Indicators *After completing these lessons I can:*	How well do I understand this skill? ☺ ☺ ☹	Comment and reflection
8.2.1 *Jane Eyre* **19th-century fiction** Date completed:	Make inferences about a character's thoughts and feelings Use the SQI method clearly Know and understand: • first person • noun phrase		
8.2.2 **'A Poison Tree'** **18th-century poetry** Date completed:	Understand how to use the IEC method to comment on: • structure • imagery • symbols • themes		
8.2.3 **Creative writing** Date completed:	Plan and write a first-person narrative Show the thoughts and feelings of my narrator Create an appropriate atmosphere in my work		
8.2.4 *The Bitter Cry of Outcast London* **19th-century non-fiction** Date completed:	Make more developed inferences Write up ideas using clear comprehension skills Show empathy by exploring issues in the role of a journalist		
8.2.5 **Professor Green on food banks** **Modern non-fiction** Date completed:	Understand and use the IEC method to comment on: • emotive language • personal anecdotes • inclusive pronouns • lists of three • imperatives		
8.2.6 **Discursive writing** Date completed:	Plan and write a debate speech focusing on an important issue Use appropriate techniques to persuade in my speech		

Year 8, Project 3: Growing Up

Lesson focus	Key Skills Indicators *After completing these lessons I can:*	How well do I understand this skill? ☺ ☺ ☹	Comment and reflection
8.3.1 *What Katy Did* **19th-century fiction** Date completed:	Read and understand a 19th-century fiction text using inference and deduction Understand how language choices add to characterisation and meaning		
8.3.2 **'I Remember, I Remember'** **19th-century poetry** Date completed:	Understand how a poet uses language features to present a speaker's feelings using: • sibilance • metaphor • anaphora • personification • plosives Understand the impact of structural features		
8.3.3 **Creative writing** Date completed:	Plan and write first person and autobiographical writing using: • emotions • chronological order • time connectives • past tense Engage the reader in my writing Use those features in my own writing to engage my reader		
8.3.4 **Anti-social behaviour** **19th-century non-fiction** Date completed:	Secure understanding of a 19th-century non-fiction text Understand how a writer can use language techniques to sensationalise their writing and express a viewpoint		
8.3.5 **Greta Thunberg speech** **Modern non-fiction** Date completed:	Understand how a point of view can be presented through persuasive and rhetorical techniques Comment on the techniques in a persuasive speech		
8.3.6 **Discursive writing** Date completed:	Write and plan an op-ed for a magazine, arguing both sides of a topic Include connectives and an informed opinion in an op-ed article		

Year 9, Project 1: The Unexplained

Lesson focus	Key Skills Indicators *After completing these lessons I can:*	*How well do I understand this skill?* ☺ ☺ ☹	Comment and reflection
9.1.1 *Dracula* **19th-century fiction** Date completed:	Explore the writer's choice of language and its effect using think, feel or imagine Develop my use of the IEC model		
9.1.2 **'The Laboratory'** **19th-century poetry** Date completed:	Interpret and comment on the narrative and characters in a 19th-century poem Confidently use the IEC model		
9.1.3 **Creative writing** Date completed:	Understand the purpose of a narrative hook and use in my own writing Create engaging characters		
9.1.4 **'"Spring Heeled Jack" in Darlington'** **19th-century non-fiction** Date completed:	Confidently: infer from the text use the SQI method Attempt to weigh up evidence and interpret a statement about the text		
9.1.5 **'Seeing is believing'** **Modern non-fiction** Date completed:	Write a clear summary of the text Attempt to weigh up evidence to give a balanced response Develop my use of SQI to include a comparison		
9.1.6 **Discursive writing** Date completed:	Confidently plan a piece of writing, considering: purpose and register hooking my reader my conclusion and call to action		

Year 9, Project 2: The Country and the City

Lesson focus	Key Skills Indicators *After completing these lessons I can:*	How well do I understand this skill? ☺ ☺ ☹	Comment and reflection
9.2.1 *Mary Barton* **19th-century fiction** Date completed:	Make more developed inferences Understand contrasts within a text Write a mini essay-style response using both the SQI and IEC methods		
9.2.2 **'Composed upon Westminster Bridge' and 'London'** **18th- and 19th-century poetry** Date completed:	In two poems, understand: language imagery structure Write a response comparing two poems		
9.2.3 **Creative writing** Date completed:	Plan and write a creative piece using contrasting: language imagery structural techniques		
9.2.4 **Account of the Peterloo Massacre** **19th-century non-fiction** Date completed:	Use the SQI method to explore ideas with empathy Use the IEC method to analyse the language and structure in an extract		
9.2.5 **Fast fashion** **Modern non-fiction** Date completed:	Use role-play skills to develop empathy with a situation Make a detailed response to an issue using our SQI method		
9.2.6 **Discursive writing** Date completed:	Plan a blog post on a key issue Write a blog post and evaluate those of my peers		

Year 9, Project 3: Crime and Punishment

Lesson focus	Key Skills Indicators *After completing these lessons I can:*	How well do I understand this skill? ☺ ☺ ☹	Comment and reflection
9.3.1 *Oliver Twist* **19th-century fiction** Date completed:	Explore how a writer presents a character's thoughts and feelings in 19th-century fiction Develop a critical evaluation of a text using both SQI and IEC.		
9.3.2 **'The Ballad of Reading Gaol'** **19th-century poetry** Date completed:	Securely use the IEC method when exploring a poet's use of structure Evaluate how a poet presents their point of view Identify and analyse language and structure in a 19th-century poem		
9.3.3 **Creative writing** Date completed:	Understand and use the conventions of crime and detective fiction, such as setting, crime and suspects, in my own writing		
9.3.4 **'The Murderer Hanged on the Sussex Downs'** **19th-century non-fiction** Date completed:	Look at how attitudes and ideas are presented in 19th-century non-fiction texts Synthesise ideas in two texts using the SQI method		
9.3.5 **'Secret Teacher: teaching in prisons'** **Modern non-fiction** Date completed:	Understand writer's viewpoint and methods in a piece of journalism Make a comparative response between viewpoints and how they are presented		
9.3.6 **Persuasive writing** Date completed:	Understand the conventions of arguing a case in court Write and present speeches for the prosecution and the defence in a mock trial		

From *The Wizard of Oz* (1900)

Dorothy lived in the midst of the great Kansas prairies, with Uncle Henry, who was a farmer, and Aunt Em, who was the farmer's wife. Their house was small, for the lumber to build it had to be carried by wagon many miles. […]

When Dorothy stood in the doorway and looked around, she could see nothing but the great gray prairie on every side. Not a tree nor a house broke the broad sweep of flat country that reached to the edge of the sky in all directions. The sun had baked the plowed land into a gray mass, with little cracks running through it. Even the grass was not green, for the sun had burned the tops of the long blades until they were the same gray color to be seen everywhere. Once the house had been painted, but the sun blistered the paint and the rains washed it away, and now the house was as dull and gray as everything else.

When Aunt Em came there to live she was a young, pretty wife. The sun and wind had changed her, too. They had taken the sparkle from her eyes and left them a sober gray; they had taken the red from her cheeks and lips, and they were gray also. She was thin and gaunt, and never smiled now. When Dorothy, who was an orphan, first came to her, Aunt Em had been so startled by the child's laughter that she would scream and press her hand upon her heart whenever Dorothy's merry voice reached her ears; and she still looked at the little girl with wonder that she could find anything to laugh at.

Uncle Henry never laughed. He worked hard from morning till night and did not know what joy was. He was gray also, from his long beard to his rough boots, and he looked stern and solemn, and rarely spoke.

It was Toto that made Dorothy laugh, and saved her from growing as gray as her other surroundings. Toto was not gray; he was a little black dog, with long silky hair and small black eyes that twinkled merrily on either side of his funny, wee nose. Toto played all day long, and Dorothy played with him, and loved him dearly.

L. Frank Baum

Learning objectives:	Resources:
• To understand some of the key ideas in an extract from *The Wizard of Oz* • To begin to present ideas and support them with reference to the text	• Extract 7.1.1 • 7.1.1 Lesson 1 PowerPoint • 7.1.1. Lesson 1 Worksheet

Getting started

• Display **7.1.1 Lesson 1 PowerPoint slide 2** and ask the students to say what they see in the picture. Ask: What do you notice about the colours used? What do you think about the landscape? What sort of place is this? Would you like to live there? Why/why not? What do you imagine the woman in the picture doing? Who is she? How is she feeling?

• Display **PowerPoint slide 1** and go over the lesson objectives. Ask the students what they already know about *The Wizard of Oz*. Introduce the idea that the novel has been adapted many times, and is well known for the Yellow Brick Road, ruby slippers and the Wicked Witch of the West. Explain that it started out as a novel, then became a film and later a stage show. Ask the students what they think these adaptations might suggest about the story (its continued relevance to audiences and popularity).

• Give out copies of **Extract 7.1.1** and display **PowerPoint slide 2**. Read the extract as a class; you might find reading the extract to the class best supports their understanding. Use the image on the slide to introduce 'the great Kansas prairies' and support the students in imagining the setting. Explain where and what the prairies are.

• Display **PowerPoint slide 3** and allow 10 minutes for the students to work through the three 'Exploring together' questions, making notes either on a copy of the extract or in their notebooks. It may also help for you to make notes that can be seen by the class. (Suggested answers: *1. A lonely, isolated place (there's not much around); a hot, dry and uninhabitable place (impact of the sun); a grey, colourless, dull, boring and lifeless place (repetition of 'gray' and the impact of the weather). 2. Uncle Henry and Aunt Em seem lifeless, miserable, intimidating, with nothing to laugh about; refer to the change in Aunt Em's appearance and Uncle Henry's personality and approach to life. 3. Students' own answers*.)

• If you have time in the lesson or as an independent learning task, it might support some of the students to draw their impression of Aunt Em and Uncle Henry and the inside of their house.

Developing skills

• Hand out copies of **7.1.1 Lesson 1 Worksheet** and ask the students to complete **Activity 1**, working in pairs. Explain the skill of skimming to get the gist of the text and scanning for specific information – in this case things that are grey. You could complete Activity 1 as a whole class as a way of modelling scanning for information; allow no more than 5 minutes for this task. (Suggested answers: *gray prairie; gray land; gray grass; gray house; Aunt Em's gray eyes, cheeks and lips; Uncle Henry is gray*.)

• The students now move on to complete **Worksheet Activity 2** in pairs or working independently. (Suggested answers: *No trees or houses; flat country that reached the edge of the sky; earth baked by the sun; the land is cracked; grass isn't green and has been burned by the sun; sun and rain ruin the paint on the houses*.)

• Display **PowerPoint slide 4** and introduce the idea of referencing or paraphrasing the text in order to develop the students' comprehension. You can use the example on the slide to support you.

• Display **PowerPoint slide 5** and continue to work as a whole group, encouraging the students to engage with the text as a way of developing their comprehension. They should verbally answer the question 'What does this quotation suggest about the sun and the rain?' with reference to the quotation on the slide. You could approach this task as a think–pair–share activity.

Trying it yourself

• Encourage the students to twork independently to complete **Worksheet Activity 3**. The activity is intended to expand their learning and pull together the whole lesson, and their responses should be a reflection of the group discussion and exploration.

Introducing older texts: *The Wizard of Oz*

You've probably noticed that Baum uses one particular adjective to describe everything: 'gray'. (We would write 'grey' in British English, but he was an American writer.)

Activity 1:

Read the passage again and use the space below to list *everything* that is described as 'gray'.

Gray prairie, ...

....

....

Activity 2:

What else does the writer say about the Kansas prairies?

Re-read the second paragraph of the extract. Jot down four other things that the writer tells us about the countryside here.

1.   ....

2.   ....

3.   ....

4.   ....

Activity 3: Trying it yourself

The writer tells us that things have been changed by their surroundings.

> Once the house had been painted, but the sun blistered the paint and the rains washed it away, and now the house was as dull and gray as everything else.

1. What does this quotation suggest about the sun and the rain? ....

....

....

2. Can you remember what else has changed? ....

....

....

Learning objectives:	**Resources:**
• To explore some of the key ideas in an extract from *The Wizard of Oz* • To learn to present and support those ideas clearly using textual references	• Extract 7.1.1 • 7.1.1 Lesson 2 PowerPoint • 7.1.1 Lesson 2 Worksheet

Getting started

• Display **7.1.1 Lesson 2 PowerPoint slide 2** and ask the students to recap and recall the previous lesson. Recall how they looked at some parts of the extract from *The Wizard of Oz*, including the writer's use of the word 'gray' and how the weather was described.

• Re-read **Extract 7.1.1** as a class. This time, it might be worth reading the extract aloud with different readers.

• Display **PowerPoint slide 1** and go over the lesson objectives.

Developing skills

• Hand out copies of **7.1.1 Lesson 2 Worksheet** and introduce **Activity 1**. Working in pairs or small groups, the students select the information in the paragraph that builds a picture of Aunt Em before and now. The aim of the activity is for the students to explore some of the key ideas in the extract while developing their ability to select correct and appropriate textual references. You might consider modelling finding information in the text as a whole group. (Suggested answers: *Aunt Em before: She had a sparkle in her eye; her cheeks and lips were red; she was a young, pretty wife. Aunt Em now: her eyes are sober and grey; her cheeks and lips are grey; she is thin and gaunt; she never smiles; she is startled by the child's laughter; she presses her hand to her heart when she hears Dorothy's voice; she can't understand what Dorothy can find to laugh at.*)

• After completing Activity 1 on the worksheet, encourage the students to feed back verbally in response to the question 'How has living on the prairies changed Aunt Em?' Encourage them to verbalise their ideas about the text; these ideas will become their 'clear statement'. As with other activities, it may support the learning if you model organising ideas by making a note of the best ideas on a visual aid that the whole class can see. (Suggested answers: *She has changed for the worse; she has lost any colour she had before; she has become grey like her environment; she isn't happy any more.*)

• Now display **PowerPoint slide 3** and break down the model answer, explaining first how the student has made a clear statement that shows how they think Aunt Em has changed, and has then used a textual reference to back up their statement.

• Working in pairs or small groups, the students now complete **Worksheet Activity 2**; if they need extra support you might prefer to complete the first part of this activity as a whole group. The aim is for the students to practice selecting and compiling ideas about the text into a clear statement sentence, then to select supporting textual references. At this point, textual reference can be paraphrasing or direct quoting; it is the process of composing the response that is most important.

Trying it yourself

• Read the 'Trying it yourself' question (**Worksheet Activity 3**) as a whole group followed by a re-read of paragraphs 3 and 4 from the extract. Ask the students what they learn about Dorothy in the final sentences of paragraph 3. (*That she is an orphan; that she was a happy child.*)

• Direct the students to complete **Activity 3** on the worksheet, replicating the model on **PowerPoint slide 3**. Those students who need extra support should be encouraged to answer from paragraph 3 using the examples of Aunt Em selected previously and considering how the last couple of sentences about Dorothy show how they are different. To stretch the students, you could ask them a more challenging question, such as: Why do you think Dorothy is different from her aunt and uncle? (**Activity 4** on the worksheet). (Suggested answer: *Dorothy is happy and laughs, unlike her aunt and uncle who are serious and sad; Dorothy hasn't turned grey like her aunt and uncle; the environment hasn't had the same effect on Dorothy as it has on her aunt and uncle.*)

Introducing older texts: *The Wizard of Oz*

Activity 1:

Read the third paragraph from *The Wizard of Oz* extract below. Think about what the writer tells us about Aunt Em in this paragraph. Find information about:

- what she was like when she first arrived on the farm
- how she is now.

Use the table below to make your notes.

When Aunt Em came there to live she was a young, pretty wife. The sun and wind had changed her, too. They had taken the sparkle from her eyes and left them a sober gray; they had taken the red from her cheeks and lips, and they were gray also. She was thin and gaunt, and never smiled now. When Dorothy, who was an orphan, first came to her, Aunt Em had been so startled by the child's laughter that she would scream and press her hand upon her heart whenever Dorothy's merry voice reached her ears; and she still looked at the little girl with wonder that she could find anything to laugh at.

Aunt Em before	Aunt Em now

Activity 2:

Question: *How has living on the prairies changed Aunt Em?*

Look back at the table of changes you completed for **Activity 1** to help you create two clear statement sentences with supporting information from the text.

1. ....

   ....

2. ....

   ....

Activity 3: Trying it yourself

Question: *How is Dorothy different from her aunt and uncle?*

Answer this question, explaining **at least two** differences and using:

- supporting sentences
- supporting textual references.

1. ....

   ....

   ....

2. ....

   ....

   ....

Activity 4: Stretch

Question: *Why do you think Dorothy is different to her aunt and uncle?*

....

....

....

....

....

From 'I wander'd lonely as a cloud' (1804)

I wander'd lonely as a cloud
That floats on high o'er vales and hills,
When all at once I saw a crowd,
A host of golden daffodils,
Beside the lake, beneath the trees
Fluttering and dancing in the breeze.

Continuous as the stars that shine
And twinkle on the milky way,
They stretch'd in never-ending line
Along the margin of a bay:
Ten thousand saw I at a glance
Tossing their heads in sprightly dance.

The waves beside them danced, but they
Out-did the sparkling waves in glee:
A poet could not but be gay
In such a jocund company!
I gazed – and gazed – but little thought
What wealth the show to me had brought.

For oft, when on my couch I lie
In vacant or in pensive mood,
They flash upon that inward eye
Which is the bliss of solitude;
And then my heart with pleasure fills
And dances with the daffodils.

William Wordsworth

Learning objective:	Resources:
• To develop confidence in exploring 19th-century poetry	• Extract 7.1.2 • 7.1.2 Lesson 1 PowerPoint • 7.1.2 Lesson 1 Worksheet

Getting started

- This lesson is aimed at encouraging students to freely explore poetry and bring their own ideas and interpretation to the tasks. Often we, as English teachers, are guilty of telling students what to think, yet poetry lends an opportunity for individual and independent interpretation – and having fun with the poem.

- Display **7.1.2 Lesson 1 PowerPoint slide 1** and go over the lesson objective. Ask the students what they already know about poetry, which poems they have read, and what makes a poem different from a novel or a newspaper. Take the opportunity to correct any misconceptions about poetry having to rhyme.

- Give out copies of **Extract 7.1.2** and read the poem to the class. You will probably find it beneficial to read the poem more than once, with a pause for thought in between.

- Display **PowerPoint slide 2** and, either as a whole group or in small groups/pairs, explore the poem using the prompts provided on the slide. Allow plenty of time for this exploration so that all students can use their imagination and feel comfortable about forming an opinion, even if its a very simple one.

Developing skills

- Hand out copies of **7.1.2 Lesson 1 Worksheet** and ask the students to work in small groups or pairs to complete **Activity 1**, which explores students' first reactions to the poem. The students can work through the prompts, which are inspired by Barbara Bleiman's method, in any order they choose. The purpose of the activity is to build their confidence in forming and sharing thoughts about poetry and then to formulate those thoughts into an oral response. Allow plenty of time for this activity, so that students have the time needed to think and explore. You might also want to build in time for feeding back as a whole class.

- Students then complete **Worksheet Activity 2**. Encourage them to pull together their learning from the previous activities to answer the questions. Prompt them to think about the language used and the image or pictures it creates using **PowerPoint slide 3**. Ask the students to consider whether the images change as the poem progresses. (Suggested answers: *1. The language and structure of the poem create a picture in the reader's mind. 2. The mood in the poem is reflective, sometimes sad and in some lines joyful.*)

Trying it yourself

- Encourage students to work on their own to complete **Worksheet Activity 3**. Their image and ideas should be a reflection of the group/pair discussion and exploration, and an opportunity to practise selecting references and using them in context.

- It might be helpful to ask some of the students to feed back and share annotations and explorations as a whole group or in pairs. Encourage those students feeding back or sharing their activity to explain *why* they made the choices they did. You can continue to use the question 'why' to delve deeper into their thinking around the poem.

Introducing 19th-century poetry: 'I wander'd lonely as a cloud'

Activity 1:

Use the prompts in the grid below, in any order you like, to explore the poem. You can look at the whole poem, parts of the poem or individual words.

What do I like?	My first thoughts are…	I'm confused by…
It makes me think…	It reminds me of…	I'm not sure…
It makes me imagine…	I want to know…	It makes me feel…

Activity 2:

Answer the questions below.

1. How does the poet, William Wordsworth, create a picture in the reader's mind?

   ....

   ....

2. What kind of mood is created in this poem?

   ....

   ....

Activity 3:

Use the space below to draw the image you see in your mind's eye when reading the poem. Label it with words or phrases from the poem that have inspired you.

7.1.2 Lesson 2 — Introducing 19th-century poetry: 'I wander'd lonely as a cloud'

Learning objective:	**Resources:**
• To explore imagery, structure and mood in 'I wander'd lonely as a cloud' by William Wordsworth	• Extract 7.1.2 • 7.1.2 Lesson 2 PowerPoint • 7.1.2 Lesson 2 Worksheet

Getting started

• Display **7.1.2 Lesson 2 PowerPoint slide 1** and go over the lesson objective.

• Ask the students to refer to their copy of **Extract 7.1.2** from the previous lesson. Ask them to re-read the poem in their heads as a recap.

• Display **PowerPoint slide 2** and work as a whole group to answer the questions. The aim is to recap and remember learning from the previous lesson as well as extend the students' thinking ahead of this lesson. Using the question prompts on the slide, establish that Wordsworth enjoys and appreciates nature; he thinks being in nature has an impact on people's mood/how they feel. Encourage the students to consider how the poet's mood changes throughout the poem: he feels sad in the opening line but is made happy and joyful by the thought of nature; he then reflects that even when he is not physically outdoors he can remember the feeling of being in nature.

Developing skills

• Project **PowerPoint slide 3** and hand out copies of **7.1.2 Lesson 2 Worksheet**. Encourage the students to work in small groups or pairs to complete **Activity 1** by reading the stanzas and underlining words and phrases to support their response to the statement. You might want to have a short group discussion first, to allow the students to share their initial responses to the statement and to select some words in order to have something on which to base their thinking. (Words and phrases that suggest Wordsworth finds nature beautiful and welcoming could include: *shine, twinkle, sprightly dance, danced, sparkling, glee, be gay, jocund company, gazed, wealth.*)

• Display **PowerPoint slide 4** and move on to **Worksheet Activity 2**. The students should develop their annotations by making notes about the effect the words have on them. You could deconstruct the example on **slide 4** by asking the students to explain their thinking and how they came to that conclusion. Alternatively, the students could complete this activity as a whole group.

• Make time for collecting student responses and to allow them to extend their notes with the ideas of others.

Trying it yourself

• Remind the students that Wordsworth was a writer who chose to live in the countryside, far away from lots of people. He believed in the power of nature to affect human beings, and he talks about his feelings in the poem 'I wander'd lonely as a cloud'.

• Encourage the students to work on their own to complete **Worksheet Activity 3**. They should use the methods they have just practised, underlining and annotating words or phrases that suggest the poet's mood in each stanza.

• **Worksheet Activity 4** is designed to encourage students to draw together their thinking and notes into two clear sentences, revisiting the skill practised in the previous week. Remind them that they should also be looking at how the structure of the poem presents the poet's mood; you might consider asking some students to explain the narrative of the poem. (Suggested answers: *1. In the first stanza he seems fed up/unhappy; 2. In the final stanza he seems content and happy/he realises that thinking of nature makes him feel better.*)

• **Worksheet Activity 5** is aimed at stretching students' thinking and bringing together ideas from the whole poem and across the week. Answers should include a comparison between the mood of the poem at the start and at the end, and may include reference to: the beauty of nature improving the poet's mood; the fact that the poet now knows to think of nature when he feels sad; his love of nature and how happy it makes him feel.

Activity 1:

'William Wordsworth finds nature beautiful and welcoming.'

Does your group agree or disagree with this statement?

Read the stanzas below and <u>underline</u> any words and phrases that support your group's response to the statement.

> Continuous as the stars that shine
> And twinkle on the milky way,
> They stretch'd in never-ending line
> Along the margin of a bay:
> Ten thousand saw I at a glance
> Tossing their heads in sprightly dance.
>
> The waves beside them danced, but they
> Out-did the sparkling waves in glee: –
> A poet could not but be gay
> In such a jocund company!
> I gazed – and gazed – but little thought
> What wealth the show to me had brought.

Activity 2:

Now add annotations to the stanzas above, to explain how the words or phrases make you feel.

Activity 3:

Re-read the first and last stanzas of the poem then underline and annotate words or phrases that suggest the poet's mood in each stanza.

> I wander'd lonely as a cloud
> That floats on high o'er vales and hills,
> When all at once I saw a crowd,
> A host of golden daffodils,
> Beside the lake, beneath the trees
> Fluttering and dancing in the breeze.

For oft, when on my couch I lie
In vacant or in pensive mood,
They flash upon that inward eye
Which is the bliss of solitude;
And then my heart with pleasure fills
And dances with the daffodils.

Activity 4:

Now write two statement sentences about the poet's mood at the start and end of the poem.

1. ....

....

....

2. ....

....

....

Activity 5:

Now write a statement sentence making a comparison between the poet's mood at the start and the end of the poem.

....

....

....

....

....

....

Learning objectives:	Resources:
• To plan a descriptive piece with a focus on setting and character • To plan and write the opening of a narrative • To hook your reader into your setting and character through carefully selected language	• 7.1.3 Lessons 1 & 2 PowerPoint • 7.1.3 Lessons 1 & 2 Worksheet

Lesson 1: Getting started

• Display **7.1.3 Lessons 1 & 2 PowerPoint slide 2**. Use the questions on the slide to encourage the students to reflect on the texts they have studied and their learning over the previous two weeks. They should re-engage with ideas around setting and how this might impact on feelings and mood. The students could respond to questions 1 and 2 as a whole class and the last question in pairs. (Suggested answers: *1. The environment was harsh and grey and made everyone in it grey and miserable. 2. At the start of the poem the poet was unhappy, but by spending time in nature his feelings changed, and he knows in the future to imagine nature when he feels negative. 3. Students' own answers.*)

• Display **PowerPoint slide 1** and introduce the learning objectives for the week's lessons.

Developing skills

• Display **PowerPoint slide 3**, which asks the students to think about two or three places they know well and could write about confidently. Some students may benefit from choosing and describing only one place, but it may help both the speaker and listener in tuning into the language and tone if the speaker describes different places. For example, the listener could consider whether the speaker changes their voice or struggles to describe one place in an interesting way. To secure the pace of the activity, you could establish a one-minute time limit for talking about each place.

• Hand out copies of **7.1.3 Lessons 1 & 2 Worksheet** and display **PowerPoint slide 4**. The students should aim to complete **Worksheet Activity 1** individually as far as possible. You might want to take time to review the five senses with some students. This activity should be used to formalise initial ideas about the setting of their story, which will be built on and refined in the following activity.

• Display **PowerPoint slide 5**. Allow pairs of students time to share and review each other's ideas. Both the reviewer and the writer should use the points on the slide as a checklist.

• Display **PowerPoint slide 6** and introduce the next step in planning. Students should use the bullet points to support thinking, but encourage them to be imaginative. Take time to reflect on the model character on the slide. Ask: Why might the boy be dressed the way he is? How does the description of his dog link with him? What might hook you in to this character? Students then work individually to complete **Worksheet Activity 2**. If it helps, they can name their characters, then draw and label them.

• Display **PowerPoint slide 7**. Using the bullet points on the slide, students develop their ideas about their characters. They might benefit from sharing some of the characters and settings with the whole group and receiving wider feedback. **Worksheet Activity 3** should be used to consolidate the students' reviews and feedback; it will also act as a reminder and starting point for reflection next lesson.

Lesson 2: Developing skills and Trying it yourself

• Display **PowerPoint slide 8**. Use the questions on the slide, along with feedback from the previous lesson, to encourage reflection on the plans the students have made and how they might improve them. You might want to set a strict time limit for this activity so that students have maximum writing time later.

• Display **PowerPoint slide 9**. Pairs discuss their wider story and how they will end the opening. Some students may benefit from making notes to support them in completing **Worksheet Activity 4**.

• Display **PowerPoint slide 10** and talk through the success criteria before students begin to write their story opening. Leave the list displayed on the board for reference during the writing activity. Depending on the length of the lesson, allow around 20 minutes for writing including 5 minutes for editing.

• Share the best pieces of writing, examples of interesting language, and good examples of creating a mood and hooking the reader in so that they want to read the rest of the story.

Activity 1:

Use the space below to create a spider diagram or mind map of words and images that create an impression of the place where your story will be set.

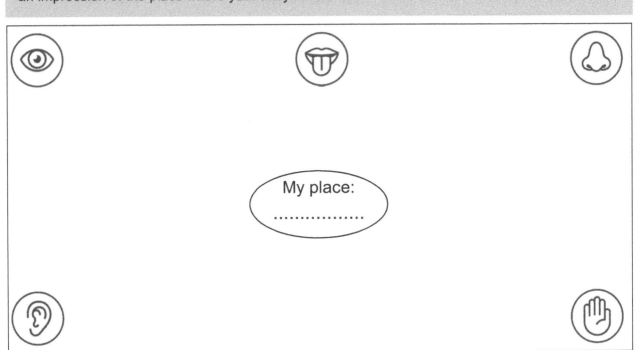

My place:
....

Activity 2:

Use the character outlines below to plan details of your characters.

1. A positive about my setting: ....

2. Language that my partner liked: ....

3. How to improve my setting: ....

4. A positive about my characters: ....

5. Language that my partner liked: ....

6. How to improve my characters: ....

7. Feedback on my overall idea: ....

....

Activity 4:

Plan your story using the planning grid below.

The place – describe it ....

....

....

Why are you/the character(s) there? ....

....

....

How do you/they feel? ....

....

....

Link this back to the setting or against it ....

....

Something happens… ....

....

....

From 'Making a Fossil Hunter', *All the Year Round* (1865)

Her father used to employ the church holidays in picking up along the beach pretty pebbles and shells, fossil and recent, and "veterberries," and "John Dory's bones," and "ladies' fingers," and other "curies," as they were called. **Lyme and its neighbour, Charmouth**, were then on the old coach-road, and the passengers mostly liked to take away a specimen or two, which they got either from Anning or from a Charmouth "fossiler," called the Cury-man, or "Captain Cury," from his trade in curiosities. In August 1800, little Mary Anning was taken to see some horse-riding in the Rack field. A thunderstorm came on: those in charge of her hurried her under a tree; a flash of lightning struck the party, killing two women on the spot, and making the child insensible. A warm bath restored her to consciousness, and, strangely enough, she who had been a very dull girl before, now grew up lively and intelligent. She soon got to accompany her father in his rambles. "Fossiling," however, does not appear to have paid so well as steady carpentry, for the family went down the hill. The father died of **consumption**, and Mary, at ten years of age, was left very badly off. Just then a lady gave her half-a-crown for a very choice ammonite. This encouraged her to take collecting as a regular means of life. But she soon proved something more than a mere "fossiler." [...]

In 1811, she saw some bones sticking out of a cliff; and, hammer in hand, she traced the position of the whole creature, and then hired men to dig out for her the **Lias** block in which it was embedded. Thus was brought to light the first Icthyosaurus (fish-lizard), a monster some thirty feet long, with jaws nearly a fathom in length, and huge saucer eyes. [...] People then called it a crocodile. Mr. Henley, the lord of the manor, bought it of the enterprising young girl for twenty-three pounds. It is now in the British Museum.

Anon

Lyme and its neighbour Charmouth: Lyme Regis and Charmouth, two towns on the Dorset coast, famous for cliff fossils
consumption: a Victorian name fur tuberculosis, a wasting disease of the lungs
Lias: a kind of stone, common around Dorset

Learning objective:	**Resources:**
• To read and understand key information in a 19th-century non-fiction extract	• Extract 7.1.4 • 7.1.4 Lesson 1 PowerPoint • 7.1.4 Lesson 1 Worksheet

Getting started

* Display **7.1.4 Lesson 1 PowerPoint slide 1** and introduce the learning objective. Explain that this is the same era in which Wordsworth wrote 'I wander'd lonely as a cloud'. The students may have some knowledge of the Victorians, so it is worth asking them to share anything they know first. You could reference: the conservative dress and point of view; the abolition of slavery; Charles Darwin publishing *On the Origin of Species* (1859) (this last point is relevant for the lesson and worth raising).

* Hand out copies of **Extract 7.1.4**. Read the extract through out loud while the students listen.

* Now hand out copies of **7.1.4 Lesson 1 Worksheet** and display **PowerPoint slide 2**, which leads into **Worksheet Activity 1**. Ensure the students have the equipment they need for highlighting or underlining.

* Read **Extract 7.1.4** again, encouraging the students to highlight any words they don't understand (you might want to limit the number of words to avoid over-highlighting). Students then complete **Worksheet Activity 1** in pairs, choosing five of the words they highlighted and deciding on their meaning. Allow around 5 minutes for this activity and then share some of the words and meanings with the class, to support shared learning. You might want to consider modelling working out a word by looking at the words around it or the wider sentence. For example, the phrase '"veterberries," and "John Dory's bones," and "ladies' fingers," and other "curies,"' is challenging, but by reading further into the text the students should be able to see that they are all old-fashioned names for different fossils.

Developing skills

* Display **PowerPoint slide 3**. As students work through the questions, reassure them that if they are able to answer then they understand the text better than they might think. (Suggested answers: *1. The extract is about a woman who collects fossils with her father and then goes on to collect fossils on the beaches, selling her finds. She then finds a larger dinosaur skeleton, the first of its kind. 2. Family pastimes; hobbies; poverty; nature; history. 3. A young girl who found the first Ichthyosaurus. 4. Students' answers might reference dragons/monsters/crocodiles.*)

* Display **PowerPoint slide 4** and use it to support understanding of what a fact is and how it is different from an opinion. You could use examples such as: *It is a fact that the school day starts at 9 a.m.; it is some students' opinion that the start time is too early.*

* Some of the students may benefit from another whole-class reading of the first paragraph of **Extract 7.1.4** before completing **Worksheet Activity 2**. Use the information on the slide to explain that the students don't have to select exact references from the text – they can summarise them in their own words (paraphrase). The objective of this task is to support understanding and exploration of the text. Take time to share the facts as a class, and encourage the students to add to their own lists.

Trying it yourself

* Display **PowerPoint slide 5** and use it to revisit the discussion about the Victorian era at the start of the lesson. Pose questions such as: Why might the Victorians be scared or nervous of the discovery of science? How do you think Mary Anning felt? How did the woman who bought the fossil from her feel? This should lead into a short discussion about how the writer felt.

* **Worksheet Activity 3** should be completed individually where possible and used to consolidate the skills of the lesson. As above, the activity is aimed at supporting understanding and the students can be encouraged to paraphrase. (Suggested answers: *'little Mary Anning' – use of 'little' suggests sympathy; 'those in charge of her' makes it sound like they caused her harm through their actions; 'the family went down the hill' suggests the family wealth or good luck didn't last; 'The father died...Mary, at ten years of age, was left very badly off' – suggests Mary's sad life, and the writer seems to feel sorry for her by including it; it's a rags to riches story/a story of success from nothing.*)

Introducing 19th-century non-fiction: 'Making a Fossil Hunter'

Activity 1:

Write down five unfamiliar words from the extract and what you think each word means.

Word	Meaning

Activity 2:

Re-read the first paragraph of **Extract 7.4.1**.

What information can you find about Mary Anning's early life? List at least five facts you have discovered.

1. ....

2. ....

3. ....

4. ....

5. ....

Activity 3:

The writer of the article seems to feel sympathy for Mary in the first paragraph. Find three pieces of information from the text that support this idea.

1. ....

....

2. ....

....

3. ....

....

Learning objective:	Resources:
• To begin to understand how the writer may present their views	• Extract 7.1.4 • 7.1.4 Lesson 2 PowerPoint • 7.1.4 Lesson 2 Worksheet

Getting started

* Hand out copies of **7.1.4 Lesson 2 Worksheet**. The students complete **Activity 1** by recalling information from **Extract 7.1.4** from the previous lesson. Allow time for pairs to share and then for a wider group sharing (either in a small group or with the whole class). By the end of the activity the students should have recalled most of the text and made notes. This activity should be completed at pace and might benefit from a timer or set time for each element.

* Follow Activity 1 with a whole-class reading of **Extract 7.4.2**, as a reminder and to consolidate learning.

* Display **7.1.4 Lesson 2 PowerPoint slide 1** and introduce the learning objective for the lesson.

Developing skills

* Display **PowerPoint slide 2**. Ask the students whether they know anything about the phrase 'reading between the lines'. Can they explain what it means? Once students arrive at a clear definition, offer them an opportunity to put it in context. You could give them the following example: *After having a meeting, I come back into the classroom stomping my feet and slamming the door. I shout at the class and tell everyone to work in silence and not speak to me. If you're reading between the lines: What mood am I in? How do you think my meeting went? How do you know?* Encourage the students to develop their explanation with this last question.

* Now move on to discuss the modelled example on **PowerPoint slide 2**, working through the elements step by step. Ask the students for feedback on the two questions, then explore what the statement and the writer's choice of language imply. (Suggested answer: *The writer is implying that Usain Bolt is not just a runner, he is the greatest sprinter of all time.*)

* Leave **PowerPoint slide 2** displayed and move on to **Worksheet Activity 2**. Encourage the students to complete the sentence starting 'The writer is implying…' by practising the skill of reading between the lines and interpreting the language used. (Suggested answer: *The writer is implying that Mary Anning is not just a fossil-hunter but a great fossil hunter, more skilled and better than any others.*)

* Display **PowerPoint slide 3** and allow the students a few minutes to discuss the statement and form their own opinion; they might start to look for evidence in the text and this should be encouraged. The statement can be proved and students who don't agree should be challenged, to avoid misconception.

* Display **PowerPoint slide 4** and work though the information on the slide as a whole class. Review the meaning of the word 'enterprising' in pairs; this is a good opportunity for dictionary work. The students then move on to complete **Worksheet Activity 3**. (Suggested answer: *The writer's use of the word 'enterprising' presents Mary's work in a positive light. It suggests that she can think for herself, even though she is still a young girl, and that she is business-like.*)

* Display **PowerPoint slide 5**. Explain the modelled SQI (statement + quotation + inference) response, focusing on how it infers the writer's point of view. Ask the students how this compares to the answer they gave to **Worksheet Activity 3** (*it uses evidence from the text and follows a clear structure*).

Trying it yourself

* Continue to display **PowerPoint slide 5**; the students can refer to it while completing **Worksheet Activities 4 and 5**. The students can paraphrase from the text or quote directly; it is their ability to select good evidence and start to infer the writer's point of view that is important in these tasks.

* **Activity 5** contains sentence starters to structure the student's response, but encourage students who don't need this structure to answer on paper using only the model for support. On completion of Activity 5, the students should peer-assess, checking that their partner has included all the elements of the SQI model from **PowerPoint slide 5** and that their inference is clear and detailed.

Introducing 19th-century non-fiction: 'Making a Fossil Hunter'

Activity 1:

- Recall five events from the extract 'Making a Fossil Hunter'.
- Compare your list of events with your partner's list. Add any events they remembered that you didn't.
- Finally, listen to others share their events and add any that you missed. Have you got the whole extract covered now?

My five events from the extract	Events from my partner	Events from the group
1.		
2.		
3.		
4.		
5.		

Activity 2:

Explain what the writer is implying about Mary Anning in this statement:

The writer says that Mary Anning was 'more than a mere "fossiler"'.

(Remember: 'fossiler' means a 'fossil-hunter'.)

The writer is implying ....

....

....

Activity 3:

Consider the statement: *The writer describes Mary as an 'enterprising young girl'.*

What does this say about the writer's point of view? Is the writer presenting Mary's work in a positive light?

....

....

....

....

Find two pieces of information from the extract that suggest the writer thinks Mary is good at what she does. Copy them out below.

1. ....

....

....

2. ....

....

....

Activity 5:

Write a short paragraph responding to the statement: *The writer thinks Mary is good at what she does.*

The writer sees Mary as good at fossil-hunting.

Firstly, the writer says ....

....

....

This suggests..

....

....

Secondly, the writer says ....

....

....

This suggests..

....

....

'Sir David Attenborough and a macabre murder mystery in Lyme Regis' by Sarah Marshall

"I was fascinated by fossils and dinosaurs – I still am. I still collect fossils if given the chance."

There are plenty of ammonites and prehistoric jewels to be discovered along Britain's coastlines, and amateur fossil hunters will no doubt be inspired by the latest Attenborough instalment. But what should they be looking out for? Recalling an afternoon spent fruitlessly searching for fossils of crabs in a remote area of northern Queensland, Australia, Attenborough admits it's not easy.

"There was a chap with a sheep station on the coast and he'd say, 'there's one' then hand it to me, 'and here's another'. I thought – what's wrong with me? I can't find anything. It was infuriating. Then suddenly I saw one, and my eye was in. It is indescribable. There are some elements – that glint, some shape – that give you a clue."

However – and wherever – people choose to engage with their environment, Attenborough finds it heartening: "If people don't understand the unity of life, they'll just go along and turn the whole place into a concrete jungle and we'll expire. A child has not yet been born who doesn't find the natural world interesting. If people lose that interest and lose that knowledge, we're heading for real trouble."

———————————

Protecting the environment is a fundamental concern, but anger and protest were never drivers for a young fossil collector fascinated by every element of life on earth. "Look, I would much rather not have to grind an axe about plastic and pollution. I feel a sense of responsibility that I've got to. But given the choice, if everything was all right with the planet, I'd be delighted to just make beautiful programmes of interesting things happening in the natural world. Everyone enjoys that." Although an impassioned conservationist and learned naturalist, Attenborough is, deep down, an entertainer. "The natural world is infinitely varied and infinitely beautiful. Wherever you look there's a new story," he delights, and it becomes obvious why for the past 60-plus years he's never stopped. "If you're bored by nature, what's left?"

From *The Telegraph*, 7 January 2018

Learning objectives:	**Resources:**
• To use the theme of the environment to understand a modern text • To begin to explore how language is used to present thoughts or feelings	• Extract 7.1.5 • 7.1.5 Lesson 1 PowerPoint • 7.1.5 Lesson 1 Worksheet

Getting started

* Display **7.1.5 Lesson 1 PowerPoint slide 2** and use the image of David Attenborough as a tool for inferring. The purpose is to re-engage students with the inference activities they completed last lesson, as well as the theme of nature. Some students may recognise David Attenborough and it may benefit the class for this information to be shared. (Suggested answers: *1. He is happy; he enjoys nature; he feels relaxed and comfortable in nature; he wants to sit down in that landscape. 2. He is happy to have the meerkat on him; he wouldn't harm nature. 3. The meerkat trusts him; he seems happy and relaxed; his posture and pose is relaxed and comfortable.*)

* Display **PowerPoint slide 1** and introduce the learning objective.

* Hand out copies of **Extract 7.1.5** and read it through as a whole class. On first reading, the students should just listen; for a second reading you might want to encourage them to read it themselves. Point out that *The Telegraph* is a newspaper. Ask the students to share what they know about newspapers and what they would expect to see in a newspaper (interview) as an inroad to the text.

Developing skills

* Hand out copies of **7.1.5 Lesson 1 Worksheet** and ask the students to complete **Activity 1** in pairs or individually. It is worth spending some time taking feedback from these questions, in particular questions 3 and 4, with a focus on what the *purpose* of a text means and what students have *inferred*, asking them how and why they have come to the conclusions they have. (Suggested answers: *1. It continues the theme of nature/the natural world; it talks about fossils. 2. It's modern and easier to understand; it's about current topics; it's an interview. 3. To show us how David Attenborough feels about the environment and nature. 4. The writer admires/likes/respects/looks up to David Attenborough.*)

* Display **PowerPoint slide 3**. For this third reading of the extract, encourage the students to either read silently or out loud in pairs or small groups. The aim of the first question is to encourage them to think about the form of a newspaper article and interview, and the fact that there are two different focuses. (Suggested answers: *1. The first part of the interview focuses on a past experience, whereas the second part is about the future and the environment. 2. Yes: dinosaurs and fossils; protecting the environment.*)

* Now direct the students to complete **Worksheet Activity 2**. Prompt them to discuss whether the opening sentence of each section supports their understanding and summary, like a topic sentence. What did they need to do to add information and summarise? Did they pick out the key points or look at the main pieces of information, or did they look at David Attenborough's and the writer's main opinions?

* The students then complete **Worksheet Activity 3**, selecting and copying words and phrases from the text that show what David Attenborough thinks and feels about nature.

Trying it yourself

* Display **PowerPoint slide 4** and talk the students through the SQI method, then display the modelled response on **PowerPoint slide 5**. Using the quotation from the article, encourage the students to select and zoom in on the words that show Attenborough's feelings ('fascinated', 'I still am', 'given the chance'). Then walk the students through the modelled SQI example, referring back to the quotation to help them see how the word 'fascinated' has led the student to infer how strongly Attenborough feels about fossils.

* The students now work through **Worksheet Activity 4** independently. The main aim here is to encourage them to structure their answer. They should use the quotations they have gathered over the lesson. Conclude by asking the students how easy they found it to write the paragraph, and to explain to their neighbour what it means to infer from the text.

Activity 1:

Read **Extract 7.1.5** then note down your answers to the following questions.

1. How do you think this text relates to the other texts you've read in this project?

   ....

   ....

2. What makes this text different to the others?

   ....

   ....

3. What do you think is the purpose of this text?

   ....

   ....

4. The text mainly presents David Attenborough's views. Can you **infer** what the writer thinks about Attenborough?

   ....

   ....

Activity 2:

Write two sentences **summarising** what each section of the text is about.

1. The first section is about ....

   ....

   ....

   ....

2. The second section is about ....

   ....

   ....

   ....

Activity 3:

Using the two sections of the text, complete the spider diagram below, adding words or phrases that give you a sense of what David Attenborough **thinks or feels about nature**.

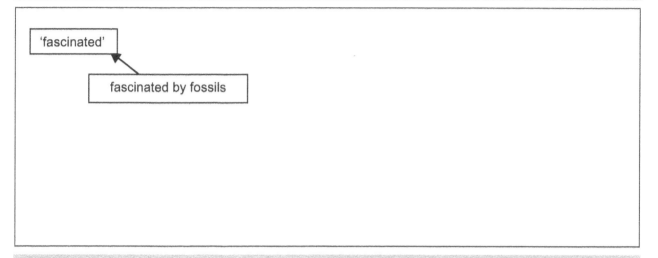

Activity 4:

How does David Attenborough feel about nature?

- Using the quotations you have collected in Activity 3, complete the first paragraph using the sentence prompts.
- If you can, complete a second paragraph without the prompts.

Statement: *David Attenborough feels* ....

....

Quotation: *He says* ....

....

Inference: *This suggests* ....

....

....

Second paragraph: ....

....

....

....

....

....

7.1.5 Lesson 2

Introducing connected modern non-fiction: Exploring connections and themes

Learning objectives:	Resources:
• To explore how the writer shows feelings about nature	• Extract 7.1.5
• To introduce the IEC method (identify, exemplify, comment)	• 7.1.5 Lesson 2 PowerPoint
	• 7.1.5 Lesson 2 Worksheet

Getting started

• Display **7.1.5 Lesson 2 PowerPoint slide 1**. Introduce the learning objectives and ask the students to recall what the text from the previous lesson was about and how the writer and interviewee felt. (*David Attenborough interview about nature; fossils and the environment. Attenborough feels passionate about fossils and nature; both feel strongly about the environment.*)

• Display **PowerPoint slide 2** and ask the students if they know what direct speech is (*words someone else has said*). Work through the discussion points as a whole class or in pairs. (Suggested answers: *1. Text messages; in schoolbooks; lists; homework tasks; emails; in code; students probably write in a different way for each. 2. Most people speak differently to the way they write. 3. Context, place and who you're speaking to change the way you speak. 4. For example, you might raise your voice if you are angry or very happy; you may speak more quietly if you feel sad, shy and nervous.*) You could also prompt the students to consider when they might select specific language to make their feelings clear. Answers may vary from speaking/persuading situations to pieces of writing. Accept all answers as long as the students can explain why they chose the language they did to make their feelings clear.

• Re-read **Extract 7.1.5** together as a whole class or individually.

Developing skills

• Display **PowerPoint slide 3** and work thought the example on the slide as a class. Explain what a rhetorical question is (a question that doesn't require an answer) and ask why David Attenborough might use it here (*he's making a statement with his question, almost daring the reader to suggest there is something boring about nature*). Answer the discussion prompt as a whole class or in pairs. (Suggested answers: *1. If someone could be bored by nature then there's nothing left to offer them. 2. It emphasises the huge value that Attenborough places on nature and how strongly he feels about it.*)

• Hand out copies of **7.1.5 Lesson 2 Worksheet** and ask the students to complete **Activity 1** in pairs or individually. Share answers as a class and ask how and why they reached the interpretations they did. (Suggested answers: *Concrete jungle: never-ending tower blocks and buildings made of concrete that are as large and vast as a jungle. Grind an axe: to express a strong personal opinion about something.*)

• The students now complete **Worksheet Activity 2**. Direct them to use the second section of **Extract 7.1.5**; it might support some students to model the first selection for them. The main aim is to encourage inference. After completing the activity, ask the students to share their ideas.

• Now display **PowerPoint slide 4** and talk through the IEC method. Point out that 'identify the feature' relates to recognising words and phrases, but explain that while it's great to name a feature, as with the rhetorical question on **slide 3**, it's also fine to simply identify it as descriptive language. Remind the students that 'exemplify' refers to a quotation, and that for 'comment' they need to consider what the writer's words make them, as the reader, think, feel or imagine while they read.

Trying it yourself

• Display **PowerPoint slide 5** and discuss the modelled example, referring back to the quotation to help students see how the description of the fossils has led to the comment about what it makes the reader imagine. You could ask them to close their eyes and listen to the quotation and see what comes to mind.

• The students now work through **Worksheet Activity 3** independently. The main aim is to encourage them to structure their answer. Encourage them to use the quotations they have found over the lesson.

• Conclude by asking the students how easy they found the paragraph to write, and to explain to their neighbour what part of the paragraph they found the most challenging. If they can only complete 'Identify' and 'Example' at this point, there will be opportunity to improve 'Comment' in future lessons.

Activity 1:

David Attenborough uses some common **idioms**. These are phrases in common use, such as 'every cloud has a silver lining'.

What do these idioms mean?

- concrete jungle
- grind an axe.

Rewrite them in a way that would be easy to understand.

Concrete jungle: ....

....

....

Grind an axe: ....

....

....

Activity 2:

Using the second section of the text, complete the table below with up to four words or phrases that show what David Attenborough thinks or feels about nature and the environment.

Words or phrases	What they suggest about his thoughts and feelings

How does David Attenborough feel about nature?

- Using the quotations you have collected in this lesson, complete the first paragraph using the sentence prompts.
- If you can, complete a second paragraph without the prompts.

First paragraph:

Identify a feature: *The writer uses* ....

....

Example: *An example of this is* ....

....

Comment: *This makes me think/feel/imagine* ....

....

....

Second paragraph:

....

....

....

....

....

....

....

....

Learning objectives:
- To introduce the elements of discursive writing
- To use some of these elements in a speech
- To plan a persuasive letter
- To consider the elements of discursive writing and introduce the concept of formality and informality

Resources:
- 7.1.6 Lessons 1 & 2 PowerPoint
- 7.1.6 Lessons 1 & 2 Worksheet

Lesson 1: Getting started

- Display **7.1.6 Lessons 1 & 2 PowerPoint slide 1** and introduce the learning objectives. Explain that discursive writing presents an argument; it is non-fiction and usually has more than one point of view. Ask where the students might find non-fiction writing that shares a point of view (*newspapers, speeches, letters, autobiographies*). Ask them to consider the word 'discursive': does it sound similar to or refer to any other word? (*discuss*) What do we do when we 'discuss' something? (*talk about it in detail*)

- Display **PowerPoint slide 2**. Working in pairs, the students come up with short attempt to persuade you of something – if a chocolate bar is inappropriate in your setting, please amend the task. The aim is to get the students to have fun around persuading. Build in time for some or all pairs to present their case.

Developing skills and Trying it yourself

- Display **PowerPoint slide 3** and hand out copies of **7.1.6 Lessons 1 & 2 Worksheet**. Read through the slide then introduce **Activity 1**. Encourage pair work or a whole-group discussion around the difference between *persuade* and *argue*. (Suggested answers: *1. Argue; 2. Persuade; 3. Persuade; 4. Argue.*)

- Display **PowerPoint slide 4** and ask the students to complete **Worksheet Activity 2**. Encourage them to be creative in the way they develop the information. Allow time for the students to cover all ideas.

- Display **PowerPoint slide 5** and ask the students to complete the task in their notebooks. They should collate their ideas into a short speech (or the notes to help them give a speech). Remind them to use the checklist on the slide, to include the devices they've developed so far and to keep their writing concise.

- The students then give their short speech to the class. Keep **PowerPoint slide 5** displayed and use the checklist to offer feedback. This can be peer feedback or self-assessment. This works best if you can choose one pair as being the most persuasive and explain why, or get the class to vote for the most persuasive pair and ask for explanations for their votes.

Lesson 2: Getting started

- Display **PowerPoint slide 1** and revisit the learning objectives for the week. Then display **PowerPoint slide 6** and ask the students to recall their learning from the previous lesson. Move on to introduce the task for this lesson and allow the students some thinking time to choose the topic for their letter. They can work in pairs or individually; encourage them to be imaginative and to adapt the tasks to your setting.

Developing skills and Trying it yourself

- Display **PowerPoint slide 7**. Encourage pair work or a whole group discussion around the difference between the two letter openings. Invite the students to give reasons for their choice and to explore why one is more appropriate. Consider: Who would the informal opening be appropriate for? (*classmates or peers*) When might you be informal? (*when talking to friends, family, classmates or peers, or when it's clear the occasion is suitable*) When should you be formal? (*when you want to be taken seriously; when addressing someone you want to impress or someone you don't know or should show respect to*).

- Display **PowerPoint slide 8**. The writing frame provided as **Worksheet Activity 3** supports this planning task. Encourage the students to be creative in the way they plan and what they include. Allow enough time for them to cover all ideas. They could work in pairs or individually to plan their writing.

- Display **PowerPoint slide 9** and go over the final writing task for the week, which the students complete in their notebooks. They should work alone where possible, to ensure they have some extended writing and are thinking about how to turn a plan and ideas into a response.

Activity 1:

Review scenarios 1–4 below and decide which are intended to:

- persuade (get a reader to agree with you)
- argue (get you to consider both points of view).

1. World Book Day should be about reading not dressing up. ....

2. You should vote for me to be young mayor. ....

3. The students at this school should choose which subjects are taught...

4. Sport is the best hobby a child could have. ....

Activity 2:

Use the space below to make notes about the elements of discursive writing.

1. **Facts:** things that can be proved ....

   ....

   ....

2. **Opinions:** what someone thinks ....

   ....

   ....

3. **Repetition:** saying something more than once ....

   ....

   ....

4. **Emotive language:** language that appeals to people's emotions ....

   ....

   ....

5. **Statistics:** numbers to help prove your thinking ....

   ....

   ....

Activity 3:

Use the writing frame below to plan your letter. What will you include in each part?

Introduction: What you are asking for and why.

....

....

....

....

....

Paragraph 1: The first reason your headteacher should agree.

....

....

....

....

....

Paragraph 2: Address anything that might go against your request (e.g. cost, missing lessons).

....

....

....

....

Conclusion: Remind your headteacher what you want and why they should agree.

....

....

....

....

....

From *The Water Babies* (1863)

Once upon a time there was a little chimney-sweep, and his name was Tom. That is a short name, and you have heard it before, so you will not have much trouble in remembering it. He lived in a great town in the North country, where there were plenty of chimneys to sweep, and plenty of money for Tom to earn and his master to spend.

He could not read nor write, and did not care to do either; and he never washed himself, for there was no water up the court where he lived. He had never been taught to say his prayers. He never had heard of God, or of Christ, except in words which you never have heard, and which it would have been well if he had never heard. He cried half his time, and laughed the other half. He cried when he had to climb the dark flues, rubbing his poor knees and elbows raw; and when the soot got into his eyes, which it did every day in the week; and when his master beat him, which he did every day in the week; and when he had not enough to eat, which happened every day in the week likewise. And he laughed the other half of the day, when he was tossing halfpennies with the other boys, or playing leap-frog over the posts, or bowling stones at the horses' legs as they trotted by, which last was excellent fun, when there was a wall at hand behind which to hide.

As for chimney-sweeping, and being hungry, and being beaten, he took all that for the way of the world, like the rain and snow and thunder, and stood manfully with his back to it till it was over, as his old donkey did to a hailstorm; and then shook his ears and was as jolly as ever; and thought of the fine times coming, when he would be a man, and a master sweep. [...] And he would have apprentices, one, two, three, if he could. How he would bully them, and knock them about, just as his master did to him; and make them carry home the soot sacks, while he rode before them on his donkey, with a pipe in his mouth and a flower in his button-hole, like a king at the head of his army.

Charles Kingsley

Learning objectives:	Resources:
• To understand some of the key ideas in an extract from *The Water Babies* • To present and support those ideas clearly	• Extract 7.2.1 • 7.2.1 Lesson 1 PowerPoint • 7.2.1 Lesson 1 Worksheet

Getting started

• Display **7.2.1 Lesson 1 PowerPoint slide 2** and ask the students to say what they see in the picture. Ask: What could be happening here? Who might the man be? Who might the boy be? What is the relationship between them? What does the boy seem to be carrying? What do you notice about the weather conditions? How does the boy look? Is he happy/sad, etc.? What about the way he is dressed?

• Display **PowerPoint slide 1** and go over the learning objectives for the lesson.

• Give out copies of **Extract 7.2.1**. Read the extract from *The Water Babies* around the class, choosing three or four students to read the passage aloud. Remind the students that this text is set in the 1800s. Ask them what things are different within the text compared to life today. You may need to explain some of the unfamiliar terms or aspects that are not in a student's contemporary frame of reference, such as 'the court where he lived', 'the dark flues', 'leap-frog', 'halfpennies' and 'apprentices'.

• Ask the students to work in pairs looking at **Extract 7.2.1** and working on the 'Exploring' questions on **PowerPoint slide 3**. Allow 10 minutes for the students to work through the five questions and make notes, either on the extract sheet or in their notebooks.

• Take feedback as a whole class. Ideas might include: *1. Fairy stories usually begin this way, although this does not continue like considering how Tom is treated. 2. Tom seems to be quite young, as he still wants to play with the other boys. 3. Probably not – he can't read or write and he works as a chimney sweep rather than going to school. 4. His job seems very difficult and dangerous; you can develop the discussion here by asking the students to imagine the experience and talk about what the job of a chimney sweep entailed. 5. Tom's childhood does not seem happy, though he seems to think his life is normal and just gets on with it.*

Developing skills

• Hand out **7.2.1 Lesson 1 Worksheet** and ask the students to complete **Activity 1** working individually. Allow approximately 5 minutes for this task. Share ideas as a class to check understanding and clarify any misconceptions.

• Using **PowerPoint slide 4**, remind the students that for effective comprehension skills they need to provide evidence or proof of their ideas using supporting quotations from the text. (If you have already worked on Project 7.1 this will be a recap.)

• Now use the modelling on **PowerPoint slide 5** to show a statement in a student's own words, together with a supporting quotation. Spend a moment looking at the way the quotation is embedded and punctuated.

Trying it yourself

• Direct the students to complete **Worksheet Activity 2**. They need to replicate the model using the six statement sentences they gathered for Activity 1. Continue to display the modelling slide (**PowerPoint slide 5**) as a guide.

Activity 1:

Make a list, in your own words, of six things we discover about Tom. Write them in short, clear statement sentences. An example has been done to get you started.

1. *Tom lives in a large and busy town in the north.*

2. ....

3. ....

4. ....

5. ....

6. ....

Activity 2:

Find a supporting quotation for each of the six statement sentences you wrote in Activity 1. You could highlight them on your extract. Write the statements and the supporting quotations below, presenting them with the correct punctuation. Use this model to help you:

Tom seems to live in poor conditions, as we learn that 'he never washed himself, for there was no water up the court where he lived'.

1. ....

....

2. ....

....

3. ....

....

4. ....

....

5. ....

....

6. ....

....

Learning objectives:	Resources:
• To draw inferences from some of the key ideas in an extract from *The Water Babies* • To present those inferences clearly	• Extract 7.2.1 • 7.2.1 Lesson 2 PowerPoint • 7.2.1 Lesson 2 Worksheet

Recap and reflect

• Ask the students to recap on what they did in the previous lesson before re-reading **Extract 7.2.1** with different readers. Take the opportunity to ask the students the meaning of any unfamiliar vocabulary from last time.

• Go over the lesson objectives on **7.2.1 Lesson 2 PowerPoint slide 1**.

• Hand out copies of **7.2.1 Lesson 2 Worksheet** and introduce **Activity 1** by telling the students:
The writer uses an interesting contrasting sentence to describe Tom's life. He says: 'He cried half his time, and laughed the other half.' Then direct the students to work in pairs for 5–10 minutes to complete Activity 1 by selecting and organising into the table the things that might make Tom cry and the things that might make him laugh. Encourage the students to use short, clear statement sentences like those they used in the previous lesson for **7.2.1 Lesson 1 Worksheet Activity 1**.

• Share ideas as a class. Answers might include: *Tom cried: when he had to climb the dark, narrow chimneys; when he skinned his knees and elbows on the rough brickwork; when the soot from the chimneys went into his eyes; when he was beaten every day; when he was hungry. Tom laughed: when he was playing games with the other boys; when he played leap frog; when he was throwing stones and trying to trip up the horses.*

Developing skills

• Display **PowerPoint slide 2**, which looks at the key skill of inference. Explain to the students the importance of this skill using the bullet points on the slide.

• Now return to the students' answers for the retrieval activity (**Worksheet Activity 1**) and begin to draw out some inferences from the points the students collated. Use the suggestions listed on **PowerPoint slide 3** to guide whole-class responses.

• Display **PowerPoint slide 4** and introduce the comprehension task, 'What do we learn about Tom's life as a chimney sweep in Victorian England?' Use the modelled examples on **PowerPoint slides 4 and 5** to break down how to organise the three parts of the SQI response: clear statement sentence; supporting quotation from the text; inference to show understanding. The students now move on to complete the modelled SQI paragraphs in **Worksheet Activity 2**; allow around 10 minutes for this task.

• Display the image of the 'master sweep' on **PowerPoint slide 6**. Invite the students to comment on the impression they have of the master sweep from the image. If possible, capture some of those impressions on the whiteboard. Do those impressions have anything in common with the 'master sweep' Tom describes in the extract? Ask the students to select and highlight two possible quotations from their extract that might back up the ideas they have had about the sweep. Share some of those ideas.

Trying it yourself

• Direct the student to **Worksheet Activity 3**. Allow them 5 minutes to work in pairs to gather some inferences from the quotations and record them alongside the extracts.

• Display **PowerPoint slide 7** and introduce the final task, 'What do we learn about the way child chimney sweeps were treated by their masters?' as a way of bringing together the comprehension skills developed in this lesson. Remind the students of the three key elements of building their answer (statement sentences, supporting quotations, inferences) and expect more than one idea to be used in the response.

Activity 1:

Look back at the passage with your partner and organise the information about Tom into:

- things you think would make him cry
- things you think would make him laugh.

You could use a table like the one below.

Things that might make Tom cry	Things that might make Tom laugh

Activity 2:

What do we learn about Tom's life as a chimney sweep in Victorian England?

- Work together to create two clear statement sentences in response to the question.
- Once you are happy with your sentences, find a supporting quotation to back up each one.
- Finally, add in your inference for each supporting quotation.

1. Statement sentence: ....

   ....

   Quotation: ....

   ....

   Inference: ....

   ....

2. Statement sentence: ....

   ....

   Quotation: ....

   ....

   Inference: ....

   ....

As we read on in the text, we find out more about what it was like to be the 'master sweep'.

- What inferences can you draw from the quotations below? Note down your inferences alongside the quotations.
- Use the following questions to help you.

1. Who do you think the master sweep was? ....

2. Does he pay his sweeps fairly? ....

3. Do you think he treated the child chimney sweeps well or badly?

   ....

4. Do you think Tom's ambition to be a master sweep is a good one? Why? Why not?

   ....

'plenty of money for Tom to earn and his master to spend'

'when his master beat him, which he did every day in the week'

'How he would bully them, and knock them about,
just as his master did to him'

'The Chimney Sweeper', from *Songs of Innocence* (1789)

When my mother died I was very young,
And my father sold me while yet my tongue
Could scarcely cry " 'weep! 'weep! 'weep! 'weep!"
So your chimneys I sweep & in soot I sleep.

There's little Tom Dacre, who cried when his head
That curled like a lamb's back, was shaved, so I said,
"Hush, Tom! never mind it, for when your head's bare,
You know that the soot cannot spoil your white hair."

And so he was quiet, & that very night,
As Tom was a-sleeping he had such a sight!
That thousands of sweepers, Dick, Joe, Ned, & Jack,
Were all of them locked up in coffins of black;

And by came an Angel who had a bright key,
And he opened the coffins & set them all free;
Then down a green plain, leaping, laughing they run,
And wash in a river and shine in the Sun.

Then naked & white, all their bags left behind,
They rise upon clouds, and sport in the wind.
And the Angel told Tom, if he'd be a good boy,
He'd have God for his father & never want joy.

And so Tom awoke; and we rose in the dark
And got with our bags & our brushes to work.
Though the morning was cold, Tom was happy & warm;
So if all do their duty, they need not fear harm.

William Blake

Developing readings of 18th-century poetry: 'The Chimney Sweeper'

Learning objectives:	Resources:
• To understand the key ideas in a poem through exploring structure • To understand the key ideas in a poem through exploring imagery	• Extract 7.2.2 • Extract 7.2.1 • 7.2.2 Lesson 1 PowerPoint • 7.2.2 Lesson 1 Worksheet a • 7.2.2 Lesson 1 Worksheet b

Getting started

• Display **7.2.2 Lesson 1 PowerPoint slide 2** and ask the students what seems to be happening in the picture. Ask: Is this a rich or a poor area? Who might the woman in the picture be? What do you notice about the little boy and the little girl? How do you feel about their expressions? Who do you think the man might be? What is he handing over to the woman? What do you make of the way the neighbours are looking on? What do you notice about the little boy near the cart?

• Then distribute copies of **Extract 7.2.2** and read William Blake's poem 'The Chimney Sweeper' aloud. Explain that the poem is taken from *Songs of Innocence and Experience*, a collection of poetry exploring different sides of life in 19th-century England.

• Display **PowerPoint slide 1** and go over the learning objectives for the lesson.

• Then display **PowerPoint slide 3** and ask the students to work together in pairs to think about the four questions on the slide. They should note down their thoughts and ideas as annotations around the first stanza of the poem.

• Take ideas as feedback from the whole class. Ensure that the students realise that children could be 'sold' into an apprenticeship or job, and that the picture on **PowerPoint slide 2** seems to show this type of transaction taking place. Aim to discuss the level of poverty that might make a parent do this. Do students think the woman is a parent or is she looking after orphans (like Mrs Mann in *Oliver Twist*)?

Developing skills

• Remind the students of the extract from *The Water Babies* they looked at in Week 1 (**Extract 7.2.1**). If the extracts are in their books, ask them to place *The Water Babies* extract side by side with this poem.

• Then display **PowerPoint slide 4**. Working in the same pairs, the students should explore the extract using the four questions on the slide. Students should note that: *the poem is organised into lines not sentences; each section has four lines; the ends of lines rhyme in pairs; there are 24 lines; some of the lines have an equal number of syllables – mainly 11.*

• Follow this up by displaying **PowerPoint slide 5** and handing out copies of **7.2.2 Lesson 1 Worksheet a**. The students might observe that this poem takes the structure of a song or a nursery rhyme and is very simple and child-like (you could remind them that the poem comes from a collection called *Songs of Innocence*). Take any sensible responses as to why the poem might have this simple, child-like structure – for example, to reinforce the innocence of the sweepers and how young some of them were. Ask the students how this makes them feel about the child sweepers. Do they think Blake could have been doing this on purpose? Why?

• Move on to look closely at the section of the poem about Tom's dream, and introduce the idea of imagery using **PowerPoint slide 6**. Re-read the section and ask the whole class for ideas based on the question prompts on the slide. At this stage, take students' initial thoughts and impressions, as the ideas will be explored in more depth in the next lesson (7.2.2 Lesson 2).

Final task

• Hand out copies of **7.2.2 Lesson 1 Worksheet b**, which provides a storyboard template. Ask the students to sketch into the storyboard whatever they see in their mind's eye or imagination when they think about the lines below the boxes. Remind them in conclusion that the images they have created in their storyboards are evidence of them responding to the imagery in the poem, and are an illustration of the 'effect' the poem has had on them.

Developing readings of 18th-century poetry: 'The Chimney Sweeper'

Activity 1:

Read questions 1–4. Working in pairs, look closely at the poem 'The Chimney Sweeper' and then note down your ideas below.

1. What is interesting about the pattern created by the rhyme scheme here?

   ....

   ....

   ....

2. For what reasons might the poet have chosen this pattern? (It didn't happen by accident!)

   ....

   ....

   ....

3. Does this pattern feel familiar? Does it remind you of anything from childhood?

   ....

   ....

   ....

4. Could there be a reason for this too? Make some suggestions.

   ....

   ....

   ....

Final task: Using the template below, create a storyboard of the imagery William Blake creates of Tom's dream.

- Think carefully about what is described in the lines of the poem.
- Use your imagination and what you see in your mind's eye.

Draw sketches to illustrate all of the key lines in the storyboard.

That thousands of sweepers, Dick, Joe, Ned, & Jack, *Were all of them locked up in coffins of black;*	*And by came an Angel who had a bright key,* *And he opened the coffins & set them all free;*
Then down a green plain, leaping, laughing they run, *And wash in a river and shine in the Sun.*	*They rise upon clouds, and sport in the wind.*

Developing readings of 18th-century poetry: 'The Chimney Sweeper'

Learning objectives:	Resources:
• To develop skills of making inferences and supporting ideas • To show developing understanding of key ideas and the writer's intention	• Extract 7.2.2 • 7.2.2 Lesson 1 Worksheet b • 7.2.2 Lesson 2 PowerPoint • 7.2.2 Lesson 2 Worksheet

Getting started

• Re-cap and re-read the poem 'The Chimney Sweeper' from the previous lesson (**Extract 7.2.2**). Ask the students to look back at their storyboards from **7.2.2 Lesson 1 Worksheet b** and, if possible, share some of their ideas. (You could use a visualiser for this if you have one available.)

• Display **PowerPoint slide 1** and the objectives for the lesson, commenting on how 'intention' refers to why a writer might have written a text – what is their 'message' or 'moral'?

Developing skills

• Hand out copies of **7.2.2. Lesson 2 Worksheet**. The students work in small groups to complete **Activity 1**, exploring the lines from the poem and adding their inferential ideas as annotations.

• Ask each group to feed back in turn. Ideas you may want to draw out include: *The scale of the use of child labour in the 19th century ('thousands') – this didn't just affect a small number of children; the use of the short, working-class monosyllabic names to give the boys an identity but with common names – there could have been any number of 'Dick, Joe, Ned, & Jack'; The gruesome image of the chimney as a 'black coffin', suggesting death and that the job could lead to the death of some children from getting stuck, inhaling fumes, etc.; The idea that freedom for some of the children only came with death and that their only escape would be their death and transformation into an 'angel' as they 'rise upon clouds'.*

• Display **7.2.2 Lesson 2 PowerPoint slide 2** and ask the students how this image relates to the couplet from the poem 'And the Angel told Tom, if he'd be a good boy, / He'd have God for his father and never want joy.' Ask: What is Blake implying here about the children who died young as a result of their difficult and dangerous work? Do you think Blake is fine about children being rewarded in 'heaven' for their hard work, or is he trying to make us see how wrong it was that children's lives could be cut short? Ask the students to consider whether William Blake thought this treatment of children was right or wrong. Is he making a point about child labour in his poem? Lead the student responses to see that this poem is a protest against the way child labourers were treated at the time.

• Ask the students to work in pairs on **Worksheet Activity 2**. The students consider the four statement sentences, which begin to form critically evaluative statements, and find a relevant quotation from the poem to support each one. (Suggested answers: *1. 'my father sold me…'weep!''; 2. 'Tom Dacre, who cried when his head…was shaved'; 3. 'thousands of sweepers…coffins of black'; 4. 'He'd have God for his father and never want joy.'*)

Final task

• Display **PowerPoint slide 3** and go over the final task, which encourages the students to show their understanding of the ideas and the interpretation of the text in a creative way. They have to put themselves in the shoes of the poet and write a letter in character. The opening sentence is provided to help the students to make a start. Encourage them to note the formal register of the letter opening. They need to write three or four statement sentences explaining the main ideas from the poem in the first paragraph, then write a second paragraph explaining the contextual intention of the poet. You could frame this for students by asking: Why did Blake write the poem – what did he want his readership to realise about child labour? What is the 'moral' of the little story within the poem?

Activity 1:

- Look back at the images you created on your storyboard of Tom's dream.
- Read the key quotations from 'The Chimney Sweep' below, which use powerful **imagery**.
- Annotate each quotation with the inferences you can draw from them. What does each one suggest or imply about the life of a chimney sweep? (Use the prompt questions to help you.)

That thousands of sweepers, Dick, Joe, Ned, & Jack

(Quote 1 prompt: What is implied about the number of child labourers? Why give them names?)

Were all of them locked up in coffins of black

(Quote 2 prompt: Why use the colour black and the shape of a coffin? What does this remind you of? How dangerous was it to be a chimney sweep?)

And by came an Angel who had a bright key,

And he opened the coffins & set them all free

(Quote 3 prompt: When might someone believe they were going to be visited by an angel? Do you really think Blake means set free here or something more tragic?)

Then down a green plain, leaping, laughing they run,

And wash in a river and shine in the Sun.

(Quote 4 prompt: What is suggested here about the kind of life children should have?)

> Then naked & white, all their bags left behind,
>
> They rise upon clouds, and sport in the wind.

(Quote 5 prompt: What does this suggest the little chimney sweeps might become one day?)

Activity 2:

- With a partner, look at the statements below and discuss whether you agree with them.
- Then find and note down a quotation from the poem that could support each idea.

1. William Blake is angry with parents for selling their children even if they are desperately poor.

....

....

....

2. William Blake is outraged that masters could treat their child sweepers so badly.

....

....

....

3. William Blake is shocked and appalled that innocent children could be forced into labour that might kill them.

....

....

....

4. William Blake disagrees strongly with the Church promising a better life after death, and feels it should be helping children while they are alive.

....

....

....

7.2.3
Lessons 1 & 2

Developing creative writing: Planning creative writing from a picture

Learning objectives:
- To gather ideas from a picture
- To understand how to present the thoughts and feelings of a character
- To plan a piece of creative writing
- To write from a character's perspective or point of view

Resources:
- 7.2.3 Lessons 1 & 2 PowerPoint
- 7.2.3 Lesson 1 Worksheet
- sugar paper and marker pens

Lesson 1: Getting started

- Display **7.2.3 Lessons 1 & 2 PowerPoint slide 2** and ask the students to look closely at the photograph of the young Victorian girl in a factory/mill setting. Then display **PowerPoint slide 3** and invite the students to work in pairs or small groups to respond to the questions on the slide; they should record their ideas and observations in their notebooks. Alternatively, this activity could be used as a whole-group starter. Take feedback, moving between the questions on **slide 3** and the larger image of the girl on **slide 2**. The students' answers here are their own imaginings.

- Display **PowerPoint slide 1** and go over the learning objectives for the lessons.

Developing skills

- Using the task on **PowerPoint slide 4**, invite the students to look more closely at the girl in the photograph on **slide 2** and 'zoom in' on key details. The students can then work together in groups of three or four with marker pens and sugar paper to create an identity for her. Ask them to use the prompt questions on the slide to create a character that is more fleshed out. Allow around 10 minutes of thinking, planning and jotting time. If lesson time allows, ask each group to share their identity ideas.

- Now the students have some ideas about the identity of the girl in the picture, they will be creating a story around the character they have created. Display **PowerPoint slide 5** and introduce the writing task: 'A day in the life of a 19th-century mill girl'. Explain that to present an effective piece of creative writing about their character, the students need to think about how they might organise or structure their writing. You could relate this back to the work the students did on the structure of Blake's 'The Chimney Sweeper' in Week 2, if applicable. Using **slide 5**, show that there are different ways to present a character's experience in prose using a diary form, a third-person narrative and a first-person narrative. Ask the students to point out any differences they notice between the three modelled examples.

- Keeping **PowerPoint slide 5** displayed, use **7.2.3 Lesson 1 Worksheet Activity 1** to support the students in thinking more deeply about the structure of their work. They need to choose which structure to use for their own work (**Worksheet Activity 2**); all three structures could be effective, so there is no right or wrong answer to this task – let the students know the preference is theirs.

- Now display **PowerPoint slide 6** and ask the students to work individually on planning a minimum of three and a maximum of five key ideas for their piece of writing. Each student should already have a clear identity for their character from their group work, and will have chosen their structure. Now they need to create a sequence of ideas to form the outline of their piece. Use the ideas on **slide 6** to help them to get started, and prompt them with further questions: What is the girl doing at the window? What is she thinking about? What things will we find out about her or her life before the mill? How did she come to be working at the mill? How does she feel about her life? What are her hopes and dreams? These individual plans are the desired outcome for Lesson 1.

Lesson 2: Developing skills and Trying it yourself

- Ask the students to recap on their previous work and look closely at their plans from 7.2.3 Lesson 1.

- Using **PowerPoint slide 7**, recap on the term 'imagery' from the lessons in Week 2, and reiterate the use of adjectives as descriptive words. Encourage the students to add clusters of adjectives to their paragraph plan, using the bulleted points on **PowerPoint slide 8** as a guide. Allow 10 minutes for students to complete this vocabulary exercise.

- Display **PowerPoint slide 9** and allow the students 30–40 minutes of quiet writing time for their final piece of work. Allow time at the end for the reflection and self-assessment on **PowerPoint slide 10**.

Developing creative writing: Planning creative writing from a picture

Activity 1: Thinking about structure

Look closely at extracts A, B and C below, then note down your thoughts and responses to the questions.

A. Diary entry

> *5:30 a.m.: I was so tired when I woke up this morning and the room was so cold...*

B. Third-person narrative

> *Agnes stared out of the huge windows to the beautiful river and the lovely trees outside in the summer sun.*

C. First-person narrative

> *Today I would give anything to be outside in the lovely spring sunshine. Instead, here I am...*

1. Which of the extracts should be organised into paragraphs? ....

2. Which could be organised into sections by different times? ....

3. Which might allow you to use more description? ....

4. Which would allow you to show the girl's personal views and experiences? ....

   ....

5. Which would show the girl in the past and which in the present? ....

   ....

Activity 2: Conclusion

Which structure do you think would be most effective to use for the task 'A day in the life of a 19th-century mill girl'? (You may have different opinions on the answer.)

....

....

From 'Transcript of the Examination of Thomas Priestley'

I am 13 years of age, I have no father, he has been dead for more than 2 years, he was one of the Turnkeys at Newgate. I have been informed that for about 5 years since I was taken to Hackney Workhouse. I was there about 2 years and then I consented before the Magistrate at Worship Street Office to go as apprentice to the Cotton Manufactory of Samuel Greg, which is situated at Styal in Cheshire. I was bound with others from this office and went to the said cotton manufactory; when we came there, we were, after a day's rest, set to work, I was the same as the others to attend 2 machines for spinning cotton, each of which spun about 50 threads, my business was to supply these machines, to guide the thread occasionally and to twist them when they snapt, and I soon became perfect in these operations, also learned to take the machinery to pieces and apply the oil, a matter that required some care. In this manner I have been employed all the while that I have been in the cotton manufactory of Mr Greg aforesaid – during the time working, and there was a great deal of cotton in the machine, one of the wheels caught my finger and tore it off, it was the forefinger of my left hand. I was attended by the surgeon of the factory Mr Holland and in about 6 weeks I recovered.

We slept in long rooms, the girls on one side of the house and the boys on the other. There were a good many beds in each room and we had clean sheets oftener than once a month, our blankets and rugs were perfectly clean. The floors of the rooms were kept very clean, the rooms were whitewashed once a year, and were aired every day, we had clean shirts every Sunday, and new clothes when we wanted them. Our diet consisted of the following articles, with porridge for breakfast and supper throughout the week, we had plenty of it and brown bread with it.

Our working hours were from 6am in summer and winter until 7 in the evening. We had only ten minutes allowed for our breakfasts, which were always brought up to the mill for us and we worked that up at night again – 2 days in the week we had an hour allowed us for dinner, while the machines were oiled, for doing this I was paid a halfpenny a time, and other days we were allowed half an hour for dinner, when the boys worked overtime, they were paid 1d per hour.

2 August 1806

7.2.4 Lesson 1	Developing ideas from 19th-century non-fiction: 'Transcript of the Examination of Thomas Priestley'

Learning objectives:	Resources:
• To understand the ideas in an extract of 19th-century non-fiction • To present and support those ideas clearly	• Extract 7.2.4 • 7.2.4 Lesson 1 PowerPoint • 7.2.4 Lesson 1 Worksheet

Getting started

- Hand out copies of **Extract 7.2.4**, explaining to the students that a transcript is a record of what someone has said, but in writing – like an interview. Explain that here, Thomas Priestley, a young boy, is interviewed about his life and experiences working as an apprentice in a cotton mill in Cheshire. Read aloud Thomas's account.

- Display **PowerPoint slide 1** and go over the learning objectives for the lesson.

- Now display **7.2.4 Lesson 1 PowerPoint slide 2** and ask the students to work in pairs or small groups to consider the questions on the slide, to gather their initial ideas and ensure their basic understanding. This could also be done as a whole-class starter activity with you guiding the questions.

- Take feedback on the questions, making sure the students understand what the workhouse was and why people would have to go there (i.e. if they were in abject poverty with nowhere else to turn). It is also important to define what an apprentice was in Thomas's time, and to ensure that the students understand that children could be 'bound' to an apprentice agreement for many years.

- Display **PowerPoint slide 3** and use the information and questions on the slide to flesh out students' understanding and perception of the context here. Many students will not realise that cars or trains were not in use in 1806. Ensure the students understand that children were widely employed in factories as cheap labour.

Developing skills

- Using **PowerPoint slide 4**, ask the students to focus on the photograph – which looks quite pleasant – and to complete the mind-mapping activity on the slide. Prompt the students to consider things like the greenery, fresh air and blue skies after living in London, a big city. Allow 5 minutes for this task.

- Then display **PowerPoint slide 5**, which shows a contrasting image of the inside of the mill. Encourage the students to use their senses and complete a second mind map, again allowing 5 minutes for the task. Prompt them to look at the space between the machines and to think about the sound and speed of those machines at work. What dangers can they foresee?

- Now continue this exploration using **7.2.4 Lesson 1 Worksheet Activity 1**. Take feedback from individual students following the listing exercise.

- Display **PowerPoint slide 6** and recap with the students what an inference is. It may be useful to remind them of their work in Week 1 on *The Water Babies*. Explain to them how their work so far in the lesson has all been 'inferential', or deduced by reading between the lines of the text.

- Use the modelling on **PowerPoint slide 7** to recap and remind the students of the core method for answering comprehension tasks, pointing out the three elements (clear statement sentence; supporting quotation from the text; an inference that shows understanding). Explain to them that the inference should not simply be a repetition of the statement but should show the development of their thought. The statement could be factual; the inference is something deduced. Also point out that the statement and inference should not simply paraphrase their chosen quotation, as this does not demonstrate their own understanding.

Trying it yourself

- The students now to complete the final task, which is detailed on the worksheet (**Worksheet Activity 2**), showing all their comprehension skills in response to the task about Thomas's experiences.

7.2.4 Lesson 1 Worksheet — Developing ideas from 19th-century non-fiction

Activity 1:

Look closely at the photographs of Styal Mill below.

Imagine you are an apprentice like Thomas, on your first day at the mill. List as many words as you can that might describe your first impressions of:

- what you can see in the mill
- what you can hear in the mill
- what your own personal feelings might be.

....

....

....

....

Activity 2:

What do you understand about Thomas's experience of coming to work at Styal Mill in the 19th century?

Answer this question using all of your comprehension skills. Remember to:

- present two or three clear statement sentences to answer the task
- select two or three snippets from the text to use as supporting quotations
- add in some of your inferences from your mind-mapping activity, to show your understanding of Thomas's experiences. You could begin these with:
  This implies that...   This suggests that...   This tells us that...
- make sure your inference is not just repeating your statement or your quotation – the inference should be in your own words and show what you understand.

Learning objectives:
- To understand the ideas in an extract of 19th-century non-fiction
- To present and support those ideas clearly
- To begin to comment on the experiences of others in the past

Resources:
- Extract 7.2.4
- 7.2.4 Lesson 2 PowerPoint
- 7.2.4 Lesson 2 Worksheet

Getting started

- Recap on the previous lesson's work. You could use this opportunity for students to peer-assess the comprehension work from the previous lesson by looking at each other's SQI (statement + quotation + inference) constructs. Ask the students to identify in the margin where their peers have managed to use all three skills and label the answers with the skills where they see them.

- Display **PowerPoint slide 1** and go over the learning objectives for the lesson, then ask the students to re-read **Extract 7.2.4**.

Developing skills

- Encourage the students to further develop their understanding of the extract by focusing on the details of Thomas's day. They could work in pairs to locate and select the information from the extract about his daily schedule. Allow 15 minutes for students to do this, using **7.2.4 Lesson 2 Worksheet** to create a timeline. Ask the students to consider what the apprentices might have had to do between 7:30 p.m. and bedtime. Take class feedback on all possible ideas and ask the students to self-mark where appropriate.

- Display **PowerPoint slide 2**. Ask the students to skim through the text again and work on identifying any positive aspects of Thomas's experience. Ask: How might the mill have been a better experience in some ways than the workhouse? The students might be encouraged to think about the regular meals, the clean laundry and beds, and the wages (though small). It might also be useful to point out that apprentices were given a rudimentary education and link this to the 7:30 p.m. bedtime slot.

- Encourage the students to create a clear list of statement sentences in their notebooks in preparation for the final task.

Trying it yourself

- Display **PowerPoint slide 3** and go over the final task: *What do you understand about life as an apprentice in a mill in the 19th century? Explain whether you think life for the apprentices was good or bad, or a mixture of both.*

- Encourage the students to write a longer comprehension response using at least three different ideas in response to the question. Recap on the skills of the SQI (statement + quotation + inference) method using the bullet points on the slide. Ask the students to evaluate and make a decision as to whether the experience was good, bad or a mixture of both; this should be reflected in the points they make in their response.

Activity 1: Thomas's day

Using the information that Thomas gives you and your own ideas, what do you imagine a typical day for Thomas might have been like?

Complete the daily schedule below.

5:30 a.m.: *Get up and get washed and dressed in work clothes. Walk over to the mill.* ....

....

6:00 a.m.: ....

....

8:00 a.m.: ....

....

8:10 a.m.: ....

....

5:00 p.m.: ....

....

7:00 p.m.: ....

....

7:30–9.30 p.m.: ....

....

9:30 p.m.: ....

....

'Child labour "rampant" in Bangladesh factories', by Michael Safi

Most mornings, 15-year-old Iqbal arrives for his job at a Dhaka panel beaters at about 10 a.m., working on cars for up to 13 hours before he can go home. The teenager, who earns less than £60 a week, has been working these hours since the age of 12, when his family's financial problems forced him out of school and into a full-time job.

A major study suggests his case might be typical of Bangladesh's poorest young people. A survey of 2,700 slum households, carried out by the Overseas Development Institute, found that child labourers living in slums worked an average of 64 hours each week – many in supply chains connected to the world's most popular brands.

The survey [...], found 15% of children aged between six and 14 did not go to school and worked full-time. Two-thirds of girls from slum areas who were working full-time were employed in Bangladesh's $30 bn (£24 bn) clothes manufacturing industry, which is one of the world's largest despite an extremely poor safety record.

The manager of one unnamed garment factory told researchers that, while he was aware children aged 11 and 14 should not be working, he did not think of their employment as illegal. He also admitted that many of his employees did not carry identification cards that would verify their age.

[...] The extent of child labour in Bangladesh's textile industry was laid bare in July when a nine-year-old boy was brutally killed at one of the largest spinning factories. Police probing the case said they found a quarter of the workforce at the factory outside Dhaka were children. [...] The chief executive of Save the Children, Kevin Watkins [...] said: 'There are very significant levels of child labour in products that end up in shops in the UK and elsewhere.'

The study also found that more than 36% of boys and 34% of girls said they had experienced 'extreme fatigue' on the job. It said that families were usually keen for their children to remain in school, but were unable to afford to live without the extra income, albeit meagre.

From *The Guardian*, 7 December 2016

Developing connections with modern non-fiction

Learning objectives:	Resources:
• To understand and make connections between child labour in the 19th century and today • To use developing comprehension skills to understand key ideas in a broadsheet article	• Extract 7.2.5 • 7.2.5 Lesson 1 PowerPoint • 7.2.5 Lesson 1 Worksheet • sugar paper and marker pens

Getting started

* As a whole group starter, ask the students to consider the statistic on **7.2.5 Lesson 1 PowerPoint slide 2**: there could be up to 168 million children still employed as child labourers today. Can they visualise that number? Ask them to compare that to the number of people in a typical school assembly and then a football stadium. Take points from the class as to how they feel about that and how life might be for other children around the world. Relate the idea of child labour still being a problem, even though we assume it's something that happened long ago – such as in the texts and images from the 19th century that students studied in weeks 1–4 (*The Water Babies* by Charles Kingsley, 'The Chimney Sweeper' by William Blake, the image of the mill girl, and the apprentice's account of life at Styal Mill).

* Display **PowerPoint slide 1** and go over the learning objectives for the lesson.

Developing skills

* Organise the class into groups of three or four. Give out copies of **7.2.5 Lesson 1 Worksheet** and show the students the images on **PowerPoint slides 3**, **4** and **5**. Pause to point out some of the details on each slide before asking the students to work in their groups to answer **Worksheet Activity 1**. Groups could collate their ideas on sugar paper with marker pens. Allow approximately 10 minutes for the students to complete this task.

* Take feedback from the groups in turn, perhaps asking one group to focus on one question from Activity 1 and so on. Ensure that students understand key ideas such as: the fact the jobs are all difficult – either manual labour or using machinery; the jobs seem very dangerous; the children have no safety equipment; the children are often dirty and in poor clothing, and look tired or sad and depressed; the labourers are both boys and girls, and seem to range from extremely young children to teenagers; there seem to be no adults supervising the children. Encourage the students to make links in question 4 with the hard, tiring, dangerous work described in weeks 1–4 and the unhappiness the children were experiencing then. In terms of differences, the students should note the geographical differences and, of course, that these images are from the present day.

* Now give out copies of **Extract 7.2.5**. Read the extract aloud to the class, making links between the ideas the students have just come up with and the facts in the article. Explain that *The Guardian* newspaper article is a report into children from poor households working in factories overseas.

* Ask the students to read the opening of the extract again and to work individually on **Worksheet Activity 2**. You may wish to check that the students are presenting the answers in sentences and that they have identified four key facts about Iqbal and noted that a 64-hour working week means children would be working at least nine hours each day if they did not have a day off.

Trying it yourself

* Briefly recap with students the SQI (statement + quotation + inference) comprehension method they worked on in weeks 1–4.

* Display **PowerPoint slide 6** and allow the students the remaining lesson time to complete the four more difficult comprehension tasks in their notebooks using the SQI method.

* If time allows, you could share some of the students' ideas and inferences at the end of the lesson.

Activity 1:

In small groups, explore the following images, which are also shown on **PowerPoint slides 3, 4** and **5**. Then think about the following questions and note down:

- your thoughts and feelings
- what you can infer from the images.

1. What type of work is being done in each of the images? How might it feel to do those jobs every day?

   ....

   ....

   ....

2. How do you think the children in the images are feeling? What might they be thinking? What do you think their lives are like?

   ....

   ....

   ....

3. What shocks or surprises you most about the images? Is it the fact the children are working? Is it the type of work they are doing? Is it their ages? Is it the looks on their faces?

....

....

....

4. What do these photographs remind you of? Can you see any similarities between the experiences of the children here and the children you have read about in previous lessons? What are some of the main differences between these children and the ones you have thought about in your previous lessons?

....

....

....

Activity 2: Exploring and understanding the ideas in the article

Present your answers to the following questions in short, clear statement sentences.

1. What do you learn about Iqbal in the opening paragraph of the article? Select four different things that you find out.

....

....

....

....

2. How many hours do children work on average in the poorest areas of Bangladesh? How many hours each day does this suggest children may be working?

....

....

....

Learning objectives:	Resources:
• To understand key aspects of language in a news article • To think about the effects of language in a non-fiction text	• Extract 7.2.5 • 7.2.5 Lesson 2 PowerPoint • 7.2.5 Lesson 2 Worksheet • sugar paper and marker pens

Recap and reflection

- Ask the students to look back at their work from the previous lesson and to re-read *The Guardian* article on child labour in Bangladesh factories (**Extract 7.2.5**).

- Then, using **7.2.5 Lesson 2 PowerPoint slide 2**, ask the students whether they feel the article agrees or disagrees with child labour. Take a few suggestions and encourage the students to say why.

- Display **PowerPoint slide 1** and go over the learning objectives for the lesson.

Developing skills

- Using **PowerPoint slide 3**, explore with the students some of the key techniques that are used, not just in this article but often in writing that expresses a point of view. Explain that these techniques can be used in articles, speeches, charity campaigns, etc., to help get readers on side.

- Hand out copies of **7.2.5 Lesson 2 Worksheet** and work through the definitions of the key terms. Then ask the students to work in pairs to complete **Activity 1** by exploring the article, finding two examples of each of the first three techniques and adding them on the worksheet. Allow 5–10 minutes for this task then take feedback from around the room so the students can mark their own responses.

- Now look again at the definition for 'emotive phrases' on the worksheet. Ask the students what the word 'emotive' reminds them of (*emotions*). Use **PowerPoint slide 4** to fully define the term.

- The students now work in pairs or small groups to complete the task on **PowerPoint slide 4**. They can write their responses in their notebooks or, if in groups, on sugar paper with marker pens. Ask the students to write the emotive phrase in the centre and mind map everything that the phrase makes them think of, see in their mind's eye, imagine or feel. Allow approximately 10–15 minutes to allow students to think about all five phrases, monitoring the time and moving students on to the next phrase after 2 or 3 minutes. Share ideas from around the class for each phrase.

- Now use **PowerPoint slide 5** to model to the students how to write up analytical points about language. Explain that the ideas connected to their thoughts and feelings are the *effect* the language has on them – their response to that phrase or technique as a reader. Talk the students through the method here: an aspect of language has been identified (emotive language), an example has been given ('living in slums') and a comment has been made that encompasses the student's thoughts and feelings and what they imagine. In this way each student can build a sensible and clear comment on effect.

Trying it yourself

- Now display **PowerPoint slide 6** and move on to the final task, which asks the students to write up their thoughts and ideas following their analysis of the remaining four emotive phrases (phrases 2–5 on **PowerPoint slide 4**). In this instance, the students could make a comment on effect that shows what they think of, feel or imagine, but encourage them to add more than one idea to their comment to show their development of thought. The students can use the model on **PowerPoint slide 5** to help them organise their ideas.

Developing connections with modern non-fiction

Definitions of key techniques:

*   *Factual information*: Information in a text that is definitely true and can be proved. This helps to convince a reader that what they are reading is reliable.

*   *Shocking statistics*: Things that use a number or a percentage to show the scale of something. Statistics can be used to make a situation seem more shocking to a reader.

*   *Quotations from real people*: Things that someone has really said. These often come from eyewitnesses to an event or experts in the subject. They help to make the point of view in an article more convincing.

*   *Emotive phrases:* phrases in a text that makes you feel a particular emotion to get you on side and to encourage you to share the point of view of the writer.

Activity 1:

Re-read **Extract 7.2.5** and identify two examples of each of the following techniques.

1. Factual information:

    a) ....

    ....

    b) ....

    ....

2. Shocking statistics:

    a) ....

    ....

    b) ....

    ....

3. Quotations from real people:

    a) ....

    ....

    b) ....

    ....

Learning objectives:
- To understand more key techniques for persuasion
- To plan for an effective speech presenting a point of view
- To write and present an effective speech presenting a point of view

Resources:
- 7.2.6 Lessons 1 & 2 PowerPoint
- 7.2.6 Lesson 1 Worksheet a
- 7.2.6 Lesson 1 Worksheet b
- sugar paper and marker pens

Lesson 1: Recap and reflection

- Organise the class into pairs. Display **7.2.6 Lessons 1 & 2 PowerPoint slide 2** and ask the students if they can define the terms from the previous lesson: factual information, shocking statistics, quotations from real people and emotive language. Remind the students that these are persuasive tools used frequently when presenting a point of view, but they are not the only ones.

- Display **PowerPoint slide 1** and go over the learning objectives for the lessons.

- Display **PowerPoint slide 3** and read the text from the anti-slavery website aloud. Ask the students if they can see any of the techniques from the previous lesson. They may spot the quotation from a real person and examples of emotive language.

Developing skills

- Organise the class into small groups. Hand out copies of **7.2.6 Lesson 1 Worksheet a**, which provides the students with a copy of the charity web page from **PowerPoint slide 3**. Then, using **PowerPoint slide 4**, explain four more key persuasive techniques that writers use for effect to present a point of view: commands, direct address, repetition and presenting a solution.

- Allow students 20 minutes to work in groups to answer the five exploratory questions on **Worksheet a**. Leave the definitions on **PowerPoint slide 4** displayed while they work. The students should record all their findings in their notebooks or on sugar paper. Move around the groups to facilitate.

- Allow some time for the students to feed back on these key exploratory questions. (Suggested answers: *1. It makes readers put themselves in the position of the enslaved person/creates empathy; 2. The quotation brings home the fact this is really happening to young individuals / adds credibility; 3. Each one seems to designed to make us see the different experiences of others in our mind's eye and make us think about the different ways people are being badly treated or exploited; 4. Direct address reiterates the point made in question 1; it makes the reader empathise/consider their own life by comparison and is particularly effective with the references to young children, as readers remember their own childhood; 5. There are a number of emotive phrases: '17 hours a day', 'kept isolated', 'exploited and abused', 'stifling heat', 'no shade from the sun', 'dust in your eyes', 'hands blistered', '8 years old'*).

- Now present the students with the final speech-writing task using **PowerPoint slide 5**.

- Hand out copies of **7.2.6 Lesson 1 Worksheet b**. Using the worksheet and the information on **PowerPoint slide 6**, allow the students 15–20 minutes of planning time for their speech.

Lesson 2: Getting started

- Ask the students to recap on their previous work and look closely at their plans from Lesson 1. Refer them to **PowerPoint slide 6** to ensure they have covered all these aspects in their plans.

- Students could work in pairs for 5 minutes to check their partner's plan and make additional suggestions.

Trying it yourself

- Allow the students approximately 30 minutes of quiet writing time for their speech.

- A fun way to conclude and assess this aspect of the project is to set up a mock UN Conference. Organise desks into a horseshoe shape and create a space at the front for each speaker. Ask for student volunteers to present their speeches to mock UN delegates, whose job is to decide at the end of the session whose speeches were most persuasive and whose solutions could be most viable.

Activity:

Re-read the web page and then answer the questions below in your groups.

---

anti-slavery   Slavery today   What we do   Our impact   Take action

Imagine...

"I was working for about 17 hours each day. I had to work for several months without pay, and I had no way of communicating with my parents."

Sophia, 16, exploited while working in a private home in Tanzania.

Imagine leaving your family home, like Sophia did, to travel to another city and stay in a stranger's home to work all day. Imagine you were kept isolated from the outside world, exploited and abused. This is the reality for children forced into domestic work in Tanzania.

Imagine yourself in stifling heat, with no shade from the sun, dust in your eyes and blocking your throat, your hands blistered from molding bricks for hours every day. Now imagine you are only 8 years old. This is the reality for children working in India's brick kilns.

Or imagine, if you can, growing up in a place where your family and your whole community are treated as slaves by traditional masters. This is the reality for children from communities of slave descent in Niger.

It is very difficult to imagine ourselves in situations like this – but it is easy to do something to help. You can help a child in slavery by donating today.

© www.antislavery.org

1. Look at the opening command to 'Imagine'. What does that make the reader do straight away? Why might this be a good way of getting the reader's attention?

2. What does the quotation from a real person – in this case Sophia – make you realise? What is her life like? How do you feel about this?

3. Look at the sentences that begin with the word 'imagine'. Why are there five sentences that begin in this way? What does repeating the word 'imagine', but using different people's experiences, help the reader to see?

4. Why does the web page use the words 'you' and 'your' so much? What do you think the charity here is trying to get you to do?

5. What examples of emotive phrases can you find on the web page? Which is the most emotive for you as a group? Decide why and note down everything it makes you all think of, feel or imagine.

Developing persuasive writing skills: Planning a short speech

Activity:

- You have all been asked to make a short speech at a United Nations Children's Conference, giving your point of view on child labour today.

- If the speeches are convincing enough, the governments of UN countries will work together to end child labour and help all children into education.

- Complete the planning grid below with your ideas for your speech.

Who will hear my speech? Should I be formal or informal?	
First line for impact: (How will I get everyone's attention straightaway?)	
Persuasive idea 1: Key technique to include:	
Persuasive idea 2: Key technique to include:	
Persuasive idea 3: Key technique to include:	
What is my idea for a possible solution? What will be my request to my listeners?	

From *Around the World in 80 Days* (1872)

Passepartout, on waking and looking out, could not realise that he was actually crossing India in a railway train. The locomotive, guided by an English engineer and fed with English coal, threw out its smoke upon cotton, coffee, nutmeg, clove and pepper plantations, while the steam curled in spirals around groups of palm-trees, in the midst of which were seen picturesque bungalows, viharis (sort of abandoned monasteries), and marvellous templates enriched by the exhaustless ornamentation of Indian architecture. Then they came upon vast tracts extending to the horizon, with jungles inhabited by snakes and tigers, which fled at the noise of the train; succeeded by forests penetrated by the railway, and still haunted by elephants which, with pensive eyes, gazed at the train as it passed.

At half-past twelve the train stopped at Burhampoor where Passepartout, was able to purchase some Indian slippers, ornamented with false pearls. The travellers made a hasty breakfast and started off for Assurghur, after skirting for a little the banks of the small river Tapty, which empties into the Gulf of Cambray, near Surat.

The train stopped at eight o'clock, in the midst of a glade some fifteen miles beyond Rothal, where there were several bungalows, and workmen's cabins. The conductor, passing along the carriages, shouted, "Passengers will get out here!"

Phileas Fogg looked at Sir Francis Cromarty for an explanation; but the general could not tell what meant a halt in the midst of this forest of dates and acacias.

Passepartout, not less surprised, rushed out and speedily returned, crying, "Monsieur, no more railway!"

Jules Verne

Learning objectives:	Resources:
• To be able to retrieve basic ideas/information from a prose text and make statements • To be able to support statements with embedded quotations	• Extract 7.3.1 • 7.3.1 Lesson 1 PowerPoint • 7.3.1 Lesson 1 Worksheet

Getting started

- Project **7.3.1 Lesson 1 PowerPoint slide 2** and ask the students where the place in the picture might be and how they know. Use the prompts on the slide to guide discussion. Further questions could include: What is suggested by the vibrant colours? How many people might live here? What does this suggest about life in this area? Steer the discussion towards suggestions as to where it could be.

- Show the lesson objectives on **PowerPoint slide 1**. Ensure the students understand the difference between retrieving and inferring information from a text – retrieval is the starting point to understanding a text and will often be factual, whereas inference will go beyond the literal information provided, 'reading between the lines'. To infer, students need to interpret clues and these will be subtler than the facts. (You could refer the students back to Projects 7.1 and 7.2, where these skills were introduced.)

- Give out copies of **Extract 7.3.1** and read it together as a class. Identify the foreign place names (Rothal, Burhampoor, etc.) and character names (Passepartout, Fogg, Sir Francis Cromarty). Focusing on the first paragraph, ask the students how India is described. (Possible answers: *Plantation crops such as coffee and palm suggest a hot climate; Vihari is an Asian word; monasteries suggests a religious nation; jungle, snakes, tigers, elephants indicates Africa or Asia; Indian architecture is mentioned.*)

- Now ask pairs to work on the 'Exploring together' questions on **PowerPoint slide 3**. Ideas to discuss during feedback might include: *1. There are three sentences. 2. 19, 59, 48. (Note that students would never be asked to count sentences or words in an exam, but it is useful here as a stepping stone to recognising and analysing structure.) 3. Long sentences create the rhythm of the train on the tracks; this suggests a long, fast journey without stopping. 4. It suggests many sights that pass quickly by.*

Developing skills

- Hand out copies of **7.3.1 Lesson 1 Worksheet** and ask the students to complete **Activity 1** individually. Allow 5–10 minutes for this task, including a chance to check their answers with a partner. The students should select: *1. Plantations – cotton, coffee, nutmeg, clove, pepper. 2. Buildings – bungalows, viharis (abandoned monasteries), ornamental architecture. 3. Jungle – snakes, tigers, elephants.*

- Now display **PowerPoint slide 4** and talk together about how using embedded quotations is sophisticated and allows the writing to flow naturally.

- Display **PowerPoint slide 5** to model this key skill. Discuss which student version on the slide sounds most natural and why. The students need to see how the words of the quotation form part of the student's own sentence. Common errors to look out for are: students repeating the quotation in their own sentence; the grammar of their own sentence not fitting with the grammar of the quotation (for example, writing 'The train is "threw out its smoke".') Establish that the students may have to change the structure of their sentence (tense/viewpoint, etc.) to ensure the embedded quotation flows.

Trying it yourself

- The students now complete **Worksheet Activity 2** by embedding quotations in their responses, using the information from the chart they completed for Activity 1. Take feedback from some of the students to check progress and understanding. They can be supported by working in pairs and highlighting the information they are going to use in the text. Students could begin by writing a sentence that gives the evidence in their own words before changing it to a quotation. Alternatively, they could start the other way around by first writing the quotation in quotation marks and then adding their own words around it.

- Share successful examples after 10 minutes working, to support any students who are struggling.

Securing supported comprehension of the 19th-century novel

Activity 1:

Fill in the chart below with what can be seen from the window of the train.

1. On the plantations	2. The buildings	3. In the jungle

Activity 2:

What do you learn about the view from the train in the first paragraph of the extract?

Write three answers with an embedded quotation in each, to show what can be seen:

1. on the plantation   2. of the buildings   3. in the jungle.

1. ....

....

....

....

2. ....

....

....

....

3. ....

....

....

....

Learning objectives:	Resources:
• To make secure inferences from reading • To use the SQI method (statement + quotation + inference) confidently	• Extract 7.3.1 • 7.3.1 Lesson 2 PowerPoint • 7.3.1 Lesson 2 Worksheet

Recap and reflection

• Project **7.3.1 Lesson 2 PowerPoint slide 2**. Ask the students how they can tell the train in the picture is older (*size of carriages, open windows and doors, decoration*), powered by steam (*no evidence of electricity; age and appearance*) and what it would be like to travel on (*noisy, breezy, danger of falling out, exciting, picturesque views, smell of steam*).

• Re-read **Extract 7.3.1** from the previous lesson and discuss the following questions as a class: What would you smell/see/hear/feel on a journey like that in the picture/extract? How would it differ from a modern train journey? What problems could a steam train have? (Suggested answers: *You would smell steam, see the landscape, hear the steam engine, feel the rhythmic movement; the main differences are the steam power and the bumpy ride; problems might include noise, running out of coal, fire risk, pollution, smell, dirt.*)

• Display **PowerPoint slide 1** and discuss the lesson objectives. Recap on the differences between retrieval and inference from 7.3.1 Lesson 1, and explain the SQI (statement + quotation + inference) method. Remind the students that inference interprets and adds information to the quotation rather than just repeating it or explaining its meaning.

Developing skills

• Hand out copies of **7.3.1 Lesson 2 Worksheet** and ask the students to complete **Activity 1** by explaining inference. The students could use dictionaries or be given examples such as, 'if I arrive wet with a broken umbrella, what might you think?'

• The students then complete **Activity 2** on the worksheet by matching the textual inferences with the correct evidence. (Answers: *inference a – 2; b – 6; c – 4; d – 1; e – 3; f – 5.*)

Trying it yourself

• Remind the students of inference, then ask them what in the extract suggests that the train journey is exciting and dangerous. (Suggested answer: *The wild animals are scared away by the approaching train, suggesting the characters would be endangered if the train stopped near the jungle; there is an unexpected stop but no actual train station: the danger is inferred.*)

• Now display the SQI model on **PowerPoint slide 3**, in response to the question, 'How does the writer suggest the train journey is dangerous?'

• Continue by displaying **PowerPoint slide 4**, to stretch the students by reminding them how they embedded quotations in the previous lesson.

• Ask pairs to use this model to write one SQI paragraph in their notebooks, showing how the writer suggests the journey is long. They could use evidence of the train having travelled through the night, or references to time. To stretch those working at a higher level, encourage them to embed quotations or write individually. Take feedback from the students to check understanding. Support them by sharing good examples, providing sentence starters and highlighting information in the text.

Final task

• Display **PowerPoint slide 5** and ask the students to work independently in their notebooks for the final task. They should use their completed inference and evidence table from the worksheet as well as the paragraph they just completed in pairs. You can support students by sharing good practice, writing an opening together, and writing SQI in their margin to structure their response.

Jules Verne gives lots of information in the text without actually stating it, so the reader has to make **inferences**. For example, if your teacher arrived dripping wet with a broken umbrella, you might **infer** that it is raining outside.

Activity 1:

Write down an explanation of inference below.

Inference means ....

....

....

Activity 2:

Match up the inference in the left column with the correct evidence from **Extract 7.3.1** in the right column. Draw a line to show where they match.

Inference	Evidence from Extract 7.3.1
a) The train passes where wild animals live.	1. 'Passepartout, on waking and looking out...'
b) The railway track is still under construction.	2. 'Jungles inhabited by snakes and tigers, which fled at the noise of the train.'
c) The train driver was in a hurry to reach his destination.	3. 'The general could not tell what meant a halt in the midst of this forest of dates and acacias.'
d) The passengers had been travelling through the night.	4. 'The travellers made a hasty breakfast.'
e) The train had not stopped at a station.	5. 'Phileas Fogg looked at Sir Francis Cromarty for an explanation.'
f) It was a surprise when the train stopped, as it was not scheduled.	6. 'workmen's cabins'

'From a Railway Carriage' (1885)

Faster than fairies, faster than witches,

Bridges and houses, hedges and ditches;

And charging along like troops in a battle

All through the meadows the horses and cattle:

All of the sights of the hill and the plain

Fly as thick as driving rain;

And ever again, in the wink of an eye,

Painted stations whistle by.

Here is a child who clambers and scrambles,

All by himself and gathering brambles;

Here is a tramp who stands and gazes;

And here is the green for stringing the daisies!

Here is a cart runaway in the road

Lumping along with man and load;

And here is a mill, and there is a river:

Each with a glimpse and gone forever!

R. L. Stevenson

Learning objectives:	Resources:
• To explore how the poet uses key images to present ideas • To explore the use of comparative techniques to create imagery and their effect	• Extract 7.3.2 • 7.3.2 Lesson 1 PowerPoint • 7.3.2 Lesson 1 Worksheet

Getting started

• Display **7.3.2 Lesson 1 PowerPoint slide 1** and discuss the learning objectives.

• Then display **PowerPoint slide 2** and use the questions to guide discussion. (Suggested answers: *1. Passengers would see the rural landscape and people, the property on the hill and the river under the bridge. 2. The men may be working in the fields/farming. 3. The train is steam-powered.*) Ask the students how they can work out that this picture is from the 19th century (*steam train, field workers, a sketch not a photograph*). Further questions might include: How might this view be different to a 19th-century city view? (*pollution, industry, factory workers, buildings*) Where might this train be going? (*another city, delivery of coal*) What sort of people may travel on it? (*businessmen, families, workers*). Explain how the Industrial Revolution changed landscapes and establish that trains became common transport in the 19th century.

• Give out copies of **Extract 7.3.2** and read the poem 'From a Railway Carriage' together as a class.

Developing skills

• Hand out copies of **7.3.2 Lesson 1 Worksheet**; the students work in pairs to complete **Activities 1** and **2**. Discuss together what the landscape in the poem is like and how we can tell that it is not modern. Feedback could include: *Solid structures – bridge, houses, stations, cart, road, mill; Nature – hedges, ditches, meadows, hill, plain, brambles, green, daisies, river; People – child, tramp, man.* The students should notice that the column for 'Nature' is the longest, which tells us the train was whizzing through a very natural landscape. Ask the students how they feel about that. How might people at the time have felt about this great iron monster spoiling the peace? Encourage the students to notice that the things the train passes are all either static or moving slowly or awkwardly.

• Display **PowerPoint slide 3** and focus on the quotation from the poem that makes the comparison 'Faster than fairies, faster than witches'. Take ideas from the class connected to the ability to fly with wings and broomsticks/to travel at speed. Encourage them to see how the speed of the train might have been viewed as almost 'magical' at the time – perhaps compared with space travel today.

• Display **PowerPoint slide 4** and remind the students of the definition of a simile. Students could work in pairs to answer the four questions on the slide, working on the similes in lines 3 and 6 of the poem. In feedback, as well as commenting on noise/power, etc., encourage the students to notice that the similes are not pleasant images – do they destroy the peace or cause havoc? For question 4, the students should identify the phrases 'in the wink of an eye' and 'whistle by', and perhaps 'gone forever'.

• Display **PowerPoint slide 5** and ask the students to work individually to highlight the things or people moving slowly, before taking class suggestions for questions 2 and 3. The students should see the speed of the train as a real contrast to the people and the natural world, and consider how it might be seen as something magical or monstrous from the outside, even though it is exciting and fun to journey inside the train.

Trying it yourself

• Explore the contrasting images of speed and stillness in the poem through the final creative task (**Worksheet Activity 3**). Use the instructions on the worksheet to guide the students. An illustration could be done in class time or a collage task set as homework to allow for more time and thought.

Securing the understanding of key ideas in 19th-century poetry

R. L. Stevenson was a Scottish poet and writer who lived from 1850 to 1894, when a lot of travel would have been by train and train travel was a relatively new form of transport.

These trains ran on steam, not electricity like today, and would have made a distinct 'choo' noise as the steam left the valves under pressure.

Activity 1:

With your partner, sort the sights seen from the railway carriage window in the poem into the three categories below. An example answer is given in each column to get you started.

Solid structures	Nature	People
Bridge	Hedge	Child

Activity 2:

Now answer the following questions with a partner.

1. Which of your columns is longer? What does this tell us about the railway journey?

....

....

....

2. How does the movement of the train make a big contrast to the places and people it passes?

....

....

....

Activity 3: Final task

- Choose one of the images from the poem that shows the train is moving fast.
- Choose one of the images from the poem that shows someone or something being still or moving slowly.
- Create an illustration, drawing or collage to show the contrast between the two images.
- Include the phrases or lines from the poem in your illustration.

7.3.2 Lesson 2 — Securing the understanding of key ideas in 19th-century poetry: 'From a Railway Carriage'

Learning objectives:	Resources:
• To explore how writers use structure to present key ideas • To present analytical points using the IEC method	• Extract 7.3.2 • 7.3.2 Lesson 2 PowerPoint • 7.3.2 Lesson 2 Worksheet

Recap and reflection

* Display **7.3.2 Lesson 2 PowerPoint slide 1** and recap the learning objectives.

* Re-read **Extract 7.3.2** 'From a Railway Carriage' and recap the previous lesson through questions such as: How did the poet create the impression of the train? What key images can you remember? What techniques can you remember?

* Share successful illustrations and collages from the final task on **7.3.2 Lesson 1 Worksheet**.

Developing skills

* Display **7.3.2 Lesson 2 PowerPoint slide 2** and remind the students of the key information using the bullet points on the slide. Allow them 5 minutes to work with a partner to identify the verbs in the poem. Note that all the verbs are in the present or present continuous tense, except 'gone'. Discuss together why they think the poet made these choices (*it gives the sense of the journey happening in the here and now, creating movement and immediacy*).

* Explain that it is not just the tense of the verbs that creates movement in the poem, but also the patterns the poet creates. Hand out copies of **7.3.2 Lesson 2 Worksheet** and allow the students 5–10 minutes to explore this idea for themselves using **Activity 1**, then take feedback. Consolidate the students' ideas using **PowerPoint slide 3**. Draw conclusions that the metre and couplets help to create the 'sound effect' of the train on the tracks, linking this with the 'choo' noise made by a steam engine.

* Move on to explain to the students that when they analyse how a writer has created a particular effect, they need to write about the features they use to do so. Display **PowerPoint slide 4** and recap on the IEC (identify, exemplify, comment) method.

Trying it yourself

* Introduce the final task (**Worksheet Activity 2**) using **PowerPoint slide 5** to model the IEC method. Allow 20–25 minutes for the students to work on this final task, which guides them into writing an analytical paragraph with support. If more support is needed, you could give time to gathering examples from the text that match the bullet-point list of techniques as a whole-class exercise. Some of the students may benefit from paired writing for their first paragraph before working independently thereafter. Reinforce understanding that the comment on effect is about the effect on the students themselves and what the technique makes them think or imagine, rather than on an 'imaginary' reader. You can extend and challenge students by asking them to consider the cumulative effect of the poet's methods through writing paragraphs that comment on how more than one technique is used in specific lines; for example, line 9 uses alliteration, internal rhyme and assonance as well as rhyming with line 10.

* Ask the students to peer-assess one another's final outcome; they can use the bullet list of techniques on **Worksheet Activity 2** and the modelled example of the IEC method on **PowerPoint Slide 5** as checklists.

* End the week by returning to the lesson objectives on **PowerPoint slide 1** and checking that the students understand the IEC method enables them to explore 'how' rather than just 'what'.

Activity 1:

With your partner, look at the first line of the poem on **Extract 7.3.2**.

1. Which other line in the poem does it rhyme with?

   ....

2. How many syllables or 'beats' does it have?

   ....

Now look at the second line of the poem.

3. How many syllables or 'beats' does it have?

   ....

4. What do you notice about what the first line has in common with the second line?

   ....

   ....

   ....

Now look at the rest of the poem.

5. What do you notice about each 'pair' of lines?

   ....

   ....

   ....

6. Why do you think the poet might have chosen this pattern or structure for this particular poem? Does this pattern seem to 'match' in any way with what the poem is about?

   ....

   ....

   ....

   ....

Activity 2: Final task

How does the poet create the speed and excitement of a railway journey in the poem?

In working on the poem you have learned that the poet uses techniques like:

- comparison
- similes
- contrasts
- verbs in the present tense
- verbs in the present continuous tense
- rhyming couplets
- a very precise metre.

Choose three of the techniques that you have found most interesting and effective in creating the impression of the speedy railway journey, and use them to complete the task using the sentence starters below.

In this poem the writer uses ....

....

An example of this is..

....

This creates the impression of the speeding train, as it makes me imagine....................................

....

Another technique the writer uses is...

....

An example of this is..

....

This gives a sense of excitement, as it makes me think that...

....

A final technique that I think is very effective is ....

....

My example of this is ....

....

This creates the effect of how speedy and exciting the journey is, as it makes me imagine ....

....

Securing creative writing: Writing a narrative with descriptive features

Learning objectives:	Resources:
• To explore narrative voice and descriptive features • To plan and write a three-paragraph narrative using similes, adjectives and a distinctive narrative voice	• 7.3.3 Lessons 1 & 2 PowerPoint • 7.3.3 Lessons 1 & 2 Worksheet • thesaurus/dictionary per student/pair

Lesson 1: Getting started

* Display **7.3.3 Lesson 1 PowerPoint slide 2**, which shows Singapore through a plane window. Ask the students: Where is this view from? What are we looking at? What colours do you see? What types of buildings are there? What time of day is it? Extend by asking: Who might visit this place and why? (*business people, tourists, family*) What else would you expect to see there? (*locals, industry, transport*) What activities might a person do in this place? (*work, visit landmarks, eat out, shop*)

* Display **PowerPoint slide 1**. Discuss the learning objectives and explain that these lessons will guide the students in planning a descriptive piece of writing based on the picture on **PowerPoint slide 2**. Prompt them to define nouns (*naming words*), verbs (*action or doing words*) and adjectives (*describe a noun*).

Developing skills

* Give out copies of **7.3.3 Lesson 1 Worksheet** and ask the students to complete **Activity 1** individually or in pairs. Support them by sharing ideas in groups or by providing key words such as family, job, travel.

* Use **PowerPoint slide 3** to discuss how the narration can have a different effect depending on the choice of narrator. Questions could include: What are the limits of telling your own story as a first-person narrator? What is the advantage of having a narrator who we don't trust to tell the truth? What does adding a narrator's thoughts bring to the writing? (Possible answers might include: *It builds suspense if we don't trust the narrator; adding their thoughts tells us additional information we might not see in the narrative and can foreshadow events.*)

* Allow the students the opportunity to add to their plan following discussion. They could use the narrative viewpoints suggested on the worksheet or ideas of their own.

* The students now complete **Worksheet Activity 2**, which can be done alongside **PowerPoint slide 3**. A thesaurus could be used to challenge the students to select vocabulary forming semantic fields at a higher level. Support students by suggesting the semantic fields of colours, size, cities, busy and night.

Trying it yourself

* The students complete **Worksheet Activity 3**, deciding which colour each adjective describes; they should use a dictionary if required. Extend by using displays and objects in the room as examples of colours unknown to the students.

* Display **PowerPoint slide 4** and revise similes. Discuss the three examples on the slide before the students try **Worksheet Activity 4**; they should do this while viewing **PowerPoint slide 2**. Support them by creating examples based on what they can see in the room.

* Discuss the modelled opening on **PowerPoint slide 5** using the annotations as starting points. Further questions could include: What information is held back in [5]? (*decision*) What is the effect if we start with [5]? (*suspense*) How could we change this to a third person narrator and what would be the effect? (*I becomes he/she; less personal but scope to comment about character*)

Lesson 2: Final task

* Ask the students to return to their plans from **Worksheet Activity 1**; they can use this plan for their writing or create a new plan on a separate piece of paper. Display **PowerPoint slide 1** again, to remind the students of the objective to include adjectives and similes in their writing. Remind them of the worksheet activities, and encourage them to use these in their final piece of writing.

* In the remainder of the lesson time, the students write their final three-paragraph piece using the picture on **PowerPoint slide 2**. You can support the students with sentence starters for each paragraph, five adjectives they could include, and paired writing of their first sentence.

Creative writing works best when the plot is simple. You will be writing around 300 words in your final piece (three paragraphs of 100 words each), so the focus is on the quality of your writing. A plan will help with this.

Below are three ideas for writing about the picture on **PowerPoint slide 2**.

Idea 1	Idea 2	Idea 3
You or someone else has left home to start a new life in a city in a different country. This could use a third-person opening.	You or someone else has come to this city in search of a specific person/object and are determined to find it. This could use an unreliable 'shady' or dishonest narrator.	You or someone else is returning home to this city after many months away, and have missed this place. This could include the narrator's inner thoughts.

Activity 1:

Complete the table below by writing a brief plan in bullet points for one of the ideas given above. Include what is happening, what can be seen, who is involved and their feelings.

Introduction: • describe the view • establish the character • introduce the situation.	
Development: • how the person feels about being there • conflict/problems with being there.	
Resolution: • any decisions the character has made to come to terms with their situation • how the writing will end.	

A **semantic field** is a group of words linked by their meaning. For example, a suitable semantic field to describe a picture of the ocean could include words linked with water, such as wet, foamy, ripple, tide, blue, waves, crash, blue.

Activity 2:

Look again at the view from the aeroplane window in the picture on **PowerPoint slide 2**. Write down three suitable **semantic fields** to describe this scene.

1. ....

   ....

2. ....

   ....

3. ....

   ....

The picture on **PowerPoint slide 2** shows a variety of colours. You can make your writing interesting by varying the **adjectives** (describing words) used to describe these colours.

Activity 3:

Decide which colour each adjective below describes and write the adjective in the correct column.

crimson   amber   sapphire   ruby   azure   navy   scarlet   turquoise

Indigo   rust   burgundy   gold   peach   lemon   maroon

Red	Blue	Yellow	Orange

A **simile** is a comparison that uses either the word 'like' or the word 'as'.

Activity 4:

- Look again at the view from the aeroplane window in the picture on **PowerPoint slide 2**.
- Finish similes 1 and 2.
- Then write a completely new simile to describe the view.

1. *Skyscrapers stretched upwards like* ....

   ....

   ....

2. *A blue glow as* ....

   as..

   ....*settled over the city.*

3. ....

   ....

   ....

   ....

From *Travels in West Africa* (1897)

We hadn't gone 200 yards before we met a current coming round the end of a rock reef that was too strong for us to hold our own in, let alone progress. On to the bank I was ordered and went; it was a low slip of rugged confused boulders and fragments of rocks, carelessly arranged, and evidently under water in the wet season. I scrambled along, the men yelled and shouted and hauled the canoe, and the inhabitants of the village, seeing we were becoming amusing again, came, legging it like lamp-lighters, after us, young and old, male and female, to say nothing of the dogs. Some good souls helped the men haul, while I did my best to amuse the others by diving headlong from a large rock on to which I had elaborately climbed, into a thick clump of willow-leaved shrubs. They applauded my performance vociferously, and then assisted my efforts to extricate myself, and during the rest of my scramble they kept close to me, with keen competition for the front row, in hopes that I would do something like it again. But I refused the encore, because, bashful as I am, I could not but feel that my last performance was carried out with all the superb reckless abandon of a **Sarah Bernhardt**, and a display of art of this order should satisfy any African village for a year at least. At least I got across the rocks on to a lovely little beach of white sand, and stood there talking, surrounded by my audience, until the canoe got over its difficulties and arrived almost as scratched as I; and then we again said farewell and paddled away, to the great grief of the natives. [...]

[...] It was getting dark and the water worse, and the hill-sides growing higher and higher into nobly shaped mountains, forming, with their forest-graced steep sides, a ravine that, in the gathering gloom, looked like an alley-way made of iron, for the foaming Ogowe.

Mary Kingsley

Sarah Bernhardt: A French actress in the 19th century

Learning objectives:	Resources:
• To use inference to interpret 19th-century non-fiction • To show secure understanding of the SQI method	• Extract 7.3.4 • 7.3.4 Lesson 1 PowerPoint • 7.3.4 Lesson 1 Worksheet

Getting started

• Display **7.3.4 Lesson 1 PowerPoint slide 2**. Tell the students the picture is of African rapids, then use the following questions to guide discussion: How deep do you think the water is? What would be the danger here? How could a person travel down or across this river? What animals might live in this water? Extend the discussion by asking: What does 'rapid' mean when describing speed? (*very quick*) What does it suggest about the water here? (*that it is fast-flowing and dangerous*) Why do you think sailing on rapids is a modern sport? Discuss thrill-seekers, adrenaline, pushing boundaries and technological advancements.

• Display the lesson objectives on **PowerPoint slide 1** and read **Extract 7.3.4** together as a class.

• Use the 'Exploring together' questions on **PowerPoint slide 3**, starting with dictionaries to find meanings of new vocabulary. Responses may include: *2. 'Confused' boulders suggests no pattern in position, shape, size (stretch by introducing personification here); 3. Clapping audience is impressed by Mary as a strong female, pleased with her success; 4 and 5. Mary feels proud (she describes danger), enjoys the attention (intends to amuse them), yet shy (won't repeat it), scared (physical effort).* Contextualise 'native' as an inhabitant born in a specific place such as Africa.

Developing skills

• Hand out copies of **7.3.4 Lesson 1 Worksheet**. Discuss the different roles of the occupants of the boat in the picture, guiding the students to differentiate between native African workers (*bare-chested, standing with poles*) and foreign travellers (*seated, wearing more formal dress and hats*).

• Discuss what might be seen/heard/felt by those in the boat or by the photographer (*river/nature sounds; wonder what the fuss is about; feel special or think Mary must be special*). Ask the students to consider the extent to which Mary Kingsley is an explorer if she is seated while native Africans propel the boat. Who might her companion be? (*guide/writer/family*)

• Ask students working in pairs to complete **Worksheet Activity 1**. (*Mary is seated higher in the boat.*) Feed back ideas, allowing the students to consider the uniqueness and impact of an English lady exploring Africa in the 19th century and what the reactions of the local people might have been. Consider Victorian support for colonialism in contrast to our modern view that Victorian beliefs that African nations were 'uncivilised' were racist.

Trying it yourself

• Display **PowerPoint slide 4** and recap on inference skills. Explain to the students that they are going to use the facts that Mary Kingsley gives in Extract 7.3.4 to write about her experiences. You may want to discuss Mary's experience more here by asking: What were the hazards? (*rocks, fast water, unknown/ unexplored territory*) How were visitors treated? (*They were helped, applauded, talked to, befriended.*)

• Show the modelled example on **PowerPoint slide 5** and recap the SQI (statement + quotation + inference) method, as well as how to embed quotations.

• Now ask the students to complete the final task (**Activity 2**) on the worksheet using the SQI method. Display **PowerPoint slide 5** throughout. You could support the students by highlighting evidence on **Extract 7.3.4** with them or by providing sentence starters; students could also work in pairs for support. They can be stretched by completing more than two SQI sequences or by developing inferences with more than one idea.

The photograph below was taken in 1895. It shows the English writer of **Extract 7.3.4**, Mary Kingsley, travelling down the Ogowe River in Gabon, West Africa. Parts of the river are very steep but also shallow. This creates fast-flowing water where rocks are exposed. These are known as the Ogowe rapids, and as well as being highly dangerous, in places they are impossible to travel through.

Activity 1:

Look at the people in the boat in the picture above.

- Which person do you think is Mary? Label her.
- In the chart below, bullet point the thoughts and feelings of the people in the picture.

1. The two seated travellers	2. The workers who are standing up

Activity 2:

What do you understand about Mary Kingsley's experience of travelling through the Ogowe rapids in the 19th century from the extract?

In your answer:

- write a clear statement sentence that answers the question – **S**
- select a relevant quotation from the extract to support your statement – **Q**
- use inference to show your understanding of Mary's experiences (you could use some of your ideas from Activity 1 here) – **I**.

Then repeat the bullets with a different statement **(S)**, a different quotation **(Q)** and a different inference **(I)**.

....

....

....

....

....

....

....

....

....

....

....

....

....

....

....

....

....

<table>
<tr>
<td>

Learning objectives:
- To be able to make secure inferences from reading about a writer's thoughts and feelings
- To understand and empathise with different viewpoints through role play
- To present those viewpoints using a persona

</td>
<td>

Resources:
- Extract 7.3.4
- 7.3.4 Lesson 2 PowerPoint
- 7.3.4 Lesson 1 Worksheet
- 7.3.4 Lesson 2 Worksheet

</td>
</tr>
</table>

Recap and reflection

- Ask the students to discuss the differences in the pictures of the boats on **7.3.4 Lesson 2 PowerPoint slide 2** and **7.3.4 Lesson 1 Worksheet**. For each image, ask: How many people are in the boat? What are they wearing? Why are bright colours used? What sort of boat are they in? What is the purpose of their activity? Guide the students to comment on the safety equipment and purpose-built boat hired for adventure on **PowerPoint slide 2**, compared to the much longer, slimmer, more basic boat, hired for exploration (and with more occupants), on the worksheet. Further questions to prompt discussion could include: Who is most prepared? How would the feelings of those in the modern boat differ from or match the feelings of those in the boat Mary hired for exploration? Establish the modern purpose of thrill-seeking compared to Mary's motives of exploration.

- Display **PowerPoint slide 1** and discuss the lesson objectives. Explain how a persona allows us to take on the role of a different person and act/write as that person, expressing their thoughts and feelings, rather than from our own point of view. You could discuss modern examples that may be familiar to the students, such as *The Hunger Games*, *Percy Jackson* and *Diary of a Wimpy Kid*.

Developing skills

- Re-read **Extract 7.3.4** then hand out copies of **7.3.4 Lesson 2 Worksheet** and ask the students to complete **Activity 1**, highlighting words Mary uses to link to the theme of performing on stage. The students consider why Kingsley compares her actions to a performance. (Suggested answers: *1. amuse, elaborately, applauded my performance, front row, encore, performance, display of art, my audience. 2. Shows how Mary feels exposed/laughed at/embarrassed/like she's making a fool of herself, but also how she reacts positively to this and plays to the crowd, perhaps enjoying the attention.*)

Trying it yourself

- Direct the students to complete the role-play activity (**Worksheet Activity 2**). You may wish to develop thinking further before the role play, with questions such as: How would Mary being female be viewed? Was Mary ever in danger? Why doesn't she travel alone? Could the villagers have seen other people do this? Stretch the students by having them adopt the persona of a specific person in the picture. Support them with a word bank, sentence starters, a chosen role or by working in their group with them. Perform some of this work to the rest of the class. Peers could give feedback regarding voice projection, actions, imagination and group work.

- Now direct the students to complete **Worksheet Activity 3**, which is the final task for this lesson – writing a diary entry for one of the villagers who witnessed Mary's journey through the rapids. Display **PowerPoint slide 3** and recap on the format of diary writing as well as its purpose. Consider how it can be compared to a monologue or soliloquy on stage. Encourage the students to adopt a persona for their villager through questioning, for example: As a villager, do you approve of Mary's journey? Do you admire her or think she is foolish?

- The students complete their diary entry in their notebooks using their ideas from **Worksheet Activity 1**. Support the students with a clear three- or four-paragraph plan with sentence starters provided; ask them what they said in character in their role play; have them consider how different Mary's journey would have been in comparison to modern white-water trips. You can use **PowerPoint slide 4** as a modelled example to provide further support. Stretch the students by challenging them to write in the formal diction of the 19th century or from a child's point of view.

Securing the exploration of ideas in 19th-century non-fiction

Mary compares her actions with those of Sarah Bernhardt, who was a French actress in the 19th century.

Activity 1:

Answer the questions below.

1. Highlight or underline all the words in the extract that link with the theme of performing on stage.

2. Why do you think Kingsley compares her actions to a performance?

....

....

....

Activity 2:

Imagine you are in Gabon, Africa, when Mary Kingsley crosses the Ogowe rapids.

In groups of three or four, role-play the reaction of the villagers when Mary arrives in the village.

*   Think about whether they are impressed by her bravery, consider her foolish, don't want English strangers in their village or welcome her.
*   In your role, you could live in the village, be married to a man working on Mary's boat, have lost someone in the rapids or have been across them yourself.
*   Focus on thoughts and feelings as well as words and actions.

(The image on **PowerPoint slide 2** shows a modern boat for travelling on river rapids, while the image on **7.3.4 Lesson 1 Worksheet** shows Mary Kingsley's boat in 1897.)

Activity 3:

Using **Extract 7.3.4** and the picture of Mary Kingsley's boat from **7.3.4 Lesson 1 Worksheet**, write a diary extract for one of the villagers who witnessed Mary's journey through the rapids. Include the thoughts and tips below:

*   Mary's decision to cross the rapids
*   her behaviour and whether or not they find it amusing
*   her attitude towards her adventure
*   what was said after Mary had gone.
*   Use a first-person narrative (*I, me, my, our, us*).
*   Start with 'Dear Diary' and use the date 1897.
*   Begin with a general sentence about what has happened that day.
*   The audience is you, so you can explore and reveal your inner feelings about events.

Bear Grylls reveals how his boy's own childhood and SAS training taught him to … grin and bear it! From *Mud, Sweat and Tears* (2011)

The air temperature is minus 20°C. I wiggle my fingers but they're still freezing cold. Old frostnip injuries never let you forget. I blame my Everest climb. 'You set, buddy?' cameraman Simon asks me, smiling. The crew say the northern Canadian Rockies look spectacular this morning but I don't really notice. Beneath me is 300 ft of snow and ice. It's steep but manageable.

I leap and I'm soon sliding on my back down the mountain at 40 mph, with Simon following on a heavy wooden sledge with his camera. The ice races past inches from my head. I gain more speed and the edge of the peak gets closer. It's time to arrest the fall.

I flip on to my front and drive my ice axe into the snow, sending a cloud of white spray and ice soaring into the air. I feel the rapid deceleration as I grind the axe deep into the mountain. It works. The world hangs still. Then – bang. Simon and his sledge pile into my left thigh at more than 45 mph. There is an instant explosion of pain and I am thrown down the mountain like a doll.

A difference of one degree in the sledge's angle and it would have hit my head. It would have been my last living thought.

Instead, I am in agony, writhing and crying. They are tears of relief: I am injured, but I am alive. I see a helicopter but hear no sound before I am taken to hospital. I have been in a few since the start of my Channel 4 series *Born Survivor*.

I can see it all through closed eyes. The dirty, bloodstained emergency room in Vietnam after I severed half my finger in the jungle. The boulder fall in Costa Rica. The mineshaft collapse in Montana. The saltwater crocodile in Australia. Countless close shaves. I quietly wonder: when did this craziness become my world?

Bear Grylls

Securing connections with modern non-fiction: *Mud, Sweat and Tears*

Learning objectives:

- To begin to present key ideas with quotations and see connections between texts from the 19th and 21st centuries
- To be able to identify some of the key techniques used to convey these ideas

Resources:

- Extract 7.3.4
- Extract 7.3.5
- 7.3.5 Lesson 1 PowerPoint
- 7.3.5 Lesson 1 Worksheet

Getting started

- Display **7.3.5 Lesson 1 PowerPoint slide 2**. Ask the students who the picture is of; explain that Bear Grylls is popular on TV and radio for his adventures and explorations. Draw out that Bears Grylls is a modern-day explorer, rather like Mary Kingsley in the 19th century. Use the question prompts on the slide to guide discussion. Possible further questions include: What are the differences between modern-day explorers and 19th-century explorers? Why it is easier to document modern-day explorations? Discuss the ease of modern-day communications and improvements in transport.

- Display the lesson objectives on **PowerPoint slide 1**. Check students' understanding of 'connections' (*links, comparisons, developments, similarities, differences*) and 'key ideas' (*main, leading*).

Developing skills

- Give out copies of **Extract 7.3.5** and read it together as a class. Ask pairs to identify the key ideas and discuss what a key idea is in a text. Take whole-class feedback and write a class definition of 'key idea' (*central thought or leading point in a text*).

- Hand out copies of **7.3.5 Lesson 1 Worksheet** and ask students to read **Activity 1**. They should start by completing the left column of the chart, based on Bear Grylls' account in **Extract 7.3.5**. (Answers could include: *amount of detail, danger faced, the humorous approach, other people present*.) Then return to **Extract 7.3.4** by Mary Kingsley and complete the right side of the chart.

- Now display the 'Exploring together' questions on **PowerPoint slide 3** and ask pairs to work through them. (Suggested answers: *1. It's very cold – minus 20 °C, with 300 ft of snow and ice. 2. He speeds down the mountain on his back. 3. He is out of control, bumped, thrown about carelessly. 4. He could have died; he thinks of all the injuries he has sustained exploring.*)

- The students now complete **Worksheet Activity 2** working individually; they draw linking lines between the left and right columns in the chart they completed for Activity 1, to show similar or opposite key ideas. Allow 15 minutes for this task. Support them with **PowerPoint slide 4** and by modelling a link such as both writers presenting the danger they found themselves in. Compile a class list of relevant links; possible suggestions include: *determination to complete the expedition, love of the adventure, an admiration of nature*.

- Now ask pairs to complete **Worksheet Activity 3**. You could support the students by completing the first link and supporting quotation together, by working in pairs, by highlighting relevant quotations on the extracts or by reducing the activity to one link.

Trying it yourself

- Display **PowerPoint slide 5** to model and recap the SQI (statement + quotation + inference) method. Further questions to ask include: What do you notice about the way the quotations are used here? (*embedded*) What do they focus on? (*the writers' feelings and actions*) Are we specifically told in either extract that Bear Grylls and Mary Kingsley enjoy the challenges they face? (*no; we use inference to work this out*)

- The students now complete writing up one of their links using the SQI method, in response to the question 'What do we learn about the two writers' experiences of exploration?' Support the students by taking feedback after 5 minutes to check progress and understanding, providing sentence starters and using pairs. Stretch the students by challenging them to write further SQI paragraphs.

Securing connections with modern non-fiction: *Mud, Sweat and Tears*

Activity 1:

Complete the chart below with the key ideas from each extract. You could think about what we learn about each explorer, where they are, the kind of trip they are making or any other ideas from the extract.

Bear Grylls	Mary Kingsley

Activity 2:

Draw lines between the left and right columns in the chart you completed for Activity 1 to identify similar or different key ideas.

Activity 3:

Choose two links you made in the chart above. These can show that the texts are similar or different. Write your two chosen links below with a relevant supporting quotation for each link.

1. Link: ....

....

Supporting quotation: ....

....

....

2. Link: ....

....

Supporting quotation: ....

....

....

Learning objectives:	Resources:
• To make connections between writers' thoughts, feelings and experiences • To present those connections with secure comprehension skills	• Extract 7.3.5 • Extract 7.3.4 • 7.3.5 Lesson 2 PowerPoint • 7.3.5 Lesson 2 Worksheet

Recap and reflection

• Re-read **Extract 7.3.5** and **Extract 7.3.4**.

• Display **7.3.5 PowerPoint slide 2** and discuss the questions. Examples of humour include Mary Kingsley's slapstick humour – for example, her comment that the locals 'seeing we were becoming amusing again, came, legging it like lamp-lighters', or Bear Grylls' 'craziness' and 'wonder', suggesting he is not quite sure when his life changed but he doesn't feel regret or negative emotions about the changes. Further questions to ask include: Did both Bear and Mary enjoy their expeditions? How do you know? Is there any implicit information to help us decide? *(Yes, despite the unfavourable conditions both persevere with their expedition, words such as 'leap', 'paddled away' create a positive image.)*

• Display **PowerPoint slide 1** and discuss the lesson objectives. Students will think about how an author's writing can express their thoughts and feelings on an experience and to compare any points of connection between the two texts.

Developing skills

• Ask the students to complete **7.3.5 Lesson 2 Worksheet Activity 1**. Support them by reading the quotations aloud and considering the tone of each. (Suggested answers: *1. Alliteration of 'a', repetition of 'ing', simile; 2. Rhetorical question, personal pronoun, adverbs*) Stretch them by considering which key words indicates the writer's feelings. *(1. amusing; 2. wonder)*

Trying it yourself

• Display **PowerPoint slide 3** and identify the words in the last paragraph linked to Mary's feelings about her surroundings (*'getting dark and the water worse', the description of the ravine, 'gathering gloom'*). Ask the students what these words suggest about the way Mary Kingsley is feeling (*scared, intimidated, small compared to nature, threatened*).

• Ask the students to complete **Activity 2** on the worksheet by adding quotations for three thoughts and feelings shown in Mary Kingsley's and Bear Grylls' texts.

• Possible quotations to use for Bear Grylls are: *1. 'Instead, I am in agony, writhing and crying. They are tears of relief: I am injured, but I am alive' – showing his determination and strength. 2. 'Countless close shaves' – to show it's happened many times but he still continues so must enjoy it. 3. 'Vietnam after I severed half my finger in the jungle. The boulder fall in Costa Rica. The mineshaft collapse in Montana' – show nature's power over people.*

• Possible quotations to use for Mary Kingsley are: *1. 'They applauded my performance vociferously ... with keen competition for the front row, in hopes that I would do something like it again.' – shows her dealing with problems using humour and not giving up. 2. 'display of art of this order should satisfy any African village for a year at least.' – shows her humour so she is enjoying it as much as the audience. 3. 'At last I got across the rocks on to a lovely little beach of white sand' – shows how she appreciates her surroundings.*

Final task

• Display **PowerPoint slide 4**. Discuss the modelled SQI (statement + quotation + inference) response as an appropriate method to use with their completed key ideas from the worksheet.

• Display **PowerPoint slide 5** and ask the students to complete the final task independently in their notebooks. Support them with sentence starters, highlighted texts, pair work and further modelled examples.

Activity 1:

Using the quotations below, circle then name any techniques that the writer uses to portray exploration as a positive experience.

1. 'seeing we were becoming amusing again, came, legging it like lamp-lighters.'

   ....

   ....

2. 'I quietly wonder: when did this craziness become my world?'

   ....

   ....

Activity 2:

Read the three key points in column 1 of the chart below. Then add quotations and inferences:

• in column 2 for Mary Kingsley's text

• in column 3 for Bear Grylls' text.

1. Key points	2. Mary Kingsley extract (add quotations and inferences)	3. Bear Grylls extract (add quotations and inferences)
Determination to take part in the expedition		
Love of the adventure of an expedition		
Admiration of nature during the expedition		

7.3.6 Lessons 1 & 2

Securing discursive writing: Writing a travel article

Learning objectives:	Resources:
• To understand the main features of travel writing • To plan and write a travel article for an audience of peers	• 7.3.6 Lessons 1 & 2 PowerPoint • 7.3.6 Lessons 1 & 2 Worksheet

Lesson 1: Getting started

- Display the lesson objectives on **PowerPoint slide 1**. In pairs, ask the students to think about the possible key features of the travel writing pieces they have just worked on in Weeks 4 and 5. (Suggested answers: *facts, opinions, imagery, first person, use of comparatives, humour, anecdotes, matching features of a place that would suit travellers.*)

- Give out copies of **7.3.6 Lessons 1 & 2 Worksheet** and ask the students to complete **Activity 1**. (Answers: *A4, B2, C1, D5, E6, F7, G3*). Move on to discuss which features of travel writing might be most effective in holding the potential readers' interest (*personal informed experience, facts, range of information, honesty, new experiences*).

- Display **PowerPoint slide 2**. Ask the students to consider the headlines for potential articles about places. Discuss the features of the headlines (rhetorical question, exaggeration, imperatives, vivid description). Take further suggestions regarding which would persuade the students to visit and why.

Developing skills

- Ask the students to complete **Worksheet Activity 2**. They need to identify the features of travel writing in the paragraph using their completed list from **Worksheet Activity 1** and the answers from **PowerPoint slide 2**. Support them through pairings and a worked example if needed. Stretch students by asking them to change key sentences to a negative viewpoint or make the same point using a different feature.

- The students could extend this work by looking for more examples of travel writing online (for example, Bill Bryson, Laurie Lee and pre-20th-century writers such as Mark Twain) and identifying the features.

Trying it yourself

- Direct the students to **Worksheet Activity 3** and go over the final task. They work on a plan for a travel article for the magazine *School Summer Holiday Destinations* based on a place they have visited or would like to visit. Use the images on **PowerPoint slides 3**, **4**, **5** and **6** to help stimulate ideas and the grid on the worksheet for the planning process. Possible questions to ask for each slide are:

    Slide 3: Have you had any memorable trips to the sea in the UK or abroad? How would you describe the sea, the sand, the sky and what there was to do there? What made the beach so special for you?

    Slide 4: Have you been lucky enough to travel to an amazing city or would you like to go to one? What would be enticing about it? Try and bring to life the sights, the sounds, the smells and the colours of a hustling, bustling busy place.

    Slide 5: Do you remember a walk with family or friends or a school trip to an outdoor centre, or did a trip to your local park turn into a fantastic day out? What was special about the environment and the natural world? Describe the colours, the sounds and the atmosphere – and don't forget the picnic!

    Slide 6: Where would you travel to if you really could? What would that be like as an experience? Or maybe your own room is a messy alien landscape and you could transport your readers there!

Lesson 2: Recap and reflect, and Final task

- Recap on the plans from the previous lesson and use the images of destinations on **PowerPoint slides 3**, **4**, **5** and **6** where required as reminders. Use **PowerPoint slide 7** to offer key reminders of the techniques that need to be included in their final piece.

- Allow 30–35 minutes for students to complete the final writing task (**Worksheet Activity 3**). Give time at the end for accuracy and peer checking. If time allows, the students could read aloud some of their pieces and share with the class, deciding on the most persuasive or fun destination from this edition of *School Summer Holiday Destinations*.

Activity 1:

Draw lines to match each feature of travel writing to its intended purpose.

Feature of travel writing	Intended purpose
A Facts	**1** Statements based from a single person's perspective
B Opinions	**2** Viewpoints that are not necessarily based on fact
C First person	**3** Speaking directly to the reader
D Comparatives	**4** Key truthful information useful to the traveller
E Superlatives	**5** Comparisons to establish the differences between things
F Figurative language	**6** The highest degree of praise
G Direct address	**7** Helps you to picture the destination

Activity 2:

Read the paragraph below. Highlight and label the travel writing features it contains.

London: the place to be and be seen?

London, the capital city and jewel of Europe, with beautiful sights such as Buckingham Palace and the London Eye. Take a stroll down Oxford Street and marvel at the number of shoppers like you and me. Wear what you want – anything goes! If you're more of the adventurous sort, take an exploration into the London Dungeon, a breath-taking experience unable to be matched anywhere else in England. If you're more of the curious sort, the British Museum opens its arms to you with relics from the forgotten annals of history. Picture the heartland of British governance, Westminster itself, which sits waiting with the ability to go into the famous House of Commons and the glamorous House of Lords. Are films your cup of tea? See the sets of famous movies such as *Harry Potter* in the Harry Potter Experience; see platform 9¾ at Kings Cross Station. To all food lovers out there, here is my plea: you simply must try the greatest selection of food Europe has to offer! From Japanese sushi to American burgers, there is food no matter how picky the eater.

Truly, London is the fairy-tale destination for everyone.

Activity 3: Final task

A new travel magazine called *School Summer Holiday Destinations* has been launched, which is aimed at children aged 10–13 years. The magazine wants to encourage young people to get involved in travel, find out more about the world and contribute their own writing to the magazine.

You have been asked to write an article of approximately 350 words for the magazine, discussing a travel destination of your choice.

- You can write about a place you have been that is very vivid in your memory. Alternatively, you can write about a place that you would like to go to and imagine visiting there.
- Give your article a snappy title or headline using some of the language features you have been learning about.
- Aim for descriptive language to bring the place to life.
- Use some of the features of travel writing you have been working on in Weeks 4, 5 and 6 to really engage your readers.

My destination: ....

My headline: ....

The main features of the place: ....

....

....

....

Ideas for vocabulary and imagery: ....

....

....

....

My thoughts and feelings about the place: ....

....

....

....

My best experiences there: ....

....

....

....

From *The Time Machine* (1895)

I am afraid I cannot convey the peculiar sensations of time travelling. They are excessively unpleasant. There is a feeling exactly like that one has upon a **switchback** – of a helpless headlong motion! I felt the same horrible anticipation, too, of an imminent smash.

As I put on pace, night followed day like the flapping of a black wing. The dim suggestion of the laboratory seemed presently to fall from me, and I saw the sun hopping swiftly across the sky, leaping it every minute, and every minute marking a day. I suppose the laboratory had been destroyed and I had come into open air. I had a dim impression of scaffolding, but I was already going too fast to be conscious of any moving things. The slowest snail that ever crawled dashed by too fast for me. The twinkling succession of darkness and light was excessively painful to the eye. Then, in the intermittent darkness, I saw the moon spinning swiftly through her quarters from new to full and had a faint glimpse of the circling stars.

Presently, as I went on, still gaining **velocity**, the **palpitation** of night and day merged into one continuous greyness; the sky took on a wonderful deepness of blue, a splendid luminous colour like that of early twilight; the jerking sun became a streak of fire, a brilliant arch, in space, the moon a fainter fluctuating band and I could see nothing of the stars, save now and then a brighter circle flickering in the blue.

H.G. Wells

switchback: a road or path with sharp bends and ups and downs
velocity: speed
palpitation: rapid or irregular heartbeat

Learning objective:	Resources:
• To understand some of the key ideas in a 19th-century fiction text	• 8.1.1 Extract • 8.1.1 Lesson 1 PowerPoint • 8.1.1 Lesson 1 Worksheet

Getting started

- Display **8.1.1 Lesson 1 PowerPoint slide 2** and use the questions on the slide to engage the students in the theme of time travel. Explore their current knowledge and understanding of what time travel might be. Establish that time travel is when you travel to the future or the past. Examples could include: Dr Who travels in a TARDIS; in the film *Back to the Future* the time machine was a car.

- Display **PowerPoint slide 1** and introduce the learning objective. Point out that *The Time Machine* was written in 1895 and is a science-fiction novel. Ask the students to share what they know about the genre of science fiction and what they would expect to see in a science-fiction text (for example, aliens, advanced technology, scientific experiments, perhaps travel to or from other planets).

- Hand out copies of **Extract 8.1.1** and display **PowerPoint slide 3**. Read the introduction to the extract on the slide and then read the extract as a whole class. On first reading, students should just listen; on a second reading you might want to stop and ensure understanding, using the glossary words.

- Now hand out copies of **8.1.1 Lesson 1 Worksheet**. The students complete the task detailed on **PowerPoint slide 3** by making notes on **Worksheet Activity 1**. (Suggested answers: *Paragraph 1: Introduces the idea that time travel is unpleasant. Paragraph 2: He is in motion and is describing the sensation of travelling away from his laboratory. He describes time passing as something that happens quickly and slowly at the same time. He also describes the physical pain in his eyes. Paragraph 3: He describes the continuous motion and movement of time, but explores the beauty of colour in the passing of night and day.*)

Developing skills

- Display **PowerPoint slide 4**. The students read the quotation on the slide and answer the questions; this could be done as a whole-class or paired activity. (Suggested answers: *1. He makes time travel sound painful and physically difficult, not something enjoyable. 2. He describes it as 'excessively unpleasant'.*)

- The students then work in pairs to complete **Worksheet Activity 2**. It's worth spending some time feeding back from this task, in particular quotations 2 and 4, with a focus on the students' interpretation of the text and what they have inferred. Ask them how and why they have come to the conclusions they have. (Suggested answers: *1. Horrid or sick emoji. 2. Shock or an emoji showing speed. 3. Pained or hurt emoji. 4. Wow, amazed or happy emoji.*)

- Display **PowerPoint slide 5**. The students work in pairs or groups to discuss their responses to the questions on the slide. Prompt them to develop their answers, thoughts and feelings with reference to the text where they can. The students should be encouraged to be imaginative and creative with their responses, drawing on the text but not exclusively.

- Encourage a few of the students to share their responses to the questions on **PowerPoint slide 5** with the whole class and encourage them to offer alternative points of view. For example, the text is relatively negative about time travel – but can they see what may be positive about it?

Trying it yourself

- Students now complete **Worksheet Activity 3**. Encourage them to use their imagination as well as develop ideas from the text. This task is aimed at engaging the students in the wider character and themes of the unit. Don't worry if some go completely off text as long as they're engaged in the task and the theme. Again, encourage the sharing of ideas through whole-class feedback or in pairs.

Introducing more skills with 19th-century fiction: *The Time Machine*

Activity 1:

After reading **Extract 8.1.1**, discuss with your partner what you think is happening in each paragraph. Use the space below to make notes.

Paragraph 1	Paragraph 2	Paragraph 3

Activity 2:

Review these quotations from the text and add an emoji next to each one to show whether it sounds enjoyable or not.

Quotation	Emoji
1. 'I am afraid I cannot convey the peculiar sensations of time travelling. They are excessively unpleasant.'	
2. 'As I put on pace, night followed day like the flapping of a black wing.'	
3. 'The twinkling succession of darkness and light was excessively painful to the eye.'	
4. '...the sky took on a wonderful deepness of blue, a splendid luminous colour like that of early twilight...'	

Activity 3:

Imagine you're interviewing the time traveller from the text. Think of two questions you would ask him and the answers you think he would give.

Question 1: ....

Answer: ....

....

Question 2: ....

Answer: ....

....

Learning objectives:	Resources:
• To start to read between the lines of a 19th-century fiction text • To be able to explain your thoughts by referencing the text	• Extract 8.1.1 • 8.1.1 Lesson 2 PowerPoint • 8.1.1 Lesson 2 Worksheet

Getting started

- Display **8.1.1 Lesson 2 PowerPoint slide 2**. Prompt the students to reflect on the images by asking: Do you think these images are both illustrating the same text? What impression does each image give? What does each image make you think, feel or imagine? Explain that both images were influenced by the text *The Time Machine*. Ask: Which image do you consider to be most like the part of the text you've read? Answers will be the students' own, but most will probably choose the more dystopian image on the right of the slide.

- Display **PowerPoint slide 1** and introduce the learning objectives for the lesson.

- Then re-read **Extract 8.1.1**; you might want to encourage the students to read it out loud.

Developing skills

- Hand out copies of **8.1.1 Lesson 2 Worksheet** and ask the students to complete **Activity 1**, working individually or in pairs. It's worth spending some time feeding back on the final question from the activity, to introduce the idea of changing points of view; this will support the students with **Worksheet Activity 2** later in the lesson and the use of metaphors to show the speed of time. (Suggested answers: *1. 'peculiar sensations of time travelling', 'excessively unpleasant', 'horrible anticipation'. 2. 'The slowest snail that ever crawled dashed by too fast for me.' 3. 'night followed day like the flapping of a black wing', 'leaping it every minute, and every minute marking a day', 'the moon spinning swiftly through her quarters from new to full'. 4. Answers will be the students' own based on the quotes they selected, but they should identify that the narrator sounds disorientated or as if he's experiencing strange feelings and thoughts that contradict and confuse his mind.*)

- Display **PowerPoint slide 3** and discuss the quotation on the slide as a class. Encourage the students to give their opinion on the quotation and respond to the questions. Ask them to zoom in on words or images from the quotation that influence their thinking. (Suggested answer: *No, it doesn't sound unpleasant; what he gets to see during time travel sounds beautiful and otherworldly.*)

- The students then move on to answer **Worksheet Activity 2** in pairs or individually. The aim of this activity is to engage them in forming their own ideas about the change in the way the writer presents time travel through the language he chooses. It's worth encouraging whole-group or paired feedback so that the students are guided to zoom in on the author's language choices as a way of explaining or backing up their thoughts. (Suggested answers might include: *1. He seems to appreciate the beauty of the sky. 2. 'wonderful deepness of blue', 'a splendid luminous colour', 'streak of fire', 'a brilliant arch'. 3. Time travel is not all bad; there are a lot of beautiful things to see.*)

Trying it yourself

- Display **PowerPoint slide 4**, which describes the final task: using the ideas from the extract, the students write the next paragraph of the text in their notebooks, describing the sensation of landing in a new time. The task is aimed at engaging the students in using their imagination to continue the ideas of the author and, where they can, to maintain the same effect on the reader. This final writing task also provides an effective way of assessing the students' understanding and interpretation of the text.

- Once they have finished their paragraph, the students can use the checklist on **PowerPoint slide 4** for self- or peer-assessment. You could also ask some of the students to share their creative writing with the class.

Activity 1:

Read the extract from *The Time Machine* then answer the questions below.

1. Find a phrase in the opening paragraph that shows that time travelling is an unpleasant activity.

   ....

2. Find a phrase in the second paragraph that shows time travel can feel slow.

   ....

3. Find a phrase in the second paragraph that shows days pass very quickly when time travelling.

   ....

4. Does the time traveller sound as though he feels and thinks the same in all of these quotations?

   ....

   ....

Activity 2:

Read the following quotation from the extract then answer the questions.

> the sky took on a wonderful deepness of blue, a splendid luminous colour like that of early twilight; the jerking sun became a streak of fire, a brilliant arch, in space

1. How does the narrator's view of time travel change in this quotation?

   ....

2. Choose two phrases from the quotation that make it sound different to how the narrator previously described time travel.

   ....

   ....

3. What do these words make you think about his experience of time travel?

   ....

   ....

'The Starlight Night' (1877)

Look at the stars! look, look up at the skies!

O look at all the fire-folk sitting in the air!

The bright boroughs, the circle-**citadels** there!

Down in dim woods the diamond delves! the elves'-eyes!

The grey lawns cold where gold, where **quickgold** lies!

Wind-beat **whitebeam**! airy **abeles** set on a flare!

Flake-doves sent floating forth at a farmyard scare!

Ah well! it is all a purchase, all is a prize.

Gerard Manley Hopkins

citadel: a fortress on high ground above a city
quickgold: liquid gold
whitebeam: a tree
abele: a white poplar tree

Learning objective:	Resources:
• To explore imagery in poetry, prose and paintings	• Extract 8.1.2 • 8.1.2 Lesson 1 PowerPoint • 8.1.2 Lesson 1 Worksheet

Getting started

* Display **8.1.2 Lesson 1 PowerPoint slide 1** and introduce the learning objective. Ask the students what we mean by prose, poetry and paintings. Establish that prose refers to novels or stories, poetry is text with a different shape and rhythm, and painting is art, images or visuals without words.

* Display **PowerPoint slide 2**. Encourage the students to spend at least 1 minute just looking at the painting; they could complete a think, pair, share activity to explain what they see, or they could look away then look back to see if they notice anything different. Then hand out copies of **8.1.2 Lesson 1 Worksheet** and ask the students to complete **Activity 1**.

* Once the students have completed Activity 1, you might explain to them that the painting is *The Starry Night* by Vincent van Gogh, and that it was painted in 1889, only 12 years after the poem they're going to study in this lesson was written, and six years before *The Time Machine* was written.

* Keeping **PowerPoint slide 2** displayed, read the poem 'The Starlight Night' by Gerard Manley Hopkins (**Extract 8.1.2**) at least twice.

Developing skills

* Again keeping the image of Van Gogh's 'The Starry Night' on **PowerPoint slide 2** displayed, encourage the students to complete **Worksheet Activity 2**. Working with a partner or independently, they draw lines between the poem and the painting, to make links between the language and imagery of the poem and the physical image depicted in the painting. Allow plenty of thinking time for the students to get started with this activity.

* Take feedback. Possible answers include: *The representation of the stars in the sky in the text and the image of the 'fire folk' and the burning stars in the painting; the ground below being grey lawns and the ground being black and contrasting in the painting.*

* Display **PowerPoint slide 3**. The students should attempt the 'Exploring together' questions in pairs, making notes if they need to, but taking the opportunity to develop their explanation orally before writing down their ideas individually. (Suggested answers: *1. Blue is mostly used. 2. Students' own answers. 3. Links with the poem and painting include: use of the colour blue; the contrast with fire and luminous colours; brighter circle flickering in the blue.*)

Trying it yourself

* Display **PowerPoint slide 4**, which supports the final writing task – **Worksheet Activity 3**. The activity includes consideration of the Van Gogh painting and a linked passage from *The Time Machine* (both displayed on the slide). The students will also need their copy of the poem 'The Starlight Night' (**Extract 8.1.2**) to refer to.

* Before the students start writing, encourage them to explain their thinking by putting their thoughts and feelings about their chosen medium down on paper. Encourage them to consider the impact of a text and the different ways images can be created. For example, you could discuss how the physical image of a painting may seem easier to decode initially, yet there are still many layers and different things to see; you could also discuss the language used to create images in poetry and prose, and how on each reading the image becomes clearer in the reader's mind. You might also consider how we all read the same words in a text or poem, and see the same image when we look at a painting, but that we all take away different interpretations of what we read and see.

Activity 1:

With a partner, look at the painting on **PowerPoint slide 2** and answer the questions below.

1. What do you think this is a painting of? ....

2. What do you notice at first sight? ....

....

3. What do you notice after looking at the painting for 1 minute? ....

....

Activity 2:

Draw lines between the poem and the painting to show the links you have made. Share your ideas with a partner.

Look at the stars! look, look up at the skies!

   O look at all the fire-folk sitting in the air!

   The bright boroughs, the circle-citadels there!

Down in dim woods the diamond delves! the elves'-eyes!

The grey lawns cold where gold, where quickgold lies!

   Wind-beat whitebeam! airy abeles set on a flare!

   Flake-doves sent floating forth at a farmyard scare!

Ah well! it is all a purchase, all is a prize.

Activity 3:

Which image of the night sky do you prefer: poem, painting or prose? Why? What does your preferred image make you think, feel or imagine about the night sky?

....

....

....

....

Learning objectives:	Resources:
• To introduce language features • To begin to explore the effect of language features	• Extract 8.1.2 • 8.1.2 Lesson 2 PowerPoint • 8.1.2 Lesson 2 Worksheet

Getting started

• Display **8.1.4 Lesson 2 PowerPoint slide 1** and introduce the learning objectives. Ask the students if they can recall any language features from previous projects in Year 7 (possible answers include: *metaphor, simile, repetition, descriptive language, emotive language, sensory description*).

• Hand out copies of **8.1.2 Lesson 2 Worksheet** and display **PowerPoint slide 2**, which focuses on metaphors. The students also need their copy of 'The Starlight Night' (**Extract 8.1.2**) to refer to.

• Discuss with the students why a writer might use a metaphor. Ask: Why is it an effective method to compare one thing to another? Establish that metaphors emphasise something or help to create an image in the reader's mind by suggesting it is something else.

• Re-read the poem 'The Starlight Night' twice, to remind the students of the content. The students then complete **Worksheet Activities 1 and 2** by identifying the metaphors in the poem. (Suggested answers for Activity 1: *'fire-folk sitting in the air'; 'bright boroughs'; 'circle-citadels'; 'diamond delves! the elves'-eyes'; 'Flake-doves'.*)

Developing skills

• Display **PowerPoint slide 3** and go through the questions on the slide as a whole group, so that the students can learn from each other's interpretations. Push the students to go beyond the obvious of 'he wants you to look at the sky' and to explore why. Ask them: What does the poet want you to see? What does he see and expect that you will see? You could ask some students to consider whether what Gerard Manley Hopkins saw in the 1800s would be different to what we see today – you might consider context, how the world has changed, light pollution, aircraft, etc.

• The students now complete **Worksheet Activity 3** working with a partner or independently. Encourage them to use the learning from the questions on **PowerPoint slide 3** to start their thinking. (Suggested answers: *1. He wants us to look up at the sky and the stars. He is in awe of them and feels we should appreciate the beauty of the night sky. 2. The repetition creates a sense of urgency; it makes it seem important that we do this straight away. 3. Nature and the stars in the sky are a prize to us on Earth.*)

Trying it yourself

• Display **PowerPoint slide 4** and remind the students of the IEC (identify, exemplify, comment) method. Then display **PowerPoint slide 5** and go over the modelled IEC paragraph on the slide.

• The students complete **Worksheet Activity 4**, exploring how the poet presents the night sky. They should complete the task using the textual references they've found or decoded in the previous activities. Some of the students might benefit from using the sentence starters on the worksheet; if you would prefer the students to respond without these, you can provide additional paper.

• The students' answers will be their own but may look similar to the model answer on **PowerPoint slide 5.** You could also refer the students to the following example answer: *The poet also uses repetition, for example the repetition of 'look' in 'look, look up at the skies'. This makes me think how important it is that we take time to look up at the sky and appreciate it.*

Introducing more skills with 19th-century poetry: 'The Starlight Night'

Activity 1:

How many metaphors can you find in the poem 'The Starlight Night'? Underline them.

Look at the stars! look, look up at the skies!

   O look at all the fire-folk sitting in the air!

   The bright boroughs, the circle-citadels there!

Down in dim woods the diamond delves! the elves'-eyes!

The grey lawns cold where gold, where quickgold lies!

   Wind-beat whitebeam! airy abeles set on a flare!

   Flake-doves sent floating forth at a farmyard scare!

Ah well! it is all a purchase, all is a prize.

Activity 2:

Draw a circle around your favourite metaphor. Explain why it is your favourite. What image does it create in your mind?

....

....

Activity 3:

Complete the questions below using these two quotations from the poem.

Look at the stars! look, look up at the skies!   ...all is a prize.

---

1. What does the poet want you to do and why? ....

....

2. What does the repetition make you think or feel? ....

....

3. What does the poet think is 'a prize'? ....

....

Activity 4:

How does the poet present the night sky in 'The Starlight Night'?

- Answer this question considering the metaphors you found in the poem and the poem's opening and closing lines.
- Complete the first paragraph using the sentence prompts. If you can, complete a second paragraph without the prompts.

First paragraph:

Identify a feature: *The poet uses* ....

....

Example: *An example of this is* ....

....

Comment: *This make me think/feel/imagine* ....

....

....

Second paragraph:

....

....

....

....

....

....

....

....

....

Learning objectives:	Resources:
• To introduce a narrative structure • To explore narrative structure using a well-known text • To plan your own narrative	• 8.1.3 Lessons 1 & 2 PowerPoint • 8.1.3 Lesson 1 Worksheet • 8.1.3 Lesson 2 Worksheet

Lesson 1: Getting started

* Display **8.1.3 Lessons 1 & 2 PowerPoint slide 1** and introduce the learning objectives. Ask the students if they know what a 'narrative' is and explain that it is a story.

* Display **PowerPoint slide 2**. Ask the students what they can recall about the nursery story *The Three Little Pigs*. The students can work in pairs to retell the story, remembering as many of the details as possible. If the students struggle to recall the narrative, you might want to share the story as a group.

Developing skills

* Display **PowerPoint slide 3** and talk the students through the different elements of the narrative structure. Explain that many stories they know will follow this type of plan, where after the opening there is a rising of action towards the climax, and then a calming of the action leading to a final solution. Ask whether the solution or conclusion always has to be positive or a 'wrapping up' of the story; discuss how some stories end on a cliff-hanger or without a 'happy ever after'. Ask the students at which point on the story arc they think the characters and setting would be introduced (*the opening, or sometimes the plot/problem*).

* Now display **PowerPoint slide 4**, which gives the story *The Three Little Pigs* broken down into 10 distinct parts, and hand out copies of **8.1.3 Lesson 1 Worksheet**. Ask the students to complete **Activity 1** by plotting the different story parts against the narrative plan. Remind them that some points on the plan may have more than one event. (Answer: *Opening: I; Plot or problem: I and G; Event 1: E and D; Event 2: F and H; Event 3: B and J; Climax: C; Solution: A*)

* The students now use the model provided on **Worksheet Activity 2** to plot another narrative. They could work in pairs or small groups and share the plotting of a story. If they are struggling to think of a narrative, you could suggest commonly known fairy tales such as *Cinderella* or *Red Riding Hood*. The students can also adapt the number of events in the plan to suit their narrative. It's worth building in time to share narratives in groups or as a whole class as a way of embedding the structure.

Lesson 2: Trying it yourself

* Display **PowerPoint slide 5**. Explain to the students that they will be writing non-stop in their notebooks for 10 minutes using one of the options on the slide: they either write a story with the title 'Beyond our World' or write a story inspired by the image. Allow them a couple of minutes to decide which option they will choose and to gather their thoughts. The aim is to get the students writing creatively; they will spend time structuring and thinking about the elements of the story in the following tasks.

* Display **PowerPoint slide 1** again and revisit the learning objectives. Ask the students to recall what a narrative is and any elements of the narrative arc they worked with last lesson.

* Then revisit **PowerPoint slide 3** and remind the students of the different elements of the narrative structure. You could ask the students to recall and explain each element.

* Hand out copies of **8.1.3 Lesson 2 Worksheet** and ask the students to complete **Activity 1** by plotting out the full narrative of the story they have just come up with. The students can adapt the plan if it suits their narrative. They should try to keep the opening, plot or problem, climax and solution as the anchored points of the plan, but the number of events that lead up to the climax are adaptable. The aim of this task is to try and get students to consider their whole narrative and plan using a structure.

* Display **PowerPoint slide 6** and introduce the final task: the students now transform the information from their plan into their narrative, writing in their notebooks. If the students do not have the time to finish their writing, they should focus on hitting the success criteria on the slide: Structure your writing so that it follows a plan; Consider the order of events.

Introducing more skills with creative writing: Planning a narrative

Activity 1:

Using the story parts on **PowerPoint slide 4**, plot the events of *The Three Little Pigs* against this narrative plan.

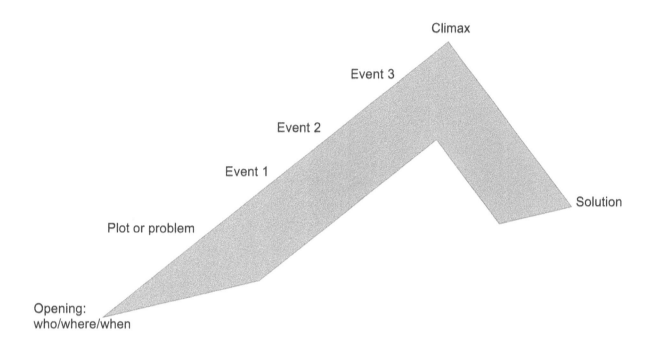

Activity 2:

Now plot the events of a story of your choice against the narrative plan below.

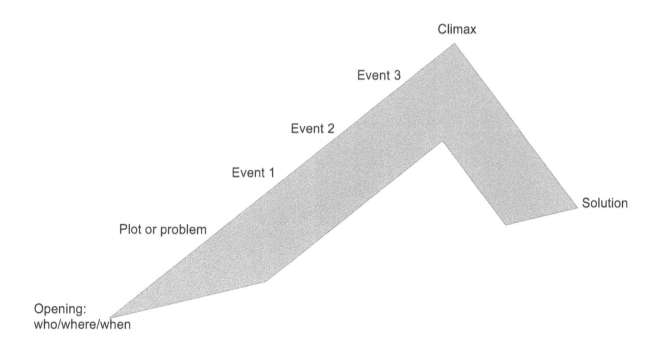

Activity 1:

Plot the events of your narrative on this plan.

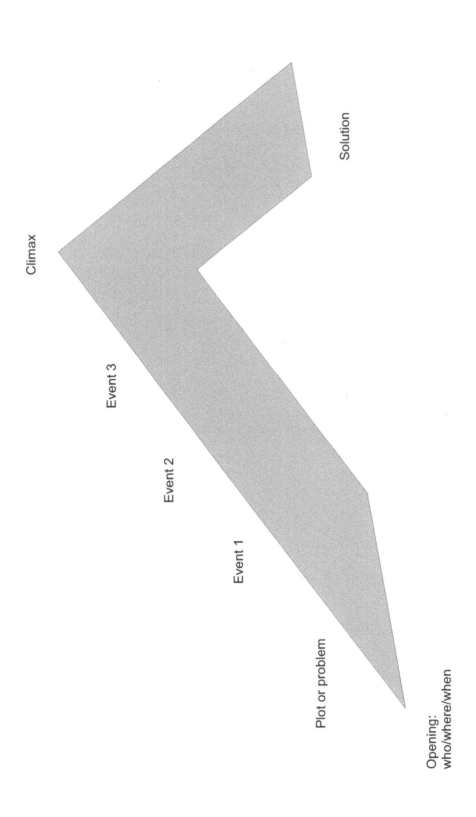

'How will the world end?' by Herbert C. Fyfe

Following in Lord Kelvin's footsteps, Professor Rees, a prominent American scientist, has been going further into the question of the exhaustion of the air supply of the world. He gives definite warning of the coming 'failure' of the air.

'Free as the air we breathe,' he writes will, in the distant future, become an out-of-date, misleading expression. Air will no longer be free, for it will be manufactured and sold like any other necessary. Those who will not work for their daily air supply, and who cannot afford to buy it, will perish, for Nature will have exhausted her supply. The artificial air will be stored up in enormous reservoirs, and to these **receptacles** applicants will come for their daily supply of oxygen. This will then be carried home and doled out to the family as part of the day's means to support life. The manufactured oxygen will be breathed in as a diver inhales the air supplied him when he sinks beneath the waves.

'Died from air starvation' will be a common verdict in the coroners' courts of the future, for 'no money, no air,' will be the rule of life. The wealthy will gain a reputation for charity by free gifts of air to the aged poor at Christmas time. Men and women will no longer be able to look at each other with eyes of love, for everyone will be clothed in a great air helmet, like a diver of to-day.

There is, however, a silver lining of hope fringing these gloomy clouds of speculation. Lord Kelvin himself is not wholly a **prophet** of evil, neither are his views of an entirely **pessimistic** nature. He looks to the agriculturist to improve his methods, so that the plant life on the globe may be able to absorb the surplus **carbonic acid gas** and release sufficient new oxygen to cope with the growing consumption of fuel.

Those sources of Nature at present allowed (except in a few instances) to run to waste – the tides, the ceaseless movement of the waves, waterfalls, solar energy, the wind, the ether, atmospheric electricity – all these in times to come will be made to supply the energy that we require for daily needs. If this be the case, we shall not die of suffocation after all.

Pearson's Magazine, 1900

receptacles: spaces used to contain things
prophet: someone who predicts the future
pessimistic: believing the worst will happen
carbonic acid gas: a solution of carbon dioxide in water

Introducing more skills with understanding older non-fiction: 'How will the world end?'

Learning objective:	Resources:
• Reading and comprehending older non-fiction	• Extract 8.1.4
	• 8.1.4 Lesson 1 PowerPoint
	• 8.1.4 Lesson 1 Worksheet

Getting started

• Display **8.1.4 Lesson 1 PowerPoint slide 2**. Encourage the students to be as imaginative as possible with this activity. They should use their notebooks to make notes, create a mind map, bullet-point ideas and/or draw images of their world of the future. Take time to share the students' worlds in small groups or across the class.

• Display **PowerPoint slide 1** and introduce the learning objective, then hand out copies of **Extract 8.1.4**, 'How will the world end?', which was published in *Pearson's Magazine* in 1900. Read through the extract once as a whole class and work through the challenging language using the glossary.

Developing skills

• Display **PowerPoint slide 3**, which gives some background context on the article, then read the extract again. After a second reading, ask the students to close their eyes and spend 30 seconds imagining the 'future' the writer is describing; encourage them to paint a picture in their mind. Ask the students what they think the article is about. Explain that the person writing the article thought we would be living in the way he describes. How does this information make them feel about the article? Could this still happen? Encourage the students to to explain their thinking.

• Now hand out copies of **8.1.4 Lesson 1 Worksheet** and ask the students to complete **Activity 1**; they should read the quotations as stimuli to answering the questions. The aim of the activity is to encourage exploration of the text alongside identifying and decoding the main points made by the author. (Suggested answers: *1. Something that is essential to our survival. 2. For example, water, gas, electricity, food. 3. Students' own answers. 4. There is something positive to be taken from the situation. 5. Plants and nature will help absorb toxic gases. 6. As well as absorbing the toxic gases, plants will also produce oxygen to save the planet. 7. We currently have hydroelectric (energy from waves), solar and wind power as common energy sources across the country.*)

• Before the students attempt question 7 on the worksheet, or while taking feedback on this question, you may wish to display **PowerPoint slide 4**, which contains images of wind, hydroelectric and solar energy. The students might find it useful to see the images to aid a discussion around renewable energy, climate change and global warming. Facilitate their discussion, prompting them to explain why renewable energy is important. Ask them to share what they know about climate change and what their opinion on it is. What can they do as an individual? What could we do as a school community?

Trying it yourself

• Display **PowerPoint slide 5**, which describes the final task. Working independently, the students write a summary paragraph explaining the key elements of the extract text. They might approach the activity in an informal way; this should be allowed if it supports them in reiterating the key points and showing a good understanding of the article. Allow around 10 minutes for writing.

• Once they have finished their paragraphs, encourage the students to peer-assess their partner's writing using the success criteria on **PowerPoint slide 5**. They could be asked to share particularly clear and concise summaries.

Activity 1:

Read the following quotations from the extract and answer the questions.

> Air will no longer be free, for it will be manufactured and sold like any other necessary.

1. What is a 'necessary'?

   ....

2. Name a 'necessary' we currently pay for.

   ....

> The manufactured oxygen will be breathed in as a diver inhales the air supplied him when he sinks beneath the waves.

3. Draw and/or describe what you imagine we'll all be wearing to enable us to breathe.

   ....

   ....

   ....

   ....

   ....

> There is, however, a silver lining of hope fringing these gloomy clouds of speculation.

4. What do you think the author means by 'a silver lining of hope'?

....

....

....

> Plant life on the globe may be able to absorb the carbonic acid gas.

5. What does this quotation suggest or imply?

....

....

....

6. Using the quotation, explain the author's plan for the future.

....

....

....

....

7. Read the final paragraph. Are any of these things happening now?

....

....

....

....

....

Learning objective:	Resources:
• To consider point of view in an older non-fiction text	• Extract 8.1.4 • 8.1.4 Lesson 2 PowerPoint • 8.1.4 Lesson 2 Worksheet

Getting started

* Display **8.1.4 Lesson 2 PowerPoint slide 1** and introduce the learning objective.

* Re-read **Extract 8.1.4** and recap and recall the text. Ask: How does the author predict people will be paid in the future? (*with air*) What is the 'silver lining' in the situation? (*plants and nature might help maintain oxygen levels*) What does the author predict wealthy people will do? (*gift air to poor people*)

* Display **PowerPoint slide 2**. Encourage the students to decode the image and the words on the placard that Greta Thunberg is holding. You can use this activity to encourage them to reflect on the strategies they use to translate and work out the words they don't know. Ask for translations of the words on the placard. When a student gives a correct translation, ask them to explain their approach; then ask if other students approached the translation differently. Once all students know the translation, encourage them to identify the connection/similarities to the English words. (Suggested answers: *1. Greta Thunberg. 2. The environment (the placard reads 'School Strike for Climate'). Students will probably know who Greta Thunberg is, and the word 'klimatet' on the placard is close to the English word 'climate'. 3. Students' own answers. 4. The protest links to the text through the theme of environment and the prediction of what the future could look like without a change in our approach to the environment.*)

Developing skills

* Display **PowerPoint slide 3** and introduce the definition of point of view. Ask the students for their point of view on topics such as homework, public transport and age restrictions on video games – or any other topic they are likely to have a view on. The students aren't expected to share their entire point of view, but by seeing that they have a point of view on these topics they will better understand the concept.

* The students move on to answer the questions on **PowerPoint slide 3**, considering their point of view in response to the statement 'We should limit everyone's travel to save the environment'. While giving and receiving pair feedback, encourage the students to comment on their ability to put across a clear point of view and the detail they add – the evidence they use, and how they develop their own argument. Remind the students of the need for balance and reflection when considering their partner's viewpoint.

* Display **PowerPoint slide 4** and introduce the definition of tone. Ask the students to consider tone of voice and when it might change. You could create a scenario where one student leaves the room and when they re-enter you state 'You're late!', first saying the words in an angry tone and then in a concerned tone, and perhaps again in a sarcastic tone. This dramatisation of tone in context can aid understanding will give you something to refer to when recalling learning.

* Hand out copies of **8.1.4 Lesson 2 Worksheet**. The students complete **Activity 1**, which focuses on tone. The students could work in pairs for the first two questions then move into independent work. Encourage them to recognise the change in tone from the first extract to the second one, and the alternative point of view presented. (Suggested answers: *1. Tone is hopeless, sombre and worst-case, disastrous. 2. 'perish', 'exhausted', 'doled out'. 3. Tone is hopeful. 4. Different: more positive about the future. 5. 'After all these in times to come will be made to supply the energy that we require', 'If this be the case we shall not die of suffocation after all'.*)

Trying it yourself

* The students now complete the final task using the writing frame provided on **Worksheet Activity 2**. Working independently, they use the prompts to write up an explanation of the writer's point of view. The main aim is for the students to decode the change in the writer's point of view.

* To conclude the lesson, display **PowerPoint slide 5** and ask the students for their own point of view on the article and climate change. They could discuss this as a whole group or in pairs before sharing their thinking with the wider group.

Activity 1:

Read the paragraphs below, which are taken from the article 'How will the world end?', and then answer the questions.

> 'Free as the air we breathe,' he writes will, in the distant future, become an out-of-date, misleading expression. Air will no longer be free, for it will be manufactured and sold like any other necessary. Those who will not work for their daily air supply, and who cannot afford to buy it, will perish, for Nature will have exhausted her supply. The artificial air will be stored up in enormous reservoirs, and to these receptacles applicants will come for their daily supply of oxygen. This will then be carried home and doled out to the family as part of the day's means to support life. The manufactured oxygen will be breathed in as a diver inhales the air supplied him when he sinks beneath the waves.

1. What tone is the author using here? ....

   ....

2. Select two words or phrases that are a good example of the tone you think the author is using.

   ....

   ....

> Those sources of Nature at present allowed (except in a few instances) to run to waste – the tides, the ceaseless movement of the waves, waterfalls, solar energy, the wind, the ether, atmospheric electricity – all these in times to come will be made to supply the energy that we require for daily needs. If this be the case, we shall not die of suffocation after all.

3. What tone is the author using here? ....

   ....

4. Is the tone in this paragraph the same or different to the tone in the previous paragraph?

   ....

5. Select two words or phrases that are a good example of the tone you think the author is using.

   ....

   ....

Activity 2:

Using your notes above to help you, explain the writer's point of view on the future of air supply.

At the start of the text the writer's point of view is ....

....

....

A quotation to show this is ....

....

....

At the end of the text the author's point of view is ....

....

....

A quotation to show this is ....

....

....

Tim Peake interview: 'I orbited the earth 2,720 times', by Joanne O'Connor

The British astronaut, 45, on how vulnerable our planet looks from space, strange floating dreams and whether we'll find life out there

I orbited the Earth 2,720 times. What strikes you most is how vast the Pacific is. If ever people said: "Where are you now?" and I didn't know, I'd just say, "the Pacific" and 9 out of 10 times we were. There are parts of the orbit where the entire planet beneath you is blue.

What goes through your mind on a spacewalk is this incredible feeling of detachedness: you're floating inside a space suit, in a weightless environment and looking through a thin visor at space or down at the planet.

From space the southern ice fields of Patagonia are absolutely stunning. It's now on my bucket list to go there. And also the volcanoes of Kamchatka, an incredibly remote but very beautiful looking landscape in eastern Russia.

Towards the end of my mission I used to have strange dreams that I was back on Earth but floating around. My body was so used to weightlessness but my mind still wanted to dream back on Earth so it put the two together.

Coming back down to Earth is much harder than going into space. Going up, you've got lots of adrenalin, you're fresh, you're fit, you're ready to go. But coming back into Earth's gravity is very punishing on the body. You feel nausea, dizziness, vertigo and your balance is shot to pieces. You have to learn how to walk again. For three or four days I just wanted to sit in a chair.

I'm a strong believer that there is life elsewhere in the universe. There are moons around Saturn and Jupiter that have icy crusts and liquid oceans beneath them so we might find single-celled microbiological life forms, either past or present, in our own solar system. We may well be very be close to finding previous signs of life on Mars within the next few years. And, of course, single-cell life forms can always develop into more complex life forms.

All world leaders should have to go into space, at least theoretically. You get a real sense of how fragile our ecosystem is, how frighteningly thin our atmosphere is, the huge areas of pollution and deforestation across continents. When we look up we see lovely blue skies, but when you're out in space, it's not warm and welcoming – it's a vast, black abyss of nothingness and you suddenly realise how vulnerable and isolated we are on this small rocky planet and that we do need to look after our home.

I'd love to go to Mars, but I have two small boys who need a dad around, so jumping on a rocket for a three-year mission wouldn't be my primary choice right now.

The Guardian, 25 November 2017

8.1.5
Lesson 1

Introducing more skills with linked modern non-fiction: Considering point of view

Learning objective:	Resources:
• To explore tone and point of view in an interview	• Extract 8.1.5 • 8.1.5 Lesson 1 PowerPoint • 8.1.5 Lesson 1 Worksheet

Getting started

* Display **8.1.5 Lesson 1 PowerPoint slide 1** and introduce the learning objective. Ask the students to recall the meanings of 'point of view' and 'tone' from the previous lesson. Ask whether they think we should spend money on space travel and exploration or on curing disease. Point out that they are developing their point of view while thinking about the topic. If they felt annoyed by the money spent on space travel they might have an angry or even aggressive tone when discussing their point of view.

* Display **PowerPoint slide 2**. Encourage the students to share their current knowledge of the form an interview takes. Establish that an interview is when one person, the interviewer, asks another person, the interviewee, questions, and that some interviews include the questions asked while others contain just the answers given. Ask what an astronaut is (someone who is specially trained to travel in outer space) and establish the students' general knowledge of what/who astronauts are. The students then work in pairs to come up with three questions for an astronaut. Allow them to have fun with this activity and come up with creative and imaginative questions. Share some of these with the class.

Developing skills

* Display **PowerPoint slide 3** and give out copies of **Extract 8.1.5**. Read the Tim Peake interview twice. Ask for the students' first impressions. Ask: We can't see the questions, but are the types of questions the interviewer asked clear from the answers that Tim Peake gives? Did anything he say disappoint you?

* After a second reading, hand out copies of **8.1.5 Lesson 1 Worksheet**. Ask the students to complete . **Activity 1**, working either individually or in pairs. Take feedback and establish that Tim Peake seems to love and feel passionate about space travel; he talks about wanting to do more and how he thinks all world leaders should do it.

* The students now move on to **Worksheet Activity 2**. They should re-read the penultimate paragraph of the extract as a whole class before attempting the questions. The purpose of this activity is to encourage independent exploration of the text, to uncover the author's point of view, and to select textual references that 'prove' the inference they have made. (Suggested answers: *1. He thinks we need to take better care of the environment. 2. 'how fragile our ecosystem is, how frighteningly thin our atmosphere is, the huge areas of pollution and deforestation across continents', 'how vulnerable and isolated we are', 'we do need to look after our home'.)*

* While sharing answers with a partner for Activity 2 question 3, the students should be encouraged to recognise that more than one textual reference might support their thinking. Ask them to consider whether some textual references are better than others, and whether the tone in some parts of the text more clearly shows how the person feels or their point of view. Remind the students that, by selecting references carefully and with consideration, their response will be clearer and more concise.

Trying it yourself

* Display **PowerPoint slide 4**. Ask the students to consider and share their response to Tim Peake's message about Earth. This could be done as a quick think, pair, share activity; alternatively, allow 30 seconds of thinking time and then select people to share at random.

* The students now complete **Worksheet Activity 3** working independently. Encourage them to use the prompts on the worksheet to respond to the student statement. The purpose of the activity is to encourage the students to form fuller responses using the SQI (statement, quotation, inference) method, to ensure they include all elements of a full response.

* To consolidate the learning, ask the students to read their response to a partner and allow a 1-minute (timed) partner discussion about the statement and their opinion, with each person in the pair talking for 1 minute.

Activity 1:

Read the Tim Peake interview then answer the questions below.

1. What is your impression of Tim Peake from this article? ....

   ....

2. How does Tim Peake seem to feel about space travel? ....

   ....

3. What information surprised you? ....

   ....

4. What do you want to know more about? ....

   ....

Activity 2:

Explore the extract from the Tim Peake interview below then answer the questions.

> All world leaders should have to go into space, at least theoretically. You get a real sense of how fragile our ecosystem is, how frighteningly thin our atmosphere is, the huge areas of pollution and deforestation across continents. When we look up we see lovely blue skies, but when you're out in space, it's not warm and welcoming – it's a vast, black abyss of nothingness and you suddenly realise how vulnerable and isolated we are on this small rocky planet and that we do need to look after our home.

1. How does Tim Peake feel about the environment? ....

   ....

2. How do you know? Select two words or phrases that show his feelings about the environment.

   ....

   ....

3. Share your choices with your partner. Have you chosen the same examples?

   ....

Activity 3:

A student reading *The Guardian* interview with Tim Peake said: 'Tim Peake makes it clear we should look after our planet or risk destroying it.'

Do you agree or disagree with the student's statement?

Explain your answer using the sentence starters below and the SQI method. Remember to:

- Give a clear **statement** sentence.
- Include a supporting **quotation** from the extract.
- Make an **inference** that interprets and adds information to the quotation rather than just repeating it or explaining its meaning.

I agree/disagree with this statement because ....

....

....

....

Evidence from the text to show this is ....

....

....

....

This quotation suggests that ....

....

....

....

Learning objectives:	**Resources:**
• To explore and compare point of view in different texts	• Extract 8.1.5 • Extract 8.1.1 • 8.1.5 Lesson 2 PowerPoint • 8.1.5 Lesson 2 Worksheet

Getting started

• Display **8.1.5 Lesson 2 PowerPoint slide 2**. Encourage the students to re-read **Extract 8.1.5** independently or with the support of a partner or small group. Follow up with a class discussion and reminder about Tim Peake's experiences and how he feels about space travel.

• Display **PowerPoint slide 1** and introduce the learning objective. Ask the students to recall the meaning of 'point of view' (someone's opinion and feelings about a topic). Establish that points of view often change across texts, especially if the writer is exploring more than one side to a topic or argument.

Developing skills

• Display **PowerPoint slide 3**. Read the extract from the Tim Peake article and use the discussion prompt to encourage pair or whole-class discussion. You could ask whether the students imagined the return to Earth from space would be more difficult, given the drama and danger of take-off.

• Then display **PowerPoint slide 4** and use the discussion prompt to explore the extract from *The Time Machine*. When comparing *The Time Machine* extract with the Tim Peake article, explore what stands out for the students between the imagined feelings of time travel and the real experiences of space travel; they could discuss this in pairs then feed back.

• Now hand out copies of **8.1.5 Lesson 2 Worksheet** and ask the students to work independently or with a partner to complete **Activity 1**. You could revisit **Extract 8.1.1** from *The Time Machine* as a class to support the students in remembering and decoding the information. (Suggested answers: *Tim Peake considers the return to Earth to be physically demanding: 'is very punishing on the body', 'feel nausea, dizziness, vertigo', 'learn how to walk again'. The time traveller finds space travel physically demanding and unpleasant: 'excessively unpleasant', 'horrible anticipation'.*)

• Ask the students to turn to **Worksheet Activity 2** and read the quotations from the Tim Peake article and *The Time Machine*. They then complete the table by exploring the similarities or differences in the way travel beyond our world is presented in each text. If you didn't complete a re-reading of **Extract 8.1.1** for Activity 1, it would be useful to re-read it as a whole class now, or you might leave the students to attempt the whole task independently, including the reading. The aim is to get the students thinking further about the texts together. Remind them that one text is a work of fiction, whereas the other text is a real account. You might choose to run this activity as pair work. (Suggested answers: *The students should be left to devise their own connections, but the most obvious similarities are: view of colour; descriptions of feeling detached or removed from normality. The differences include: Peake's description is quite terrifying whereas the time traveller's description sounds welcoming and like the night sky.*)

Trying it yourself

• Display **PowerPoint slide 5** and introduce the final task, which the students complete using **Worksheet Activity 3**. Before they start, it would be worth investing some time in a whole-group discussion, sharing findings from the previous activity and prompting a wider comparison of the two texts and the similarities and differences. Working independently, the students then use the sentence starters on the worksheet to develop their response to the question, 'What are the similarities and the differences between the real and the imaginary trips beyond our world?' The purpose of this activity is to encourage the students to develop their inferences, drawing from two texts for a longer SQI response. They should aim to complete at least one other paragraph in their notebooks without the sentence starters and lined spaces.

• To round off the lesson, you could ask the students to share their own point of view on how accurate H.G. Wells was in his imagined experience of travel beyond our world.

Activity 1:

Answer the questions below. Remember to support your opinions with quotations from the texts.

1. What does Tim Peake think and feel about the physical impact of space travel?

    ....

    ....

2. What does the time traveller think and feel about the physical impact of space travel?

    ....

    ....

Activity 2:

Read the quotations below then complete the table by exploring the similarities or differences in the way travel beyond our world is presented in each text.

Quotations from Tim Peake article:

'There are parts of the orbit where the entire planet beneath you is blue...'

'What goes through your mind on a spacewalk is this incredible feeling of detachedness'

'when you're out in space, it's not warm and welcoming – it's a vast, black abyss of nothingness...'

Quotations from *The Time Machine*:

'The twinkling succession of darkness...'

'the sky took on a wonderful deepness of blue, a splendid luminous colour...'

'I was already going too fast to be conscious of any moving things.'

Quotation from Tim Peake interview	Quotation from *The Time Machine*	Similarity or difference in the way space travel is presented

Activity 3: Final task

Does Tim Peake's real account of space travel match H.G. Wells' imaginary account? What are the similarities and the differences between the real and the imaginary trips beyond our world?

Use the writing frame below to write a paragraph comparing the Tim Peake interview from *The Guardian* (**Extract 8.1.5**) and the extract from *The Time Machine* (**Extract 8.1.1**).

Then, in your notebooks, write a second paragraph of comparison without the writing structure.

Paragraph 1:

In my opinion both writers feel ....

....

For example, the time traveller feels ....

....

A quotation to show this is ....

....

In comparison, Tim Peake feels ....

....

A quotation to show this is ....

....

This suggests ....

....

8.1.6
Lessons 1 & 2

Introducing more skills with discursive writing: Presenting a point of view

Learning objectives:
- To plan a piece of writing including a balanced point of view
- To draft and review ideas ahead of writing

Resources:
- 8.1.6 Lessons 1 & 2 PowerPoint
- 8.1.6 Lesson 1 Worksheet

Lesson 1: Getting started

- Display **8.1.6 Lessons 1 & 2 PowerPoint slide 2**. Revisit the elements of the project and consolidate the students' understanding of tone and point of view through partners sharing their definitions.

- Display **PowerPoint slide 1** and introduce the learning objectives. Explain to the students that discursive writing usually explores more than one point of view, and that even if the writer has a clear bias they tend to balance the piece of writing with a reference to or exploration of an alternative point of view. To support understanding you could refer to *The Time Machine* (**Extract 8.1.1**) or 'How will the world end?' (**Extract 8.1.4**), drawing on the fact that both writers offered negative points about the situation but then hope, enjoyment and a possible solution.

Developing skills

- Display **PowerPoint slide 3** and introduce the discursive writing task, checking the students understand what is expected of them and what they are working towards. Encourage pair work or a whole-group discussion around initial ideas based on who or what lives on the planet; things to do; things to avoid; how you travel there. **PowerPoint slide 4** contains a visual that might support some students in getting started with ideas.

- Display **PowerPoint slide 5** and hand out copies of **8.1.6 Lesson 1 Worksheet**. The students complete question 1 of **Activity 1** by developing a mind map to collate their initial ideas, using the prompts and diagram on the slide. Encourage them to add everything they can think of at this stage. Remind them that they are writing a discursive piece so they should try to be balanced, covering both the positive and negative points. Allow enough time for the students to include a wide range of ideas.

- Display **PowerPoint slide 6** and ask the students to work through the points on the slide. They should present their initial ideas to a partner, then use this to help them edit the mind map they completed for Activity 1. Encourage them to keep their writing concise and not to include anything that they're struggling to develop at the planning stage. It's key at this point that they independently check their plan to make sure it shows a balanced point of view. Ask partners to focus on this in their feedback and the students to make sure they take the feedback on board.

- The students then include an additional note about the tone they will use at different points in their writing. The aim here is to ensure the students have a clear plan from which they can write a final piece. It might support them to revisit the task instructions on **PowerPoint slide 3**.

Lesson 2: Getting started and Trying it yourself

- Display **PowerPoint slide 1** again and revisit the learning objectives. Explain that most of this session will be spent writing and transforming their plan from the previous lesson into a piece of discursive writing. Then display **PowerPoint slide 7** and revisit the elements of the writing task, allowing the students to spend around 10 minutes revisiting their plan from the last lesson using the prompts on the slide. Some of the students might benefit from a reminder of what a fact is and how you might include a quotation from, or interview with, an alien.

- Display **PowerPoint slide 8** and go through the suggestions on the slide for how the students can refine their plans. Encourage pair or whole-class discussion to support the students in grouping their ideas from their plan into topics using sub-headings. Some students might benefit from revisiting **Extracts 8.1.4** and **8.1.5** in pairs, to reflect on how the tone and point of view changes through the text.

- Display **PowerPoint slide 9**. Using their plans to support writing, the students independently complete the writing task in their notebooks or on a separate piece of paper. Allow them time to check and edit their work against the success criteria on the slide.

Introducing more skills with discursive writing

Activity 1:

Write a travel guide to another world or planet. Consider:

- who or what lives there
- things to do
- things to avoid
- how you travel to the other world
- positives and negatives about the planet.

1. Plan your writing using the mind map template below.

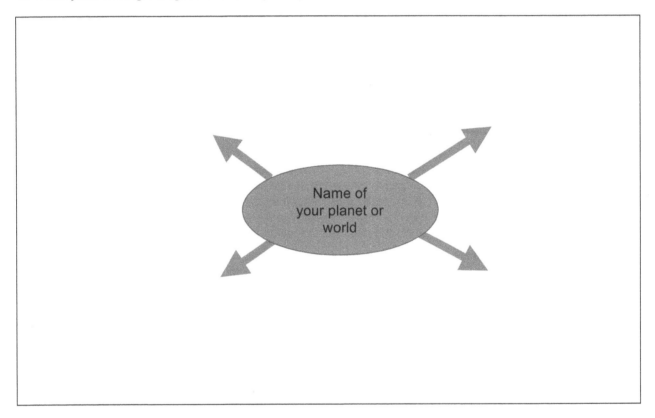

Name of your planet or world

2. Complete the notes below.

The tone I will use in most of my writing is...

....

I will change my tone when I talk about ....

....

My tone will change to ....

....

From *Jane Eyre* (1847)

Extract 1: There was no possibility of taking a walk that day. We had been wandering, indeed, in the leafless shrubbery an hour in the morning; but since dinner the cold winter wind had brought with it clouds so sombre, and a rain so penetrating, that further out-door exercise was now out of the question.

I was glad of it: I never liked long walks, especially on chilly afternoons: dreadful to me was the coming home in the raw twilight, with nipped fingers and toes, and a heart saddened by the chidings of Bessie, the nurse, and humbled by the consciousness of my physical inferiority to Eliza, John, and Georgiana Reed.

Extract 2: The said Eliza, John, and Georgiana were now clustered round their mama in the drawing-room: she lay reclined on a sofa by the fireside, and with her darlings about her (for the time neither quarrelling nor crying) looked perfectly happy. Me, she had dispensed from joining the group; saying, 'She regretted to be under the necessity of keeping me at a distance; but that until she heard from Bessie, and could discover by her own observation, that I was endeavouring in good earnest to acquire a more sociable and childlike disposition, a more attractive and sprightly manner – something lighter, franker, more natural, as it were – she really must exclude me from privileges intended only for contented, happy, little children.'

'What does Bessie say I have done?' I asked.

'Jane, I don't like questioners; besides, there is something truly forbidding in a child taking up her elders in that manner. Be seated somewhere; and until you can speak pleasantly, remain silent.'

Extract 3: A breakfast-room adjoined the drawing-room, I slipped in there. It contained a bookcase: I soon possessed myself of a volume, taking care that it should be one stored with pictures. I mounted into the window-seat: gathering up my feet, I sat cross-legged, like a Turk; and, having drawn the red curtain nearly close, I was shrined in double retirement.

Folds of scarlet drapery shut in my view to the right hand; to the left were the clear panes of glass, protecting, but not separating me from the drear November day. At intervals, while turning over the leaves of my book, I studied the winter afternoon. Afar, it offered a pale blank of mist and cloud; near a scene of wet lawn and storm-beat shrub, with ceaseless rain sweeping away wildly before a long and lamentable blast.

I returned to my book – Bewick's *History of British Birds*: the letterpress thereof I cared little for, generally speaking; and yet there were certain introductory pages that, child as I was, I could not pass quite as a blank. With Bewick on my knee, I was then happy: happy at least in my way. I feared nothing but interruption, and that came too soon. The breakfast-room door opened.

Charlotte Brontë

Developing inferential reading with the 19th-century novel: *Jane Eyre*

Learning objectives:	Resources:
• To develop skills of inference with a 19th-century novel • To build an interpretation of characters and their actions	• Extract 8.2.1 Lesson 1 • 8.2.1 Lesson 1 PowerPoint • 8.2.1 Lesson 1 Worksheet

Getting started

- Hand out **Extract 8.2.1 Lesson 1**, which is organised into **Extracts 1, 2 and 3**. Explain that, in these extracts from *Jane Eyre*, Jane is nine years old and is living with her aunt and her cousins, Eliza, John and Georgiana Reed. Read aloud **Extract 1**.

- Now display **8.2.1 Lesson 1 PowerPoint slide 2** and ask the students to respond to the questions on the slide as a whole group. (Suggested answers: *1. The students should be able to identify the first person perspective and give an example. 2. The students might note that Jane does not like the rain or having to go on long walks, especially when it's cold; that she seems to be told off by the nurse and is much smaller than her cousins. 3. Focus on some of the tricky vocabulary and see if the students can identify some of these words from their context in the sentence – for example, shrubbery from 'leafless', 'sombre' from the idea of rain clouds and 'chidings' from the fact it makes her heart sad.*)

- Display **PowerPoint slide 1** and go over the learning objectives for the lesson.

Developing skills

- Introduce the supporting information for **Extract 2** using **PowerPoint slide 3**. Ask the students to think about the three questions on the slide as you read. As you read the extract, ensure you emphasise the aunt's dialogue in a very formal and haughty voice. Take some ideas from the whole class for the questions. Ensure the students note that Jane is not 'clustered around…mama' with the others. (Suggested answers: *1. The students might pick up on the fact the children are spoilt. 2. The household seems rich, as it has servants and a 'mama' who lies on the sofa. 3. The aunt seems strict and formal with Jane and treats her differently to her own children; she seems to need to separate her from the group and point out her faults.*)

- Pair up the students for support to work on the comprehension questions on **PowerPoint slide 4**. Recap on the core SQI (statement + quotation + inference) method used throughout the Year 7 projects and reinforced in Project 8.1. Allow approximately 15 minutes for this activity.

- Take feedback. The students should identify that Jane is portrayed as badly behaved, is separated from the others and isolated, and that she appears to resent their treatment of her. More confident students may pick up on the fact that Jane is conscious the others are being spoilt from the reference to 'her darlings'; these ideas could be consolidated though whole-class feedback if necessary. In feedback, aim to see if the students have concluded that Jane is an orphan.

Trying it yourself

- Hand out copies of **8.2.1 Lesson 1 Worksheet** and support the students by reading **Extract 3** out loud, before asking them to read it again themselves. The students should work individually on this task and aim to draw some inferences on their own about Jane, selecting quotations to support their thoughts and ideas. The students may come up with ideas such as: *Jane wants to be alone or left alone; she loves books; she likes looking at picture books; she likes to be snug, safe and warm; she's interested in nature outside the window; she's reading a book about nature; she seems quiet and imaginative, not badly behaved, and enjoys her own company.*

Jane's aunt seems to treat her differently from her cousins, and **Extract 2** suggests that in some ways Jane must be badly behaved.

Activity 1:

Read **Extract 3** carefully.

- How would you describe Jane's behaviour and personality from the evidence here?
- Fill in the table below with your thoughts and evidence.

I would describe Jane as...	A quotation that suggests this is...

From *Jane Eyre* (1847)

Extract 4:

John Reed was a schoolboy of fourteen years old; four years older than I, for I was but ten: large and stout for his age, with a dingy and unwholesome skin; heavy limbs and large extremities. He gorged himself habitually at table, which gave him a dim and bleared eye and flabby cheeks. He ought now to have been at school; but his mama had taken him home for a month or two, 'on account of his delicate health.' Mr. Miles, the master, affirmed that he would do very well if he had fewer cakes and sweetmeats sent him from home; but the mother's heart turned from an opinion so harsh, and inclined rather to the more refined idea that John's sallowness was owing to over-application and, perhaps, to pining after home.

John had not much affection for his mother and sisters, and an antipathy to me. He bullied and punished me; not two or three times in the week, nor once or twice in the day, but continually: every nerve I had feared him, and every morsel of flesh in my bones shrank when he came near. There were moments when I was bewildered by the terror he inspired, because I had no appeal whatever against either his menaces or his inflictions; the servants did not like to offend their young master by taking my part against him, and Mrs. Reed was blind and deaf on the subject: she never saw him strike or heard him abuse me, though he did both now and then in her very presence, more frequently, however, behind her back.

Habitually obedient to John, I came up to his chair: he spent some three minutes in thrusting out his tongue at me as far as he could without damaging the roots: I knew he would soon strike, and while dreading the blow, I mused on the disgusting and ugly appearance of him who would presently deal it. I wonder if he read that notion in my face; for, all at once, without speaking, he struck suddenly and strongly. I tottered, and on regaining my equilibrium retired back a step or two from his chair.

'That is for your impudence in answering mama awhile since,' said he, 'and for your sneaking way of getting behind curtains, and for the look you had in your eyes two minutes since, you rat!'

Accustomed to John Reed's abuse, I never had an idea of replying to it; my care was how to endure the blow which would certainly follow the insult.

'What were you doing behind the curtain?' he asked.

'I was reading.'

'Show the book.'

Charlotte Brontë

Learning objectives:	Resources:
• To develop skills of inference with a 19th-century novel • To build an interpretation of characters and their actions	• Extract 8.2.1 Lesson 2 • 8.2.1 Lesson 2 PowerPoint • 8.2.1 Lesson 2 Worksheet

Getting started

* Recap on the previous lesson and ask the students what they remember about the character Jane Eyre. Where did we leave her and what was she doing?

* Display **8.2.1 Lesson 2 PowerPoint slide 1** and recap on the lesson objectives.

* Give out copies of **Extract 8.2.1 Lesson 2** and read **Extract 4** aloud. Explain that, in this extract, Jane's cousin John Reed interrupts Jane while she is reading quietly in the library of the Reeds' house.

* Using **PowerPoint slide 2**, focus closely on the phrases on the slide and take ideas from the class about what is implied by each. Prompt the students by asking: Does John sound like a pleasant character? Does he sound healthy? You may need to define 'gorged' and prompt the students to see he might also be greedy. You may also want to refer to the first paragraph of the text, to point out how John has been spoilt and indulged by his mother. Ask the students whether this adds to their perception of Mrs Reed from the previous lesson.

Developing skills

* Using **PowerPoint slide 3**, take some time to show the students what a noun phrase is and how the changing adjective can change our mental picture of something. Encourage them to note how, each time the adjective is changed, it creates a different picture in our mind's eye. Link this back to the extract with the use of 'bleared eye'.

* Give out copies of **8.2.1 Lesson 2 Worksheet** and encourage the students to work in pairs to complete **Activity 1**, finding examples of adjectives and noun phrases from the extract that describe John. Use the question mantra 'What do they make you think of, feel or imagine?' to keep the students focused on reader response when they add their ideas to the effects box. Allow about 10 minutes for the students to complete this activity.

* Working in the same pairs, ask the students to complete **Worksheet Activity 2** by thinking about the way that John treats his cousin Jane and jotting down notes and evidence from the extract. Develop this by asking the students to make similar notes on how Jane feels about her cousin John, again with evidence. Allow another 10 minutes to answer both questions and then take feedback. The students might note that John is a bully and is much older and bigger than Jane; that Jane is frightened of him; that Jane feels she has no one to take her side; that John's behaviour is rude and disgusting; that John is violent and abusive.

* Use the modelling on **PowerPoint slide 4** (which uses material from the previous lesson) to show the students how they can build an interpretation of a character by using the SQI (statement + quotation + inference) comprehension method coupled with a point on language and effect. Ask the students to identify each of the elements: the statement; the quotation; the inference; the feature that has been identified; the example; the comment on effect.

Trying it yourself

* Display **PowerPoint slide 5** and go over the final task with the students. You may wish to return to the model on **PowerPoint slide 4** for them follow, to help with writing a more sustained response to the task.

* If time allows, ask the students to return to the modelling on **PowerPoint slide 4** and label the different elements in their own answer in the margin, to check their success.

Activity 1:

Read **Extract 4** then complete the table below by:

- identifying three or four adjectives and/or noun phrases that are used to describe John Reed
- describing the effect they have on you as reader.

Examples of adjectives/noun phrases	What effect do they have? What do they make you think of, feel or imagine about this boy?

Activity 2:

Answer the questions below.

1. What do you understand about how John Reed is treating his cousin here? What is your evidence? Make some notes.

   ....

   ....

   ....

   ....

2. What do you understand about how Jane feels about John? What is your evidence? Make some notes.

   ....

   ....

   ....

   ....

'A Poison Tree', from *Songs of Experience* (1794)

I was angry with my friend;

I told my wrath, my wrath did end.

I was angry with my foe:

I told it not, my wrath did grow.

And I water'd it in fears,

Night & morning with my tears:

And I sunned it with smiles,

And with soft deceitful wiles.

And it grew both day and night.

Till it bore an apple bright.

And my foe beheld it shine,

And he knew that it was mine.

And into my garden stole,

When the night had veil'd the pole;

In the morning glad I see;

My foe outstretched beneath the tree.

William Blake

Developing an understanding of an 18th-century poem: 'A Poison Tree'

Learning objectives:

- To develop an understanding of the structure and sequence of a poem
- To develop an understanding of how a writer's choices create meaning

Resources:

- Extract 8.2.2
- 8.2.2 Lesson 1 PowerPoint
- 8.2.2 Lesson 1 Worksheet

Getting started

- Ask the students to write the word 'poison' in their notebooks and, with a partner, play word association with the word. What words, phrases or lyrics can they come up with in 2 minutes?

- Display **8.2.2 Lesson 1 PowerPoint slide 1** and go over the lesson objectives.

- Now hand out copies of **Extract 8.2.2** with the poem 'A Poison Tree'. Before reading, ask the students what the title of the poem suggests. What kind of a plant would a 'poison tree' be? Do they know of any poisonous plants?

- Read the poem aloud. Explain that it describes the poet's feelings towards another person. You may need to check that all students understand what the following words mean: *foe, wrath, wiles*.

Developing skills

- Ask the students to work in pairs. Allow them 5 minutes with their partner to look at **PowerPoint slide 2** and work on the questions. Then take whole-class feedback on the obvious patterns and opposites, but go on to ask the students what the difference is between the way the friend was treated and the foe. Ask: Do people treat their friends differently to their enemies? Is it different if we're angry with someone we don't like? What does the poet mean when he says that anger will 'grow'?

- Allow a further 5 minutes for the students to work in the same pairs on stanza 2 of the poem, which is displayed on **PowerPoint slide 3**. Again take feedback. Most of the students will pick up on the idea of the plant or gardening image. Explain how this comparison with the plant is *metaphorical*: the growing plant is a metaphor for the growing anger and resentment.

- Now ask the students to look at **PowerPoint slide 4**. Some of them will be able to identify the Adam and Eve cartoon, and may know from their Religious Studies lessons that the apple was a symbol of temptation. Most of the students will know of the fairy tale Snow White and that she was given a poisoned apple. In both cases the apple was *symbolic* – share this term with the students.

- Now ask the students to write down and then share their suggestions about what the apple might symbolise in the poem 'A Poison Tree'. They may suggest: *growing anger, resentment, a grudge, jealousy, mistrust, being two-faced.*

Trying it yourself

- Display **PowerPoint slide 5** and stretch the students to think about the end of the poem using the questions on the slide. Invite them to consider: the idea of the 'foe' visiting the garden; the night-time setting as ominous; the consuming of the 'poisoned' apple and the 'death' of the foe. In what ways could all of these things be metaphorical?

- Ask the students to now think about the key events and visual images in the poem. How do they help us to see the poet's message or moral? Is there a lesson to be learned from the poem?

- Go over the final task on **PowerPoint slide 5** and hand out copies of **8.2.2 Lesson 1 Worksheet**, which provides a template for the storyboard activity. The students storyboard the events in 'A Poison Tree', highlighting and illustrating the poem's images.

- As a plenary, the students could decide what they think the moral of the poem 'A Poison Tree' might be and make a note of it. They will need to consider this for the next lesson.

Developing an understanding of an 18th-century poem: 'A Poison Tree'

Final task:

Design a storyboard showing the sequence of events in the poem 'A Poison Tree'.

I was angry with my friend;
I told my wrath, my wrath did end.
I was angry with my foe:
I told it not, my wrath did grow.

And I water'd it in fears,
Night & morning with my tears:
And I sunned it with smiles,
And with soft deceitful wiles.

And it grew both day and night.
Till it bore an apple bright.
And my foe beheld it shine,
And he knew that it was mine.

And into my garden stole,
When the night had veil'd the pole;
In the morning glad I see;
My foe outstretched beneath the tree.

Learning objectives:	Resources:
• To develop an understanding of the ideas in a poem • To develop an understanding of the writer's intention	• Extract 8.2.2 • 8.2.2 Lesson 2 PowerPoint • 8.2.2 Lesson 2 Worksheet

Getting started

• Display **8.2.2 Lesson 2 PowerPoint slide 1**. Refer to the lesson objectives to show how this lesson will focus on the ideas in the poem 'A Poison Tree' and why the poet may have written this poem.

• Re-read the poem 'A Poison Tree' (**Extract 8.2.2**) aloud. Ask the students to reflect on the previous lesson and the images on their storyboard. Recap on what some of the students thought the moral of Blake's poem was.

Developing skills

• Display **8.2.2 Lesson 2 PowerPoint slide 2** and introduce the idea of themes. Ask the students to work in pairs for a few minutes to decide what possible themes the poem 'A Poison Tree' touches on. They may suggest: *friendship, anger, jealousy, resentment*.

• Now use the definition of theme on the slide (an idea that occurs through a piece of writing) to explore how things such as friendship, anger, jealousy and resentment are all 'abstracts' or abstract nouns. Ask the students if they have heard of abstract painting. Explain how abstracts are the 'big ideas' and, as such, make up many of the 'big themes' we read about in literature.

• Now display **PowerPoint slide 3** and go over the five comprehension questions with the students. Ask them to work in pairs on the questions for support, though they should each write their own answers. Before they start, use **PowerPoint slide 4** to remind them of the SQI (statement + quotation + inference) and IEC (identify, exemplify, comment) methods taught so far, to enable the students to answer the two different question types: 'what' and 'how'. Then allow the students a good 20–25 minutes to answer the five questions, writing in their notebooks.

Trying it yourself

• Now hand out copies of **8.2.2 Lesson 2 Worksheet** and ask the students to think about the possible moral of the poem 'A Poison Tree'; direct them to consider the evaluative statements in **Activity 1**. Ask the students to work individually to select some evidence from the poem to support each statement as a possible moral or key message, or the poet's intention.

• Take feedback from students on their ideas here, as these may vary. Ask the students to justify their choices and explain their thoughts.

• Finally, display **PowerPoint slide 5**. Ask the students to reflect on Blake's poem in the light of the two images. Ask: In war, who is a 'friend' and who is a 'foe'? How do we treat them? In the picture on the right of the slide, a migrant refugee looks out from a refugee camp – are migrant refugees being treated as 'friends' who need help or as 'foes'?

• Ask the students to reflect on whether Blake's poem, written in 1794, has a wider and more important message about how we treat others that is still relevant today. The students can record their final thoughts on these questions on **Worksheet Activity 2**.

Activity 1:

Select the line or lines from the poem 'A Poison Tree' that best supports each of these viewpoints.

Poet's message	Supporting quotation
In this poem, the writer's main message is that we should not let our anger get out of control.	
In this poem, the writer's message is that we treat our enemies differently to our friends and this is a bad thing in the long run.	
In this poem, the writer is trying to teach us that it is never good to bear a grudge.	
The poem shows how bad feelings can get out of control and cause lasting damage.	

Activity 2: Final task

Have you changed your mind from last lesson about the moral of the 'story' within the poem 'A Poison Tree'? Explain your thinking below.

....

....

....

....

....

....

....

....

....

....

From *Jane Eyre* (1847)

'You have no business to take our books; you are a dependent, mama says; you have no money; your father left you none; you ought to beg, and not to live here with gentlemen's children like us, and eat the same meals we do, and wear clothes at our mama's expense. Now, I'll teach you to rummage my bookshelves: for they are mine; all the house belongs to me, or will do in a few years. Go and stand by the door, out of the way of the mirror and the windows.'

I did so, not at first aware what was his intention; but when I saw him lift and poise the book and stand in act to hurl it, I instinctively started aside with a cry of alarm: not soon enough, however; the volume was flung, it hit me, and I fell, striking my head against the door and cutting it. The cut bled, the pain was sharp: my terror had passed its climax; other feelings succeeded.

'Wicked and cruel boy!' I said. 'You are like a murderer—you are like a slave-driver—you are like the Roman emperors!'

'What! what!' he cried. 'Did she say that to me? Did you hear her, Eliza and Georgiana? Won't I tell mama? but first—'

He ran headlong at me: I felt him grasp my hair and my shoulder: he had closed with a desperate thing. I really saw in him a tyrant, a murderer. I felt a drop or two of blood from my head trickle down my neck. I don't very well know what I did with my hands, but he called me 'Rat! Rat!' and bellowed out aloud. Aid was near him: Eliza and Georgiana had run for Mrs. Reed, who was gone upstairs: she now came upon the scene, followed by Bessie and her maid Abbot. We were parted: I heard the words—

'Dear! dear! What a fury to fly at Master John!'

Then Mrs. Reed subjoined —

'Take her away to the red-room, and lock her in there.' Four hands were immediately laid upon me, and I was borne upstairs.

Charlotte Brontë

8.2.3
Lessons 1 & 2

Developing more skills with creative writing: Imagining the 'red-room'

Learning objectives:
- To develop skills in creative writing by considering atmosphere, imagery, thoughts and feelings
- To plan and write an effective first-person narrative

Resources:
- Extract 8.2.3
- 8.2.3 Lessons 1 & 2 PowerPoint
- 8.2.3 Lesson 1 Worksheet
- sugar paper and marker pens

Lesson 1: Getting started

- Organise the class into small groups and give each group sugar paper and marker pens. Look at the lesson objectives together on **8.2.3 Lessons 1 & 2 PowerPoint slide 1**.

- Then, using **PowerPoint slide 2**, ask the students to spend 5 minutes generating a mind map around the word 'red'. Share ideas among the whole group. Hopefully ideas will emerge connected with danger, anger, love, passion, roses, blood, etc.

- Recap on the Week 1 lessons based on the *Jane Eyre* extracts. If it helps, ask the students to look back at their work on John Reed from Week 1 Lesson 2. Ask them what they recall and then pick up the story and read **Extract 8.2.3**. Ask the students to consider what the 'red-room' might be and why it has this name. Does it sound warm and inviting or terrifying and threatening? How do they respond to the idea of Jane being locked in? Can they remember how old Jane is? Is it fair how she is being treated?

- Display **PowerPoint slide 3** and set the creative task for the lesson. Explain that the students will spend Lesson 1 preparing for this task and will then complete it in Lesson 2.

Developing skills and Trying it yourself

- Hand out copies of **8.2.3 Lesson 1 Worksheet**, which has four extracts from novels with a Gothic element to them. Read aloud **Extracts 1** and **2**, from *The Picture of Dorian Gray* and *The Time Machine*. Keeping the students in the same small groups, ask them to complete **Worksheet Activity 1** by exploring the extracts and making notes on the atmosphere created in them. Display **PowerPoint slide 4** for the students to refer to during this task; allow about 10 minutes for them to complete it. Take feedback, which should include references to the skull, the darkness, the sinister atmosphere, the idea of the unsettled and worsening weather, the creepy silence (repeated and juxtaposed), the way the narrator's senses are on high alert, and the idea of the wind moaning like a ghost.

- Now read aloud **Extracts 3** and **4** on the worksheet, from *Dracula* and *Carmilla*, and ask the students to complete **Worksheet Activity 2**. Again, they should work in groups for 10 minutes or so using the prompts on **PowerPoint slide 5**. Take feedback, which should include identifying the first-person narrative. Push the students to see that from this perspective we are in the position of 'not knowing', like the narrator. Discuss the use of the sound adjectives in *Dracula* ('heavy step', 'rattling chains') to create fear. In *Carmilla,* consider the fact that the adults are as scared as the child, who seems to have been left to sleep in a room with a ghostly presence.

- The students now work individually to plan for their 'next chapter'. Display **PowerPoint slide 6** and ask them to plan a five-paragraph piece using the conventions of storytelling: introduction, rising action, climax, falling action and conclusion. Encourage them to 'borrow' the last line from **Extract 8.2.3** to begin their narrative and set the scene. Will the action rise as Jane is locked in and left alone? How will the tension rise? What will be the high point? How will it be resolved?

Lesson 2: Getting started and Final task

- Return to **PowerPoint slide 3** to remind the students of the final creative writing task. Ask them to reflect on their outline of the plot via the five-point plan and to make any changes or add in any stronger ideas. Then, using **PowerPoint slide 7**, ask the students to use the exploratory work from the previous lesson to flesh out their ideas and their plan. This slide could also be displayed as a skills checklist while students complete the Big Write. Give the rest of the lesson over to the final writing task.

- During the checking process and for self-evaluation, return to the checklist on **PowerPoint slide 7** and encourage the students to ask 'Have I successfully used…?'

Activity 1:

Read Extracts 1 and 2 below. Make notes on the atmosphere created in the extracts.

Extract 1:

The moon hung low in the sky like a yellow skull. From time to time a huge misshapen cloud stretched a long arm across and hid it. The gas-lamps grew fewer, and the streets more narrow and gloomy.

The Picture of Dorian Gray (1890)

Extract 2:

The darkness grew apace; a cold wind began to blow in freshening gusts from the east, and the showering white flakes in the air increased in number. From the edge of the sea came a ripple and whisper. Beyond these lifeless sounds the world was silent. Silent? It would be hard to convey the stillness of it. All the sounds of man, the bleating of sheep, the cries of birds, the hum of insects, the stir that makes the background of our lives, all that was over. As the darkness thickened, the eddying flakes grew more abundant, dancing before my eyes; and the cold of the air more intense. At last, one by one, swiftly, one after the other, the white peaks of the distant hills vanished into blackness. The breeze rose to a moaning wind. I saw the black central shadow of the eclipse sweeping towards me. In another moment the pale stars alone were visible. All else was rayless obscurity. The sky was absolutely black.

The Time Machine (1895)

....

....

....

....

....

....

....

....

Activity 2:

Read Extracts 3 and 4 below. Make notes on the thoughts and feelings of the characters in the extracts.

Extract 3:

All I could do now was to be patient, and to wait the coming of morning.

Just as I had come to this conclusion I heard a heavy step approaching behind the great door, and saw through the chinks the gleam of a coming light. Then there was the sound of rattling chains and the clanking of massive bolts drawn back. A key was turned with the loud grating noise of long disuse, and the great door swung back.

Dracula (1897)

Extract 4:

I was now for the first time frightened, and I yelled with all my might and main. Nurse, nursery maid, housekeeper, all came running in, and hearing my story, they made light of it, soothing me all they could meanwhile. But, child as I was, I could perceive that their faces were pale with an unwonted look of anxiety, and I saw them look under the bed, and about the room, and peep under tables and pluck open cupboards; and the housekeeper whispered to the nurse: 'Lay your hand along that hollow in the bed; someone *did* lie there, so sure as you did not; the place is still warm.'

Carmilla (1872)

....

....

....

....

....

....

....

....

....

....

....

From *The Bitter Cry of Outcast London* (1883)

At the top of an otherwise empty house lived a family; the husband had gone to try and find some work. The mother, 29 years of age, was sitting on the only chair in the place in front of a grate, destitute of any fire. She was nursing a baby only six weeks old, that had never had anything but one old rag round it. The mother had nothing but a gown on, and that dropping to pieces; it was all she had night or day. There were six children under 13 years of age. They were barefooted, and the few rags on them scarcely covered them. In this room, where was an unclothed infant, the ceiling was in holes. An old bedstead was in the place, and seven sleep in it at night, the eldest girl being on the floor.

In another miserable room are eight destitute children. Their father died a short time ago, and 'on going into the house to-day,' says the missionary, 'the mother was lying in her coffin.' Here is a filthy attic, containing only a broken chair, a battered saucepan and a few rags. On a dirty sack in the centre of the room sits a neglected, ragged, bare-legged little baby girl of four. Her father is a soldier, and is away. Her mother is out all day and comes home late at night, and this child is left in charge of the infant that we see crawling about the floor; left for six or eight hours at a stretch—hungry, thirsty, tired, but never daring to move from her post. And this is the kind of sight which may be seen in a Christian land where it is criminal to ill-treat a horse.

The child-misery that one beholds is the most heartrending and appalling element in these discoveries. From the beginning of their life they are utterly neglected; their bodies and rags are alive with vermin; they are subjected to the most cruel treatment; many of them have never seen a green field, and do not know what it is to go beyond the streets immediately around them, and they often pass the whole day without a morsel of food. Here is one of three years old picking up some dirty pieces of bread and eating them. We go in at the doorway where it is standing and find a little girl twelve years old. 'Where is your mother?' 'In the madhouse.' 'How long has she been there?' 'Fifteen months.' 'Who looks after you?' The child, who is sitting at an old table making match-boxes, replies, 'I look after my little brothers and sisters as well as I can.'

Andrew Mearns and William C. Preston

Learning objectives:	Resources:
• To select, retrieve and make inferences from a 19th-century non-fiction text • To write more developed comprehension answers about 19th-century non-fiction	• Extract 8.2.4 • 8.2.4 Lesson 1 PowerPoint 8.2.4 Lesson 1 Worksheet

Getting started

* Display **8.2.4 Lesson 1 PowerPoint slide 1** and introduce the lesson objectives. Emphasise the movement to more developed comprehension responses.

* Using **PowerPoint slide 2**, ask the students to identify what word class the words on the slide are (*adjectives*) and to consider the questions on the slide. The students might suggest a story about poor people; someone homeless, a refugee, etc. Develop their thoughts using **PowerPoint slide 3** – encourage them to think about a point of view that might be *empathetic* to a situation and explain what *empathy* is. Highlight how point-of-view writing can be used to draw attention to a serious issue and make the reader feel empathy and perhaps lead to a call to action.

* Now read **Extract 8.2.4** aloud to the class. Ask for the students' initial responses: what do they find most shocking?

Developing skills

* Pair up the students to complete the retrieval exercise: **8.2.4 Lesson 1 Worksheet Activity 1**. You could allocate questions 1, 2 and 3 to different pairs or with a group working at a higher level. Allow the students around 12 minutes to complete all three questions. Ensure their answers are given in clear, short statement sentences that make sense, not in notes.

* Now use **PowerPoint slide 4** to focus on three selected quotations. Allow the students 5 minutes to consider their responses to the three questions in pairs; they should note down their ideas on **Worksheet Activity 2**, using the questions on the slide for support.

* Take feedback from the class and aim to develop their initial inferences by asking them to think about the consequences; for example, yes, the second quotation implies the mother was dead – but what does this mean for the family? Who will now take care of the children and provide for them? What are the writers telling us about a society where children are left to fend for themselves? Are they implying that something needs to change? Push the level of questioning to develop the students' depth of understanding.

* Now link this inferential reading to **PowerPoint slide 5**. Encourage the students to see that while laws were in place to protect animals from ill treatment, there were no laws to protect people from society's ill treatment. Ask the students to think about why the writers produced the pamphlet and what changes they wanted to see.

Trying it yourself

* Display **PowerPoint slide 6**. The students now move on to the final task, consolidating their knowledge through three key comprehension questions. They should write their responses in their notebooks. Remind them of the SQI (statement + quotation + inference) method and check that the three elements are in place as you move around the room. The students could use the quotations and ideas from **PowerPoint slide 4** to help them get started. Where possible, encourage the students to write more than one SQI construct for each question.

Activity 1: Retrieval skills

Answer the following questions using short statement sentences.

1. List four things we learn about the family in paragraph 1.

....

....

....

2. List four things we learn about the family in the attic in paragraph 2.

....

....

....

3. List four things we learn about the 12-year-old girl in paragraph 3.

....

....

....

Activity 2: Inferential skills

What is suggested or implied by the following quotations from the text?

Quotation	What is implied
'that had never had anything but one old rag round it'	
'the mother was lying in her coffin'	
'sitting at an old table making match-boxes'	

8.2.4 Lesson 2	Developing understanding of 19th-century non-fiction: How points of view are presented

Learning objective:	Resources:
• To develop empathy and understanding of the issues in a 19th-century non-fiction text	• Extract 8.2.4 • 8.2.4 Lesson 2 PowerPoint

Getting started

• Begin by re-reading and recapping on **Extract 8.2.4** from the previous lesson. Ask the students to share some of their thoughts and ideas from the comprehension tasks set for the final task in Lesson 1.

• Display the lesson objective on **8.2.4 Lesson 2 PowerPoint slide 1** and ask the students if they remember the word 'empathy' from the previous lesson; can they define it in their own words? Explain to them that they are going to empathise even more in this lesson.

Developing skills

• Display **PowerPoint slide 2** and go over the task. Working individually, the students choose one of the families from either paragraph 1, 2 or 3 of **Extract 8.2.4** and write 10 questions they would like to ask the family based on the information given in the extract. They should write their questions in their notebooks.

• The students then pair up to take part in a role-play exercise as journalist and family member, as described on **PowerPoint slide 3**. They take turns in their pairs to ask their ten questions in role as journalist and give the answers in role as family member; they should record the responses in their notebooks. Allow about 20 minutes for both interviews to take place and for the information to be gathered. Consider pairing less confident students with those who are more confident, to allow for more developed responses overall.

Trying it yourself

• Display **PowerPoint slide 4** and introduce the final task, which requires the students to write a more developed article in the role of journalist, focusing on their chosen family from the role-play activity. The students are supported in this task by being able to use six words or phrases from the original extract – their choices here will help you to see how they select key evidence.

• Display **PowerPoint slide 5**, which contains some formal sentence openers to support the students to achieve the 'voice' of the original journalist in expressing the point of view. This slide can be displayed while the students complete the final writing task.

• If time allows, the students could read out some of their responses. Check to see that the writer's original viewpoint has been understood by the nature of the written response, and that the students have understood and can communicate back to you some of the key issues from the pamphlet. Their articles could be developed or completed for homework if necessary.

'I've spent time in Britain's food banks – the destitution these people are facing is appalling', by Professor Green

With Christmas fast approaching, many in the UK are gearing themselves up for a season of joy and excess. Ahead of the parties and gift-giving, however, I'd ask people to step back and think about the many families that will struggle to put lunch on the table on the 25th December. As seems to be the case year after year these days, food banks and charities are currently preparing themselves for the busiest Christmas yet.

But it's not just the festive period they'll have to worry about. The harsh reality is that many families deal with hunger year-round. While I've worked with a number of important charitable causes throughout my career, this is one that remains particularly close to my heart.

The statistics are startling. 14 million people in the UK live in poverty. Over 4 million of these are children. In the last year alone, The Trussell Trust, the UK's biggest food bank provider, has delivered over 1.6 million food parcels to vulnerable people, with over one-third of those given to children.

I was confronted with the extent of the problem whilst volunteering at my local food bank. I met the people at the frontline of UK hunger and discovered how easy it is to be blinded by statistics, but meeting hungry people brought the issue home. These people are living on my doorstep. It humanised the statistics and forced me to consider the underlying issues that drive people to use these services.

Assumptions are too easy to make – whether it be that these people choose not to work or struggle to budget. The truth is that finding yourself in need of this kind of support can be as simple as receiving an unexpected bill or a delay with benefit payments.

We should strive for a society that no longer needs these services – they have become an accepted part of austerity in Britain and that needs to change. There's no doubt that eradicating these inequalities is far from straightforward, but that doesn't mean we can't help to provide people with the tools to break out of the cycle of poverty. It costs virtually nothing for those among us who don't have to live that reality to raise awareness, volunteer our services for those who need it and to hold the government accountable in terms of how their policies affect the average person.

The people I met don't want to rely on these services to feed their families. We all need to do our bit to help make a change so they don't feel forced to. While the cohort of volunteers I met go over and above to offer their support, there is a responsibility on each and every one of us to do our bit – no matter how small.

Educate yourself, volunteer, and tell yourself that you have the power to lend a helping hand. Even a small act of kindness can make a difference to those in your local community.

From *The Independent*, 9 November 2019

Developing skills with connected modern non-fiction: Exploring how points of view are presented

Learning objectives:	**Resources:**
• To understand the key ideas in an issue-based article • To make inferences as to the writer's viewpoint	• Extract 8.2.5 • 8.2.5 Lesson 1 PowerPoint

Getting started

• Give out copies of **Extract 8.2.5** to the students. Many may recognise or know Professor Green from his music career, but they not be aware of his work for social justice. Read the article aloud. Explain that this is an opinion article from *The Independent* showing the rapper's views after volunteering at a food bank

• Display **PowerPoint slide 1** and go over the learning objectives for the lesson.

• Display **8.2.5 Lesson 1 PowerPoint slide 2**. Ask the students to look closely at the information in the paragraph from the extract. They need to list four things that are factual and can be seen to be convincing in their notebooks. Ask them to think about the word 'startling'. Why might those facts and statistics be startling for some people?

Developing skills

• Using the skills developed in 8.2.4 Lesson 1 for developing inferences, ask the students to work in small groups of three or four and look at the quotations from the text on **PowerPoint slide 3**. Allow them 10–15 minutes to discuss and note down the inferences and consequences they can draw from the four quotations. Support them with leading questions such as: What do the quotations help us to realise about the difficulties and challenges many people face? What do they help us to realise about our society in modern times? What might they imply about our own communities and neighbourhoods? Feed back the ideas as a whole class.

• Now test the students' inferential reading even further by focusing on the quotation on **PowerPoint slide 4**. Ask them what they make of the assumptions the author describes first? Are these common views? Where do we see and hear them? What do they imply about who is to blame for people's poverty? How does the second sentence challenge this? Which view shows more empathy?

Trying it yourself

• Display **PowerPoint slide 5** and go over the final task with the students. Allow 20 minutes or so for the students to work on this more detailed task in their notebooks. Using the SQI (statement + quotation + inference) method, ask them to use any of the ideas from the lesson in their response.

• This final task is less structured than the final task from 8.2.4 Lesson 2, so the students should make some decisions before they start as to the key focus of their statements (remind them of the focus in the previous week regarding parents and children, and responsibility). A good way to begin is to encourage the students to select and highlight the three most important and relevant quotations in the article, to use as evidence for the statement and the starting point for drawing out the inferences.

Learning objectives:	Resources:
• To develop an understanding of persuasive language techniques • To consider the effects of persuasive techniques	• Extract 8.2.5 • 8.2.5 Lesson 2 PowerPoint • 8.2.5 Lesson 2 Worksheet • sugar paper and marker pens

Getting started

• Display **8.2.5 Lesson 2 PowerPoint slide 1** and go over the lesson objectives. Ask the students to recall any of the persuasive techniques they know already, from previous work or projects in Year 7. They may recall facts, statistics, emotive language, etc.

• Re-read **Extract 8.2.5** and ask the students to note down any persuasive features they recognise as they read. (This may also work with mini-whiteboards and pens if available.)

• Ask the students to define the term 'emotive phrases' for you (the phrases in a piece of writing that evoke emotions such as shock, joy, horror and sympathy, etc.).

Developing skills

• Display **PowerPoint slide 2** and ask the students to look at the collection of emotive phrases from the Professor Green article. Working as a whole class, with you facilitating the discussion, ask the students what each phrase in turn makes them think of, feel or imagine, or how they respond to the phrase.

• Now give out copies of **8.2.5 Lesson 1 Worksheet** and organise the class into small groups of three or four, with a scribe and sugar paper and marker pens. Allow the students 20–25 minutes to complete the activity by exploring the article in their groups, using the guided questions alongside the article to facilitate the discussion. The scribe should collect their points and ideas. If time allows, each group could feed back on one or two of the guided questions.

• Suggested responses to the questions might include: *1. The image of Christmas as family time/a time of lots of food, parties and presents/all the advertisements on TV and pressure they create; sets the scene for the contrast with having to visit the food bank and not be part of these celebrations. 2. Sympathy for the fact that this is not just a problem at Christmas, but that families are struggling all year round – an on-going problem; raises sympathy and shocks us that people are going hungry. 3. Intended to startle us: something surprising but in a shocking way; suggests the readers of the paper may not be aware of the problem. 4. Gives credibility to what the writer is saying: we know he has witnessed this first-hand, so his opinion is supported by his own observations. 5. Pronouns switch to 'we' and 'us' to feel more inclusive; this suggests we all have a part to play in helping others; it makes the reader feel part of a possible solution. 6. He suggests that if you are in a position to do so, you can help by 'raising awareness', using your time to volunteer or making sure the government knows, e.g. by contacting your MP. He uses the list of three. 7. Another list of three, this time all beginning with a verb (imperative or command form) to make a call to action and get you involved in helping to solve the problem.*

• Ask the students what different techniques they have come across as a result of their exploration, then use **PowerPoint slide 3** to consolidate this. Ask the students if they can define each term on the slide and add the definitions to the whiteboard if appropriate.

• Now display **PowerPoint slide 4**, which models how to present language analysis using the IEC (identify, exemplify, comment) method through colour coding.

Trying it yourself

• Display **PowerPoint slide 5** and introduce the final task. Ask the students to use the model on **PowerPoint slide 4** to write their own points in response to the question. They should answer the question in their notebooks using two or three different features of persuasive language. Encourage them to give examples. They should also aim to comment on the effect by considering what they think of, how they feel, and how they respond to that feature themselves.

Activity:

- In your groups, explore the Professor Green article using the guided questions below to develop your discussion.
- Choose someone in your group to act as scribe and note down your points and ideas.

With Christmas fast approaching, many in the UK are gearing themselves up for a season of joy and excess. Ahead of the parties and gift-giving, however, I'd ask people to step back and think about the many families that will struggle to put lunch on the table on the 25th December. As seems to be the case year after year these days, food banks and charities are currently preparing themselves for the busiest Christmas yet.

1. What picture is created of the season in your mind's eye? Why do you think the writer begins with this?

But it's not just the festive period they'll have to worry about. The harsh reality is that many families deal with hunger year-round. While I've worked with a number of important charitable causes throughout my career, this is one that remains particularly close to my heart.

2. The writer uses emotive language here. What emotion is he trying to create and why?

The statistics are startling. 14 million people in the UK live in poverty. Over four million of these are children. In the last year alone, The Trussell Trust, the UK's biggest food bank provider, has delivered over 1.6 million food parcels to vulnerable people, with over one-third of those given to children.

3. What is the impact of using the adjective 'startling'? How is this emotive too?

I was confronted with the extent of the problem whilst volunteering at my local food bank... I met the people at the frontline of UK hunger and discovered how easy it is to be blinded by statistics, but meeting hungry people brought the issue home. These people are living on my doorstep. It humanised the statistics and forced me to consider the underlying issues that drive people to use these services.

4. What might be the impact of the writer using his personal experience here?

Assumptions are too easy to make – whether it be that these people choose not to work or struggle to budget. The truth is that finding yourself in need of this kind of support can be as simple as receiving an unexpected bill or a delay with benefit payments.

5. Up to this point, the writer uses the pronoun 'I'. What do you notice about the pronouns in this paragraph? What does that make you feel?

We should strive for a society that no longer needs these services – they have become an accepted part of austerity in Britain and that needs to change. There's no doubt that eradicating these inequalities is far from straightforward, but that doesn't mean we can't help to provide people with the tools to break out of the cycle of poverty. It costs virtually nothing for those among us who don't have to live that reality to raise awareness, volunteer our services for those who need it and to hold the government accountable in terms of how their policies affect the average person.

6. What actions does the writer now suggest we should do? How many of them are in the list?

The people I met don't want to rely on these services to feed their families. We all need to do our bit to help make a change so they don't feel forced to. While the cohort of volunteers I met go over and above to offer their support, there is a responsibility on each and every one of us to do our bit – no matter how small.

Educate yourself, volunteer, and tell yourself that you have the power to lend a helping hand. Even a small act of kindness can make a difference to those in your local community.

7. What do you notice about the actions here? How do they make you feel? How many of them are suggested – do you notice a pattern?

Learning objectives:	Resources:
• To reflect and use the issues raised through the project to complete the writing of a speech • To show competent use of the persuasive techniques studied in your own writing	• 8.2.6 Lessons 1 & 2 PowerPoint • 8.2.6 Lessons 1 & 2 Worksheet • Extract 8.2.5 (for reference)

Lesson 1: Recap and reflect

* Display **8.2.6 Lessons 1 & 2 PowerPoint slide 1** and go over the lesson objectives. Explain that this week's task will involve using the ideas, skills and techniques they have been learning about through the study of the non-fiction texts.

* Display **8.2.6 PowerPoint slide 2** to stimulate a whole-class starter discussion reflecting on the project, the texts and the issues raised. Ask the students what key issues and topics they can recall from the list of texts. Can they make any connections between the way Jane Eyre was treated by her cousin John and bullying now? What is similar? What is different? Can they reflect on the issues about anger/ resentment and how we see and treat others from Blake's poem 'A Poison Tree'? Can they recall the images of war and the refugees? Can they see any connections between the families in need in the pamphlet *The Bitter Cry of Outcast London* and the Professor Green article on food banks?

Developing skills

* Share the details of the debate task on **PowerPoint slide 3** and hand out copies of **8.2.6 Lessons 1 & 2 Worksheet**, which is provided to aid planning. Develop discussion by considering the questions in the four bullet points on the slide as a whole class, to stimulate initial thoughts.

* Now display **PowerPoint slide 4** and ask the students to select a particular focus for their own speech. They can take a topic from the list or use one of their own stimulated by the earlier discussion if they wish. Allow a few minutes for the students to consider and note down their choice on the worksheet (question 1).

* Use **PowerPoint slide 5** to recap on the key techniques the students can use in their speeches to create impact and effect.

* Then, using **PowerPoint slide 6** in connection with the Professor Green article (**Extract 8.2.5**), show the students a five-point structured plan. This structure is also provided for planning on the worksheet (question 2).

* Display **PowerPoint slide 7** and prompt the students to think about the overall tone and register they should use in their speech.

Trying it yourself

* Now allow planning and writing time. The students complete the five-point plan on their worksheet, revisiting **PowerPoint slide 6** for support. If you have ICT facilities available you could allow the students time to research and gather more facts about their chosen issue, or provide some key fact sheets yourself from internet research. If homework is scheduled, the students could compete this aspect at home.

Lesson 2: Trying it yourself

* Allow the students a good 45 minutes of writing time once they have finished their planning.

* Monitor their work around the class as they complete each paragraph of their Big Write. The students can self-check their tone using **PowerPoint slide 7** and their use of techniques using the prompts on the worksheet (question 3) as they write.

* A productive way to complete the project and celebrate success is to set up the classroom to present the debate speeches. Plan for a speaking and listening session where the students present their speeches in response to the debate motion *This house believes that we must treat others with empathy and kindness,* with the students' various angles and chosen topics from **PowerPoint slide 4**. Those students making speeches can take questions from their colleagues afterwards, if appropriate.

Activity: Final task

'This house believes that we must treat others with empathy and kindness.'

Complete the plan for your speech below.

1. What topic interests you the most from the issues we have covered?

    ....

2. Planning your structure:

Introduction	
Key idea 1	
Key idea 2	
Key idea 3	
Call to action	

3. Checklist of key techniques: place a tick by each one you manage to include in your speech.

Technique	Have I included? (✓)	Technique	Have I included? (✓)
Factual information		Commands/imperatives	
Shocking statistics		Inclusive pronouns	
Quotations from real people		Lists of three	
Imagery		Personal anecdotes/personal pronouns	
Emotive language			

From *What Katy Did* (1872)

'Well, Katy Carr, I *should* think you'd be ashamed of yourself,' said Aunt Izzie, 'wreaking your temper on your poor little sister!' [...]

So they went up stairs. Katy, left below, felt very miserable: repentant, defiant, discontented, and sulky all at once. She knew in her heart that she had not meant to hurt Elsie, but was thoroughly ashamed of that push. [...]

She went out by the side-door into the yard. As she passed the shed, the new swing caught her eye.

'How exactly like Aunt Izzie,' she thought, 'ordering the children not to swing till she gives them leave. I suppose she thinks it's too hot, or something. *I* sha'n't mind her, anyhow.'

She seated herself in the swing. It was a first-rate one, with a broad, comfortable seat, and thick new ropes. The seat hung just the right distance from the floor. Alexander was a capital hand at putting up swings, and the wood-shed the nicest possible spot in which to have one.

It was a big place, with a very high roof. There was not much wood left in it just now, and the little there was, was piled neatly about the sides of the shed, so as to leave plenty of room. The place felt cool and dark, and the motion of the swing seemed to set the breeze blowing. It waved Katy's hair like a great fan, and made her dreamy and quiet. All sorts of sleepy ideas began to flit through her brain. Swinging to and fro like the pendulum of a great clock, she gradually rose higher and higher, driving herself along by the motion of her body, and striking the floor smartly with her foot, at every sweep. Now she was at the top of the high arched door. Then she could almost touch the cross-beam above it, and through the small square window could see pigeons sitting and pluming themselves on the eaves of the barn, and white clouds blowing over the blue sky. She had never swung so high before. It was like flying, she thought, and she bent and curved more strongly in the seat, trying to send herself yet higher, and graze the roof with her toes.

Suddenly, at the very highest point of the sweep, there was a sharp noise of cracking. The swing gave a violent twist, spun half round, and tossed Katy into the air. She clutched the rope,—felt it dragged from her grasp,—then, down,—down—down— she fell. All grew dark, and she knew no more.

Susan Coolidge

Learning objectives:	Resources:
• To secure comprehension of a 19th-century fiction text • To use inference and deduction to explore character and meanings	• Extract 8.3.1 • 8.3.1 Lesson 1 PowerPoint • 8.3.1 Lesson 1 Worksheet

Getting started

• Display **8.3.1 Lesson 1 PowerPoint slide 2** and discuss the questions on the slide. Develop discussion by asking the students to talk to each other about their earliest or most memorable experience of using a swing. Bring discussion round to accidents, dangers and risks, and whether the students always take the precautions that their parents tell them to.

• Display and go over the lesson objectives on **PowerPoint slide 1** and recap on the skills of inference and deduction, establishing the need to 'read between the lines' and use what you know to work out what you don't know.

• Hand out copies of **Extract 8.3.1** and read the extract together as a class while displaying **PowerPoint slide 3**. Ask the students to consider the questions while you read, and then take feedback. Establish Katy's anger at her aunt and shame at being told off, which she feels is unjustified. This leads her to consider Aunt Izzie's swing ban as unjustified too, but she is tempted by the swing's appearance and good craftsmanship. Establish how the story builds to Katy's fall, through emphasis of the height of the swing and her daydreaming. Extend by discussing whether Katy's mood contributes to what happens. Ask whether the students have ever brought about a disastrous event because they were in a bad mood.

Developing skills

• Give out copies of **8.3.1 Lesson 1 Worksheet** and ask the students to work in pairs to complete **Activities 1** and **2**. To support the students' understanding, you could read Katy's words aloud in a petulant, arrogant manner.

• Take feedback and develop this into a discussion about Katy's character. (Suggested answers to Activity 1: *1. Katy feels Aunt Izzie always spoils their fun without good reason. 2. Katy seems arrogant, disobedient, naïve and immature, as well as angry. 3. Katy sets herself apart from/above the children; maybe she is older or considers herself better/more responsible.*) Take feedback from Activity 2 through the students acting out their chosen voices. Encourage them to put the emphasis on different words, and establish how a stress on 'I' could make Katy seem self-obsessed and arrogant, whereas a stress on 'Aunt Izzie' could create a mocking tone. Consider how a meek, quiet tone wouldn't demonstrate Katy's disobedience and would make her actions less convincing.

• Display **PowerPoint slide 4**. The students discuss their responses to the questions on the slide in pairs before feeding back. (Suggested answers: *1. The students should note the descriptions of 'first rate', the emphasis on 'new', the superlative 'nicest possible spot', 'just the right distance' and 'capital', which all suggest the swing is the best ever and perfectly positioned for Katy to try out. 2. Establish that Alexander may be a family member, friend or handyman/gardener. 3. Katy may have stormed off or see herself as not fitting in/different to her siblings.*)

Trying it yourself

• Display **PowerPoint slide 5** and remind the students of the SQI (statement + quotation + inference) method. They can note down their responses to the two questions on the slide in their notebooks or on a separate piece of paper, selecting their evidence from the first two paragraphs of the extract. The students should write one SQI paragraph for each question. More confident students could extend to two paragraphs or be encouraged to offer two alternative interpretations. Support them with the modelled example on **PowerPoint slide 6** and with further suggestions and modelling, by selecting appropriate quotations and by referring the students back to their work on tone and mood.

• Finish the lesson by taking feedback summarising what the students have learned about Katy as a character and her interactions with other characters. Conclude the discussion with consideration of whether Katy is to blame for the accident.

While we don't know much about Katy, the writer Susan Coolidge presents enough information for the reader to be able to make inferences about her character.

Activity 1:

In pairs, look at what Katy says in the opening paragraph of the extract and then answer the questions below.

1. What do you think is Katy's opinion of Aunt Izzie?

   ....

   ....

2. What is suggested about Katy's character from the use of italics in '*I* sha'n't mind her'?

   ....

   ....

3. What is suggested by Katy's reference to 'the children', even though she is still a child?

   ....

   ....

Activity 2:

* In pairs, take turns to read Katy's words aloud, experimenting with different tones of voice.
* How do you think Katy's words should be spoken and why?

....

....

....

....

....

....

<table>
<tr><td>

Learning objectives:

- To secure comprehension of a 19th-century fiction text
- To use inference and deduction to explore character and meanings
- To consider how language choices add to characterisation and meaning

</td><td>

Resources:

- Extract 8.3.1
- 8.3.1 Lesson 2 PowerPoint
- 8.3.1 Lesson 2 Worksheet
- highlighter pens

</td></tr>
</table>

Recap and reflection

- Re-read **Extract 8.3.1** and recap what was suggested about Katy in the previous lesson. Then display **8.3.1 Lesson 2 PowerPoint slide 1** and go over the lesson objectives.

- Display **PowerPoint slide 2** and discuss the questions on the slide. Question 2 could be extended into a role play between Aunt Izzie and the children. Discussion around question 3 could explore whether the extract would end differently if Aunt Izzie had explained that the swing wasn't safe/wasn't finished yet.

Developing skills

- Display **PowerPoint slide 3** and go over the task. Remind the students that a simile is a comparison that includes the words 'like' or 'as'. The students mark up their copy of the extract to identify the language features; you could provide them with highlighter pens to support this work. (Suggested answers: *1. 'very high roof'; repetition of 'higher'; 'at the top of the high arched door'; 'graze the roof with her toes'. 2. 'pigeons sitting and pluming themselves on the eaves of the barn'; 'white clouds blowing over the blue sky'. 3. 'hair like a great fan'; 'to and fro like the pendulum of a great clock'; 'it was like flying'.*)

- Take feedback and stretch the students by considering the symbolism of the high swing representing freedom from rules for Katy, or how she may consider herself above rules or above the other children. Discuss the proverb 'pride comes before a fall' and how it may be true both literally (Katy falls from the swing) and metaphorically (her arrogance leads her to pain, embarrassment and regret).

Trying it yourself

- Now hand out copies of **8.3.1 Lesson 2 Worksheet** and ask the students to complete **Activity 1**, which develops their understanding of the three similes they identified previously. Support the students by first clarifying that a pendulum is a swinging weight, usually in a clock, which keeps precise time, as its swing doesn't change. Extend this by considering how a repetitive, constant, rhythmic noise or action like this can make a person sleepy, mesmerised or even hypnotised.

- Take feedback. (Suggested answers: *1. Katy felt cooler, calmer and free from Aunt Izzie's restrictions. 2. The repetition of 'great' suggests a unique experience unlike any other; Katy feels relaxed, sleepy. 3. The idea of Katy 'flying' suggests that she feels thrilled, special, exhilarated, free, proud, defiant and triumphant.*) Extend the students' thinking by linking the symbolism in the three similes to Katy's feelings – as though she is experiencing something beyond the realms of the other children, proving Aunt Izzie wrong and showing her independence and disregard for rules. Support the students by having them compare Katy's experience to fairground rides they may have been on, or by supplying key words like 'proud' for them to match to a simile.

- Follow up this activity with **Worksheet Activity 2**, which continues the close focus on the description of Katy swinging. Guide the students towards the words 'dark', 'cool', 'dreamy', 'quiet', 'strongly', 'smartly' and 'sleepy', suggesting Katy's relaxation and pleasure, perhaps even complacency. Challenge them to identify which word class they have selected – for example, 'cool': adjective; 'strongly': adverb.

- Display **PowerPoint slide 4** and go over the students' final task, which combines the comprehension elements they have been working on with their language analysis skills (what + how). Use **PowerPoint slide 5** to model a possible opening and to demonstrate both SQI and IEC techniques. Support the students through further modelling, sentence and paragraph starters, and by referring them back to their previous work on the extract. Challenge them to consider who the writer intends us to blame for the accident and how she achieves this. This can be written as a concluding paragraph.

Activity 1:

For each simile below, explain what it tells us about Katy's feelings while she is swinging.

1. 'It waved Katy's hair like a great fan.'

   ....

   ....

2. 'Swinging to and fro like the pendulum of a great clock'

   ....

   ....

3. 'It was like flying'

   ....

   ....

Activity 2:

What other words in the description of Katy swinging tell us about her feelings?

Word	What this tells us about Katy's feelings

'I Remember, I Remember' (1827)

1

I remember, I remember,
The house where I was born,
The little window where the sun
Came peeping in at morn;
He never came a wink too soon,
Nor brought too long a day,
But now, I often wish the night
Had borne my breath away!

2

I remember, I remember,
The roses, red and white,
The vi'lets, and the lily-cups,
Those flowers made of light!
The lilacs where the robin built,
And where my brother set
The laburnum on his birthday,—
The tree is living yet!

3

I remember, I remember,
Where I used to swing,
And thought the air must rush as fresh
To swallows on the wing;
My spirit flew in feathers then,
That is so heavy now,
And summer pools could hardly cool
The fever on my brow!

4

I remember, I remember,
The fir trees dark and high;
I used to think their slender tops
Were close against the sky:
It was a childish ignorance,
But now 'tis little joy
To know I'm farther off from heaven
Than when I was a boy.

Thomas Hood

Securing understanding of 19th-century poetry: 'I Remember, I Remember'

Learning objectives:	Resources:
• To understand more language features • To explore how a poet uses language features to express a speaker's feelings	• Extract 8.3.2 • 8.3.2 Lesson 1 PowerPoint • 8.3.2 Lesson 1 Worksheet

Getting started

• Display **8.3.2 Lesson 1 PowerPoint slide 2** and use the questions to start a discussion. Extend through asking: What is the appeal of playing in mud or puddles? What do people think of a child doing this compared to a teenager doing it? Draw out the idea that childhood play and imagination is encouraged but that such frivolity tends to be frowned upon later in life. Ask the students what they miss about being a very young child and allow them to recall specific memories.

• Display **PowerPoint slide 1** and discuss the lesson objectives. Ensure that the students can differentiate between language and structure.

• Hand out copies of **Extract 8.3.2**. The students read the poem 'I Remember, I Remember' in pairs then feed back their initial thoughts on the poem's meaning. This is just to encourage independent thought and not to be corrected or commented on at this stage.

Developing skills

• Give out copies of **8.3.2 Lesson 1 Worksheet** and ask the students to complete **Activity 1**. Support them by highlighting images in the poem, through allowing pair work and by explaining key words where required. Challenge them by creating abstract pictures for the images. Develop by discussing whether the childhood images are negative or positive and how they know, drawing out the links with freedom in the poem (*birds flying, nature, light and lightness*).

• Display **PowerPoint slide 3** and go over the task on the slide. You could support the students by mind mapping a range of emotions beforehand (for example, regret, remembrance, worry, annoyance, sorrow, joy, fear, calmness, anticipation, love). In feedback, draw out the contrast between the poet's feelings about childhood and adulthood. Challenge the students to use synonyms to avoid repetition.

• Now extend this work by identifying themes in the poem through discussion, which may include: time – through the repetition of 'I remember', the tree in verse 2, 'used to' in verse 4, and connectives like 'then', 'now' and 'yet'; innocence – via images of nature, flowers, light, sun, and thinking the firs touched the sky; freedom – through images of birds, lightness and light; memories – consider the poem's first line, the use of past tense and 'used to'.

Trying it yourself

• Display **PowerPoint slide 4** and go over/introduce the different language techniques, which the students need to identify in the poem for **Worksheet Activity 2**. They complete the activity working independently or in pairs for support if preferred. You could support the students by providing selected quotations to match to the techniques, a modelled example and highlighted extracts. (Suggested answers: *Sibilance: repeated 's' sound, verse 3, lines 2–7 including 'used to swing' and 'rush as fresh' (wistful); Metaphor: verse 4, lines 3–4, 'their slender tops / Were close against the sky' (shows childhood freedom); Anaphora: repeated word or phrase at the start of successive clauses, line 1 of every verse (sorrow); Personification: verse 1, lines 3–4, 'Sun/Came peeping' (happy memory); Plosive: hard consonant sound of t/k/p/d/g/b, verse 1, line 8, 'borne my breath' (also alliteration); verse 2, line 7, 'laburnum on his birthday'; verse 3, line 7, 'pools could hardly cool' (negative feelings in the present).*)

• For their final task, ask the students to write up one of the rows of their completed table from **Worksheet Activity 2** into an explanatory paragraph detailing how the poet uses language in 'I Remember, I Remember' to express the speaker's feelings. The students should use the IEC (identify, exemplify, comment) method. Support the students with the modelled IEC paragraph on **PowerPoint slide 5**; challenge them through writing up of further rows of their table.

The poet Thomas Hood uses imagery to describe his childhood as a happy and carefree time.

Activity 1:

- Read each verse of the poem again and identify the memory the poet has of his childhood.
- Draw the images the poet describes. The first one has been done for you.

Verse 1	Verse 2
Verse 3	**Verse 4**

Activity 2:

The poet uses a variety of language devices to contrast the innocence of childhood with the restrictions of adulthood. Complete the chart below with evidence of each language technique.

Language technique	Evidence from the poem	What we learn about the speaker's feelings
Sibilance		
Metaphor		
Anaphora		
Personification		
Plosive		

Learning objectives:	Resources:
• To understand more structural features • To secure use of the IEC method when exploring how a poet uses structure to enhance meaning	• Extract 8.3.2 • 8.3.2 Lesson 2 PowerPoint • 8.3.2 Lesson 2 Worksheet

Recap and reflection

* Re-read **Extract 8.3.2**, the poem 'I Remember, I Remember' by Thomas Hood. Recap on the main ideas from the poem, drawing out the contrast of the poet's free childhood with his stagnant adulthood.

* Display and go over the lesson objectives on **8.3.2 Lesson 2 PowerPoint slide 1**. Recap on the IEC (identify, exemplify, comment) method and the differences between language and structure.

* Hand out copies of **8.3.2 Lesson 1 Worksheet** and ask the students to complete **Activity 1**. Establish that verses 1–3 end with an exclamation mark, as the speaker recalls the happiness and freedom of childhood. Consider how this contrasts with the sombre mood of the end of the poem, when the exclamation mark is replaced with the finality of a full stop.

Developing skills

* The students now complete **Worksheet Activity 2** by linking the last two lines of each verse of the poem to a relevant interpretation. Support the students by linking key words like 'fever' in verse 3 to 'sickness' (interpretation A) and 'heaven' in verse 4 to 'God' (interpretation B). (Answers: *1D, 2C, 3A, 4B.*)

* Extend the discussion in feedback by asking: What is the tone or mood of the end of each verse? *(negative/ melancholic)* What elements of childhood do we lose as we grow older? *(imagination, freedom)* What do we gain as we grow older? *(wisdom, responsibility, expectations)*

Trying it yourself

* Display **PowerPoint slide 2** and go over the list of structural features on the slide: enjambment, caesura, rhyme and syllable. The students should be guided to count the number of syllables per line and look for patterns and repetitions. Encourage them to examine the punctuation to see whether the poet wishes them to pause mid line (caesura, indicated by punctuation such as the comma in verse 1 line 7) or to continue reading into the next line without stopping (enjambment, for example verse 1 lines 3–4).

* The students then complete the task on the slide, annotating their copies of **Extract 8.3.2** by identifying the structural features listed and briefly describing the effect of each one. Support the students through pair work and by providing annotated poems and meanings to match to the techniques.

* Take feedback. (Suggested answers: *Enjambment: verse 1 lines 3–4, verse 2 lines 6–7, verse 3 lines 3–4 and 7–8, verse 4 lines 3–4 and 6–8; creates flow of memories. Caesura: verse 1 line 7; shatters happy memory and brings poet back to/contrasts with the reality of the present. Rhyme is ABCBDEFE; in each verse lines 2/4 and 6/8 always rhyme; the consistent rhyme emphasises that the poet is trapped in the never-changing present, remembering the past. Syllables alternate 8/6 per line; this repetition suggests the poet is going over the same thing again and again so is stuck in the past, which adversely affects his enjoyment of the present.*)

* Display **PowerPoint slide 3** and introduce the final task, which builds on the students' work during the lesson by asking them to show how the poet uses structural techniques to enhance meaning in the poem 'I Remember, I Remember'. They should write at least two paragraphs using the IEC (identify, exemplify, comment) method. Explain the need to show how the poet contrasts childhood freedom with the restrictions of adulthood. Use **PowerPoint slide 4** as a modelled example. Further support the students with sentence starters and discussion of the differences between childhood and adulthood.

In the last two lines of each verse of the poem 'I Remember, I Remember', the speaker comments on his life in the present.

Activity 1:

Read the poem then answer the questions below.

1. What punctuation is used at the end of verses 1–3?

   ....

2. What is the speaker's mood at the end of verses 1–3?

   ....

   ....

3. What punctuation is used at the end of the final verse and how does the poet's mood change?

   ....

   ....

Activity 2:

Match the last two lines of each verse with the correct interpretation on the right by drawing a line to link them.

Verse ending	Interpretation
1: 'But now, I often wish the night Had borne my breath away!'	**A:** The poet feels like he is sick because he misses his childhood so much.
2: 'The laburnum on his birthday,— The tree is living yet!'	**B:** The poet is saying children are more innocent and so they are closer to God.
3: 'And summer pools could hardly cool The fever on my brow!'	**C:** The poet is excited to describe a living reminder of his lost childhood.
4: 'To know I'm farther off from heaven Than when I was a boy.'	**D:** The poet thinks if he had died young, his childhood would never have had to end.

**Securing creative writing:
Presenting memories in real and
fictional autobiographical writing**

Learning objectives:	Resources:
• To recognise features of first-person and autobiographical writing • To use those features in my own writing to engage my reader	• 8.3.3 Lessons 1 & 2 PowerPoint • 8.3.3 Lesson 1 Worksheet

Getting started

• Display **8.3.3 Lesson 1 PowerPoint slide 2** and use the questions to guide discussion. Draw out the idea of memories linking like cogs or being 'sparked'. Consider how a person may remember an event the way they wanted it to happen, and discuss dementia (a reduction in brain function due to disease or injury) and amnesia (loss of memory, which may be temporary). Allow the students to give examples of memories from their own lives. Ask pairs to discuss their earliest memories and feed back.

• Display **PowerPoint slide 1** and discuss the learning objectives. Ask the students to name features of autobiographical writing (*first person; chronological with time connectives; includes names, dates and memories, as well as thoughts of the future*). Explain that these features will be explored in the lesson.

• Ask the students to consider how they can engage their readers through humour, interesting events, describing characters and settings, etc. Then use **PowerPoint slides 3** and **4** to introduce examples of autobiographical writing to support this discussion. Extend through discussion of Victorian women such as George Eliot and the Brontë sisters writing under male pseudonyms (**slide 4**).

Developing skills and Trying it yourself

• Give out copies of **8.3.3 Lesson 1 Worksheet** and ask the students to complete **Activity 1**, identifying the most and least likely features of autobiographical writing. There is no particular order but it is likely the students will put first person/past tense/connectives near the top and headline/glossary/slogan at the bottom. Support them by asking which features of autobiographical writing they used when recalling memories. Did they give facts or use humour? In what order did they tell the events and why?

• The students now work in pairs to complete **Worksheet Activities 2 and 3**, which are based on an extract from *Black Beauty* by Anna Sewell. Support them with **Activity 2** by annotating the first paragraph together. Extend by discussing what is missing (date, humour) and how many of the features of fiction and autobiographical writing are similar. For Activity 3, support the students with suggested emotions. (Suggested answers: *Activity 2: first person past tense ('I was forced'); chronology ('soon'); anecdote (whole extract); setting ('Beyond the turnpike'); point of view ('This could not go on'); time connective ('soon'), emotions ('groaned'). Activity 3: distress ('suffered dreadfully'), discomfort ('intense pain'), fear ('This could not go on'), worry ('he did not rise'), bravery ('I uttered no sound').*)

• Now introduce the writing task for the week: the students are to write an autobiographical account using the features discussed in the lesson. Display **PowerPoint slide 5** and use the prompts on the slide to help the students recall a strong memory on which to base their account. Support with paired discussion and by giving ideas such as: first day at school; a prank they played; moving house; going on holiday.

• Display the four example openings on **PowerPoint slide 6** and ask which features of autobiography they use (*all: first person; 1. connectives and chronology; 2. anecdote; 3. past tense. 4. emotion of pride*).

• The students then write an opening sentence for their planned memory, using **PowerPoint slide 7** for support. They can peer-assess the openings for features of autobiography.

Lesson 2: Final task

• The students use the second lesson to write their autobiographical account. Support them by returning to the lesson objectives on **PowerPoint slide 1**, **PowerPoint slide 7** and their completed worksheet activities. Further support could be provided by mind-mapping ideas, suggesting topic sentences, and reading extracts from Roald Dahl's *Boy* or *Going Solo*, Anne Frank's *The Diary of a Young Girl*, Jane Goodall's *My Life with the Chimpanzees*, or autobiographies of well-known figures. **PowerPoint slide 8** provides a self-assessment checklist of the required features of autobiographical writing.

Securing creative writing: Presenting memories in real and fictional autobiographical writing

Autobiography is an account of a person's life written by that person. Though it describes events and feelings that are true, the writer may still choose to exaggerate some of the details, writing it as though it is all true.

Activity 1:

Complete the diamond rank below by sorting the text features according to how likely they are to feature in autobiographical writing. You should only select nine text features from the list.

- past tense
- instructions
- imperatives
- setting
- present tense
- point of view

- anecdotes
- humour
- first-person narrative
- headline
- explaining a process

- emotive language
- dates
- connectives of time
- glossary
- facts

- feelings
- slogan
- chronological order

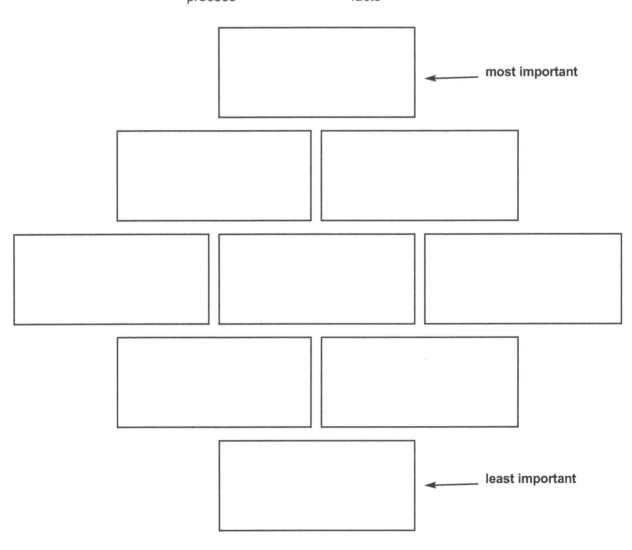

most important

least important

Anna Sewell's book *Black Beauty* tells the story of a horse's life from the horse's first-person perspective.

Activity 2:

Read the extract from *Black Beauty*. Then, using the list of the features of autobiography from Activity 1, label the extract to show those features.

Beyond the turnpike was a long piece of road, upon which fresh stones had just been laid—large sharp stones, over which no horse could be driven quickly without risk of danger. Over this road, with one shoe gone, I was forced to gallop at my utmost speed, my rider meanwhile cutting into me with his whip, and with wild curses urging me to go still faster. Of course my shoeless foot suffered dreadfully; the hoof was broken and split down to the very quick, and the inside was terribly cut by the sharpness of the stones.

This could not go on; no horse could keep his footing under such circumstances; the pain was too great. I stumbled, and fell with violence on both my knees. Smith was flung off by my fall, and, owing to the speed I was going at, he must have fallen with great force. I soon recovered my feet and limped to the side of the road, where it was free from stones.

The moon had just risen above the hedge, and by its light I could see Smith lying a few yards beyond me. He did not rise; he made one slight effort to do so, and then there was a heavy groan. I could have groaned, too, for I was suffering intense pain both from my foot and knees; but horses are used to bear their pain in silence.

I uttered no sound, but I stood there and listened.

Activity 3:

What emotions does Anna Sewell present in the extract above? Add more labels to the extract, to show where emotions are presented.

From 'A Fearful State of Things in South Lambeth: Roughs Rule the Roost'

TERRORISM reigns supreme in Lambeth. For years the organised gangs of young ruffians who infest the neighbourhood have been getting worse and worse, until now it is no exaggeration to say that the more respectable portion of the community go in fear of their lives.

Probably the worst part of Lambeth is the New Cut and the streets immediately surrounding and it is from here that the pests of South London are mostly drawn. Sometimes they move about in gangs, dodging the police from street to street, and at other times go round in twos and threes waylaying anybody and everybody who looks as if he might have – to use their own expressive phrase – anything 'wuth pinchin'.'

A favourite occupation of the younger members of the gangs is to throw the newspaper placard-boards into the small shops which abound in the neighbourhood, and then if the shopkeeper dares to say anything he will probably have a stone put through his window. 'It never used to be so,' said an Oakley Street shopkeeper. 'I've been here thirteen years, but lately the place is unbearable. In the evening I can't leave my shop a minute or I should have things stolen, and I've had my windows broken several times, and I do wish the police could do something to stop it.'

The police, however, are under considerable difficulty and seem almost powerless. About three years ago the trouble was very bad, but by vigorous measures it was stamped out, but, like a hardy weed, it has grown again, and is as vigorous as ever.

From sixteen to twenty-five is the usual age of the Hooligan, and none can say that during that time he does any appreciable amount of honest work. He preys by night, and if he comes out of his den during the day he generally slouches about comparatively harmless; it is after dark that he can be seen in all his glory. A resident who knows the gang well says:—'The thing that would stop them would be the lash. Give it them, just before they come out, so that their friends can see the effect, and I'll warrant the outrages will soon be put a stop to.'

Illustrated Police News, 30 July 1898

Learning objectives:	Resources:
• To explore and discuss ideas about anti-social behaviour in the 19th century • To secure comprehension of a 19th-century non-fiction text	• Extract 8.3.4 • 8.3.4 Lesson 1 PowerPoint • 8.3.4 Lesson 1 Worksheet

Getting started

- Display **8.3.4 Lesson 1 PowerPoint slide 1**. Go over the lesson objectives and explain that the students will be discussing the behaviour of teenagers in London in the 19th century.

- Read **Extract 8.3.4** together as a class, then display and work through the 'Getting started' questions on **PowerPoint slide 2**. Establish that the article focuses on disruptive hooligans in South London; the use of the word 'terrorism' emphasises the threat of the gangs; the shopkeepers are worried that the hooligans might throw a brick through a shop window; 'the lash' is a type of whip used as punishment.

- Display **PowerPoint slide 3** and ask the students to look carefully at the photograph. The picture shows the street gang's appearance but does not show evidence of their actions. In pairs, ask the students: Do you find this gang more or less threatening than the gangs described in the extract? Why? Imagine the gang in the picture approached you in the 19th century: list as many words as you can to describe your first impressions of their clothes, facial expressions and behaviour. Support the students with discussion of stereotypes, by defining the word 'gang' and by contextualising crime in the 19th century compared to now (for example, the contrast between pickpockets, stealing and murder in the 19th century as opposed to cyber-crime, stalking, murder, fraud, etc., today). Then hand out copies of **8.3.4 Lesson 1 Worksheet** and ask the students to complete the activity.

- Take feedback. Discuss with the students how their ideas as well as their thoughts and feelings are based on what they *imagine* by deducing details from the picture. By comparison, the extract gives some reliable factual information about anti-social behaviour in the 19th century.

Developing skills

- The writer of the newspaper article is very critical of the young gangs and their actions. Ask the students to annotate the extract, highlighting words to show where the writer is critical of the gangs (*'Hooligans', 'pests', 'occupation'*). In a different colour, they should annotate words that show the feelings of local people (*'unbearable', 'fear'*). In feedback, discuss the number of direct and indirect criticisms of the gang in the article. The students should consider the use of anecdotes and their purpose (*the shopkeepers' views and experiences reveal how the gangs' behaviour is affecting the community*). Support them by highlighting direct and indirect criticisms, and by discussing implied meanings and inferences.

- Display **PowerPoint slide 4**. Using the students' annotations from the previous task, ask them to go through the extract highlighting opinions in one colour and facts in another colour. Then have the students decide whether the article is a balance of the two. Ask if the newspaper report can be expected to be accurate and realistic (determine what is fact and what is opinion). Introduce the term 'bias'.

Trying it yourself

- Display **PowerPoint slide 5** and introduce the final task: *What do you understand about anti-social behaviour in the 19th century?* Explain that the students are to write two paragraphs in response to the question using the SQI (statement + quotation + inference) method.

- To support the students, display the model answer on **PowerPoint slide 6** and ask them how they would improve it (*they could develop the inferences to include more than one suggestion, be more specific as to how the gangs avoid the police, and provide more evidence as to why the police struggle to stop this behaviour*).

- The students then complete their own response to the question, writing in their notebooks. Keep the task instructions on **PowerPoint slide 5** displayed as they write.

Activity:

Look at each boy in the photograph on **PowerPoint slide 3**.

- Choose **one** boy from the photograph. In the table below, make notes on how he is dressed, his facial expression, the way he is standing, and the way he is looking at the camera.
- What features of the boy you have chosen can be inferred as stereotypical for a member of a 19th-century gang?

Aspect of photograph	Chosen boy	Which of these features are stereotypical for members of gangs?
How he is dressed		
His facial expression		
The way he is standing		
The way he looks at the camera		

Securing skills with understanding of 19th-century non-fiction

Learning objective:	Resources:
• To understand how a writer can use language techniques to sensationalise their writing and express a viewpoint	• Extract 8.3.4 • 8.3.4 Lesson 2 PowerPoint • 8.3.4 Lesson 2 Worksheet • thesaurus or dictionary

Recap and reflection

* Re-read **Extract 8.3.4**. Ask the students to define 'ruffian' and to suggest other words with a similar meaning (*vagabond, hooligan, scoundrel, rough*). They then find alternatives for these words using a thesaurus or dictionary (possible answers: *teenagers, young people, young men, youth*).

* Display **8.3.4 Lesson 2 PowerPoint slide 1** and discuss the learning objective. Explain that the students are going to examine how the writer uses emotive language to support his viewpoint on gangs in South London.

Developing skills

* Display **PowerPoint slide 2** and ask the students to answer the questions in pairs. Take feedback. (Suggested answers: *1. It likens the gang members to animals ('roost'). 2. The gangs are everywhere and merciless. 3. Worth stealing. 4. Crime and terrorising people. 5. Scathing/negative.*) Ask why the writer may present teenagers and young people in this way and the effect (*the gangs appear ruthless, menacing, frightening – something to be terrified of*). Ask whether the writer is sympathetic to the young men in South Lambeth and what emotive language reveals this. Establish the writer's negative viewpoint and attitude, and consider the semantic fields of pests, weeds and prey; discuss the metaphorical symbolism of these words.

* Give out copies of **8.3.4 Lesson 2 Worksheet** and ask the students to complete **Activity 1** in pairs. They should be prepared to give evidence for their point of view in feedback. Support them by highlighting negatives and positives in the article and allowing them to look up any unfamiliar vocabulary.

* Ask the students to think about what makes the article sensationalist rather than a purely factual account (*the language used is one-sided, rather than presenting a balanced viewpoint*). Establish that *Illustrated Police News* might want to push its own agenda on the difficulties of policing South Lambeth.

* Display **PowerPoint slide 3** and ask the students to complete the three sentences using the information they have understood from the report so far. (Suggested answers: *1. ...prevalent, dangerous and unruly. 2. ...scared for their livelihood. 3. ...under pressure and powerless.*)

Trying it yourself

* Display **PowerPoint slide 4** and go over the definition of emotive language. Use the questions on the slide to establish how emotive language is used effectively in the article to make South Lambeth gangs seem a pressing threat and to create horror at their unlawfulness. Explain how the emotive language might make 19th-century readers feel scared or worried about being out on the streets.

* The students now complete **Worksheet Activity 2**. Once they have completed the table, ask whether emotive language should be used in the *Illustrated Police News*; the students should give reasons for their answer. Support them by highlighting which emotions the article evokes (*anger, fear, anxiety*) and by asking whether the public expects certain publications to be unbiased and not fearmongering. The students then complete **Worksheet Activity 3**, identifying and commenting upon the effectiveness of language techniques used by the writer to sensationalise the situation.

* Display **PowerPoint slide 5** and introduce the final task. Remind the students of the IEC (identify, exemplify, comment) technique and display the modelled IEC paragraph on **PowerPoint slide 6**.

* The students then write two or three IEC paragraphs in response to the question in their notebooks. They should consider: the work covered across the two lessons; how the article has a worrying tone that creates fear for ordinary people living in South Lambeth; whether the gang members have been misrepresented and how might they defend themselves from the accusations in the news article.

Activity 1:

- Complete the table below to show the criticisms the writer makes about the gangs, supported by quotations from the extract.
- Then state which criticism is the strongest and why.

Criticism	Quotation

Which criticism is the strongest and why: ....

....

....

Activity 2:

- In the left column of the table, list four emotive language points from the extract.
- In the right column, write the point in a way that uses non-emotive language.

Emotive language point	Non-emotive statement

Using the examples of language techniques in the first column, complete the table by:

- finding an example of each technique in the extract
- explaining how the writer uses the technique to sensationalise his viewpoint of the gangs.

Language technique	Example of technique in extract	How this sensationalises the gangs
Metaphor		
Simile		
Semantic field of animals		
Emotive language		

'You did not act in time': a speech to MPs at the Houses of Parliament, 23 April 2019

Extract 1: My name is Greta Thunberg. I am 16 years old. I come from Sweden. And I speak on behalf of future generations.

I know many of you don't want to listen to us – you say we are just children. But we're only repeating the message of the united climate science. Many of you appear concerned that we are wasting valuable lesson time, but I assure you we will go back to school the moment you start listening to science and give us a future. Is that really too much to ask?

In the year 2030 I will be 26 years old. My little sister Beata will be 23. Just like many of your own children or grandchildren. That is a great age, we have been told. When you have all of your life ahead of you. But I am not so sure it will be that great for us.

I was fortunate to be born in a time and place where everyone told us to dream big; I could become whatever I wanted to. I could live wherever I wanted to. People like me had everything we needed and more. Things our grandparents could not even dream of. We had everything we could ever wish for and yet now we may have nothing. Now we probably don't even have a future anymore. Because that future was sold so that a small number of people could make unimaginable amounts of money. It was stolen from us every time you said that the sky was the limit, and that you only live once.

You lied to us. You gave us false hope. You told us that the future was something to look forward to. And the saddest thing is that most children are not even aware of the fate that awaits us. We will not understand it until it's too late. And yet we are the lucky ones. Those who will be affected the hardest are already suffering the consequences. But their voices are not heard.

Is my microphone on? Can you hear me?

During the last six months I have travelled around Europe for hundreds of hours in trains, electric cars and buses, repeating these life-changing words over and over again. But no one seems to be talking about it, and nothing has changed. In fact, the emissions are still rising.

Extract 2: We children are not sacrificing our education and our childhood for you to tell us what you consider is politically possible in the society that you have created. We have not taken to the streets for you to take selfies with us, and tell us that you really admire what we do.

We children are doing this to wake the adults up. We children are doing this for you to put your differences aside and start acting as you would in a crisis. We children are doing this because we want our hopes and dreams back.

I hope my microphone was on. I hope you could all hear me.

Greta Thunberg

Learning objectives:	**Resources:**
• To understand the writer's key ideas • To explore and comment on the writer's point of view	• Extract 8.3.5 • 8.3.5 Lesson 1 PowerPoint • 8.3.5 Lesson 1 Worksheet

Getting started

* Display **8.3.5 Lesson 1 PowerPoint** and go over the lesson objectives.

* Then display **PowerPoint slide 2** and discuss the questions, which provide the students with an opportunity to reflect on previous aspects of the project so far. Take ideas from around the class, probing the students to think about the stereotypical complaints of teenagers: they are noisy, rude, uncaring, disrespectful, obsessed with their phones, etc. The students might also be surprised that the teenagers in the article from Week 4 (**Extract 8.3.4**) were so troublesome, given all the stereotypes of children in the past being seen and not heard, and the belief that behaviour was always better in the past. For question 4, the students may name young people in the public eye or from the school community.

* Now display **PowerPoint slide 3** and see if students recognise Greta Thunberg and know that she is a climate change activist.

* Give out copies of **Extract 8.3.5** and read Greta Thunberg's speech out loud. Explain to the students that this speech was given in London at the Houses of Parliament. You may also wish to play a video of Greta giving this speech (at the time of publication versions of this speech are available to watch online).

* Now hand out copies of **8.3.5 Lesson 1 Worksheet** and ask the students to complete **Activity 1**, which is a simple retrieval exercise. The students should be able to easily pick up on Greta's age and country of origin, that she is speaking 'on behalf of future generations' and that she has a sister.

Developing skills

* Display **PowerPoint slide 4** and look closely at the selected quotations with the whole group, exploring possible interpretations of each quotation. Lead the students to question who Greta might be talking about in the first quotation (*for example, large corporations that use lots of power, power companies themselves, airlines, etc.*) and who she might be talking about in the second quotation (*those who have lost their homes or land because of climate change, maybe through flooding or deforestation – consider animal life here as well as humans*).

Trying it yourself

* The students now work in pairs to complete some inferential reading of their own using **Worksheet Activity 2**, recording their ideas and observations in the table. Take feedback.

* Using the feedback from the activities, present the final task on **PowerPoint slide 5** and ask the students to use the (now well-established) SQI method to construct a longer answer to the task on the slide. Support the students by suggesting they use the quotations from **Worksheet Activity 2** and the earlier discussion within their answer, formulating clear opening statements for their constructs.

* If time allows, once the students have completed their writing, they could share the idea they feel most satisfied with or read aloud parts of answers around the class to build a collaborative 'golden' response.

Activity 1:

List four key facts you learn about Greta Thunberg from the speech.

1. ....

2. ....

3. ....

4. ....

Activity 2:

Look at the following quotations selected from Greta Thunberg's speech.

For each quotation, discuss with a partner what it suggests or implies. Add all your ideas and thoughts to the table.

Quotation from the speech	What can be inferred or implied? What is suggested?
'you say we are just children'	
'I am not so sure it will be that great for us'	
'we probably don't even have a future anymore'	
'no one seems to be talking about it'	

Learning objectives:	Resources:
• To understand how point of view is presented • To comment on the techniques of a persuasive speech	• Extract 8.3.5 • 8.3.5 Lesson 2 PowerPoint • highlighter pens

Recap and reflection

* Display **8.3.5 Lesson 2 PowerPoint slide 1** and go over the lesson objectives.

* Display **PowerPoint slide 2** and use the prompts on the slide to recall the students' prior knowledge. Recap on persuasive and point of view texts and their techniques then ask the students to jot down as many as they can remember from prior work and/or previous lessons/projects in 1 minute. The students are likely to remember facts, opinions, rhetorical questions, perhaps direct address, imperatives or commands.

* Re-read Greta Thunberg's speech (**Extract 8.3.5**). Remind the students that this speech was given at the Houses of Parliament to MPs and lawmakers.

Developing skills

* Display the list of persuasive or rhetorical devices on **PowerPoint slide 3** and recap any the students may have missed. You could perhaps ask them to reflect on 'emotive statement' as the thing that provokes any kind of emotional response in the reader. Remind them that abstract nouns describe intangible things – things that we can't touch.

* Now ask the students to work in pairs to find at least one example of each of these persuasive or rhetorical devices in **Extract 8.3.5**; they should highlight the example and then label it with the correct term. If the students require more support, these techniques can be found in chronological order in the speech, though there are other examples too.

* Allow approximately 20 minutes for this task. The students could self-mark through whole-class feedback. (Suggested answers: *Emotive statement: 'Now we probably don't have...anymore'; List of three: 'You lied..., You gave us..., You told us...'; Direct address: 'as before'; Inclusive pronouns: 'We will...', 'We are...'; Rhetorical question: 'Is my microphone on?'; Factual statement: 'the emissions are still rising'; Repetition: 'children...childhood...children'; Abstract noun: 'hopes and dreams'.*)

* Move on to **PowerPoint slide 4** to focus on the rhetorical questions. With the whole class, ask the students to think about why these questions are so powerful. Encourage them to see how Greta refers to whether her microphone is on at two different places in the speech, repeating the idea. The students should be encouraged to explore how she is asking not to be ignored but to be properly listened to, and for the audience of MPs to act on what she is saying. Reflect on how rhetorical questions can be used to provoke a particular response in the listener or reader's mind.

Trying it yourself

* Use **PowerPoint slide 5** to set the final analytical task. The modelling on the slide uses only sentence starters for the IEC (identify, exemplify, comment) method for language analysis, encouraging the students to build on prior knowledge. The model can also be used as a starting point to support the students.

* Encourage the students to select and write about three different features of language that they feel present Greta Thunberg's viewpoint most powerfully. Allow approximately 20 minutes for this final writing task.

* Finish the lesson by sharing strong examples as a whole group.

Learning objectives:	Resources:
• To write an op-ed for a magazine, arguing both sides of a topic • To include connectives and an informed opinion	• 8.3.6 Lessons 1 & 2 PowerPoint • 8.3.6 Lessons 1 & 2 Worksheet

Lesson 1: Getting started

• Display **8.3.6 Lessons 1 & 2 PowerPoint slide 1** and go over the learning objectives. Explain that the students will be writing an op-ed for a magazine, in which they will argue both sides of the question 'Angels or devils: is this a good description of the modern teenager?'

• Discuss what an op-ed is; establish that it comes from the words 'opposite editorial' and is a piece of opinion writing usually found opposite the editorial page of a newspaper or magazine, typically written by a journalist guest writer not employed directly by the newspaper or magazine.

• Ask what a counter-argument is and why is it useful when exploring both sides of a topic. Ensure the students understand that it is the opposite argument to the one presented, and that including it gives balance and shows consideration of others' views.

• Display **PowerPoint slide 2** and recap on stereotypes. Ask: Are stereotypes useful or harmful? Is labelling a person unhelpful? Establish that stereotypes are assumptions that limit your perception of others and can be harmful; also that labelling people is a form of binary stereotyping.

• Discuss how angels and devils can be used to describe teenagers, and display **PowerPoint slide 3**. Ask for examples of 'angelic' and 'devilish' teenage behaviour (for example: *helping with chores, acting as a carer to younger children, being a school prefect; smoking, swearing, being disrespectful*). Support the students by having them position things teenagers do on a pencil line from 'angel' to 'devil', according to how good they think the act is. Discuss whether the descriptions on the slide are fair. Explain this is how an op-ed can work: giving one point of view and using counter-arguments to dismiss any contrary view.

Developing skills

• Hand out copies of **8.3.6 Lessons 1 & 2 Worksheet** and ask the students to complete **Activity 1** in pairs, with one student arguing that teenagers are angels and the other that teenagers are devils. They should not show their responses to their partner. When each pair's responses are complete, ask one student to present their ideas to their partner, who responds with a counter-argument. After the discussion, allow the students time to add the key points their partner made to their table, along with any other points they can think of. Ask: Is it unfair to describe teenagers as a whole as strictly angels or devils? Focus on whether an individual teenager can be just an angel or just a devil; you might consider examples from texts the students have read, such as Tom Riddle in *Harry Potter* or Beth in *Little Women*.

• The students then rank-order the arguments from the activity from strongest to weakest, and consider which points might be used in an op-ed column when writing about teenagers.

• Display **PowerPoint slide four 4** and use the questions to recap and revise connectives and their functions. (Suggested answers: *1. a) Contrasting; b) Emphasising; c) Comparing. 2. Examples: thus, consequently, as a result, therefore, because*; *they are useful for providing impact, cause and balance*).

• Display **PowerPoint slide 5** and use the checklist to discuss the key skills needed for an op-ed piece.

Lesson 2: Trying it yourself

• Display **PowerPoint slide 6** to model a response. Support the students with discussion of the style (*personal experience, anecdote, emotive language*) and how the writing could be developed (*facts, statistics, counter-argument, hyperbole, humour*).

• Now ask the students to select three points for and three points against the topic 'Angels or devils: is this a good description of the modern teenager?' for an op-ed article for a magazine. They complete their plan using **Worksheet Activity 2**; remind them to plan a *balanced* argument.

• The students then write their op-ed article working independently.

Activity 1:

Use the chart below to list your points on the stereotyping of teenagers.

Teenagers are angels	Teenagers are devils

Activity 2:

Use the space below to create a plan for your op-ed piece. You could use a list, a mind map, a spider diagram or any other planning technique.

From *Dracula* (1897)

By this time I had finished my supper, and by my host's desire had drawn up a chair by the fire and begun to smoke a cigar which he offered me, at the same time excusing himself that he did not smoke. I had now an opportunity of observing him, and found him of a very marked physiognomy.

His face was a strong—a very strong—aquiline, with high bridge of the thin nose and peculiarly arched nostrils; with lofty domed forehead, and hair growing scantily round the temples but profusely elsewhere. His eyebrows were very massive, almost meeting over the nose, and with bushy hair that seemed to curl in its own profusion. The mouth, so far as I could see it under the heavy moustache, was fixed and rather cruel-looking, with peculiarly sharp white teeth; these protruded over the lips, whose remarkable ruddiness showed astonishing vitality in a man of his years. For the rest, his ears were pale, and at the tops extremely pointed; the chin was broad and strong, and the cheeks firm though thin. The general effect was one of extraordinary pallor.

Hitherto I had noticed the backs of his hands as they lay on his knees in the firelight, and they had seemed rather white and fine; but seeing them now close to me, I could not but notice that they were rather coarse—broad, with squat fingers. Strange to say, there were hairs in the centre of the palm. The nails were long and fine, and cut to a sharp point. As the Count leaned over me and his hands touched me, I could not repress a shudder. It may have been that his breath was rank, but a horrible feeling of nausea came over me, which, do what I would, I could not conceal.

The Count, evidently noticing it, drew back; and with a grim sort of smile, which showed more than he had yet done his protuberant teeth, sat himself down again on his own side of the fireplace. We were both silent for a while; and as I looked towards the window I saw the first dim streak of the coming dawn. There seemed a strange stillness over everything; but as I listened I heard as if from down below in the valley the howling of many wolves. The Count's eyes gleamed.

Bram Stoker

Introducing ways to explore the 19th-century novel: *Dracula*

Learning objective:	Resources:
• To explore the language in an extract from *Dracula*	• Extract 9.1.1 • 9.1.1 Lesson 1 PowerPoint • 9.1.1 Lesson 1 Worksheet

Getting started

* Display **9.1.1 Lesson 1 PowerPoint slide 1** and introduce the learning objective. Point out that *Dracula* was written in 1897 and is a Gothic horror novel. Ask the students to share what they know about the genres of Gothic and horror, and discuss examples of texts they are familiar with, such as *Frankenstein* and *The Woman in Black*. Ask what they would expect to see in such a text. Establish that these genres include elements of mystery and fear; the setting and atmosphere is often haunted or supernatural; there is usually a villain and a lady in distress.

* Display **PowerPoint slide 2** and use questions 1 and 2 to establish the students' current knowledge and understanding of vampires and the character of Dracula. Establish via discussion that Dracula is a vampire, a form of 'living dead' that feeds off the life blood of his victims; a monstrous predator with supernatural powers, such as the ability to shapeshift (change his form, for example into a bat or smoke).

* Hand out copies of **Extract 9.1.1** and read it out loud twice. Explain that it is an extract from the fictional journal of Jonathan Harker, an accountant who has been sent to Transylvania to work with Dracula; he has arrived at the Count's castle thinking he is on a business trip.

* The students now move on to answer questions 3 and 4 on **PowerPoint slide 2**. Encourage them to share their knowledge, experience and ideas as a class. For question 3, comparisons could be made to the *Twilight* series of novels and films, and other modern versions where vampires are presented as attractive, desirable and 'other worldly'. Discuss how Bram Stoker's presentation of Dracula generates anticipation and fear, and focus in on the description of him as human but with monstrous features.

Developing skills

* Display the task on **PowerPoint slide 3**; the students highlight **Extract 9.1.1** to show words or phrases that create an image of Dracula. Allow around 5 minutes for this activity. Encourage the students to be selective in what they highlight: they should avoid highlighting whole paragraphs, instead focusing on selecting single words or short phrases.

* Now hand out copies of **9.1.1 Lesson 1 Worksheet** and ask the students to complete **Activity 1** by drawing Dracula and annotating their drawing with the words and phrases they highlighted in the extract.

* Display **PowerPoint slide 4**. The students answer the questions on the slide, working in pairs or as a whole class, before moving on to complete **Worksheet Activity 2** individually.

* It's worth spending some time feeding back from this activity, with a focus on the impact of the adjectives, and how and why the descriptive language changes their image of Dracula. You could ask the students to read some sentences aloud with and without the adjectives, and to explain the differences. Discuss how the adjectives add fear and mystery to the character: they make Dracula seem monstrous, and when they are removed he appears more human/normal.

Trying it yourself

* Display **PowerPoint slide 5**. The students work in pairs or as a whole group to explore the three quotations on the slide using the questions to help them. The task is aimed at engaging the students in a writer's language choices and their effects on the reader. Explain that the language in a text is always carefully chosen by the author to paint a particular image.

* The students now note down their responses to the task from **PowerPoint slide 5** individually using **Worksheet Activity 3**. (Suggested answers: *1. 'cruel-looking' hints at him being evil or unkind; 'Heavy moustache' creates an image of hiding his mouth because it would give away his identity. 2. 'hairs in the centre of the palm' makes us imagine a monster or animal. 3. 'shudder' shows it was his natural response to Dracula, his instinct or senses taking over.*)

Activity 1:

Draw the character of Dracula below.

- Base your image on the words and phrases you highlighted in **Extract 9.1.1**.
- Annotate your drawing with the words and phrases from the extract.

Activity 2:

- Highlight all the *describing words* in your annotated drawing of Dracula.
- Then try removing a few to see how your impression of Dracula changes.

Activity 3:

Read the descriptive sentences taken from the *Dracula* extract below. For each sentence, note down your responses to the following questions:

- Why has the writer chosen that language?
- What does the writer want me to think of or feel?
- What does the writer want me to imagine?

---

1 'The mouth, so far as I could see it under the heavy moustache, was fixed and rather cruel-looking.'

....

....

....

....

....

---

2 'Strange to say, there were hairs in the centre of the palm.'

....

....

....

....

....

---

3 'I could not repress a shudder.'

....

....

....

....

....

Learning objective:	**Resources:**
• To learn how to explain the effects of language	• Extract 9.1.1 • 9.1.1 Lesson 2 PowerPoint • 9.1.1 Lesson 2 Worksheet

Getting started

• Display **9.1.1 Lesson 2 PowerPoint slide 1** and introduce the learning objective.

• Ask the students to re-read **Extract 9.1.1**; you might want to encourage them to read it out loud, or some of the students may benefit from independent reading.

• Display **PowerPoint slide 2** and reiterate the learning at the end of the previous lesson about the writer's intentions when composing their text. Establish that, when writers are composing, whether it's a novel or a newspaper article, they select words and phrases that help create and build images of characters, objects or settings in the reader's mind. Remind the students that authors draft and redraft texts, editing constantly.

Developing skills

• Display **PowerPoint slide 3**. The students could complete the questions on the slide working in pairs or as a whole class. (Suggested answers: *1. He's interesting because he is different, but his difference is subtle and it's not clear what he is. 2. It makes you question what Dracula is; you might imagine him to be like a bat or another animal associated with vampires.*)

• Hand out copies of **9.1.1 Lesson 2 Worksheet** and ask the students to work individually or in pairs to complete the activity. It's worth spending some time feeding back on the final column from the table, to introduce the ideas and effect of the language. (Suggested answers for column 2 of the table include: *'peculiarly arched nostrils'; 'lofty domed forehead'; 'eyebrows were very massive'; 'mouth…rather cruel-looking'; 'peculiarly sharp white teeth'; 'remarkable ruddiness showed astonishing vitality in a man of his years'; 'extraordinary pallor'; 'hairs in the centre of the palm'; 'nails…cut to a sharp point'.*)

• Display **PowerPoint slide 4** and discuss the modelled response as a whole group. The aim is to engage the students in forming their own ideas and responses from their notes using the IEC (identify, exemplify, comment) method. It's worth encouraging whole-group or paired feedback to the model answer. Ask: Can you see where the student has included a feature? Could the example be more concise? Zoom in on the embedded quotations used in the comment on the effect of the language.

Trying it yourself

• Display **PowerPoint slide 5**, which outlines the final task: *How does Bram Stoker present Dracula as an interesting character in this extract?* Some of the students may benefit from a teacher-led discussion to generate ideas. Ask them: How does the author present Dracula as physically unusual or different? Why isn't Jonathan Harker more scared? What does Jonathan Harker think Dracula is?

• The students can complete the writing task in their notebooks. Those who can should try to embed quotations in the analysis of effect on the reader. Answers will be the students' own, based on the model response and IEC structure.

• Once the students have completed the final writing task, encourage them to peer-assess their answers against the success criteria on **PowerPoint slide 5**. They should offer feedback on whether their partner has included all elements from the success criteria, and in particular whether they have developed the last section of their response where they explain the effect of the writer's language choices. You might find it useful to go back to the modelled IEC paragraph on **PowerPoint slide 4** as a guide to expectations and to support feedback.

Introducing ways to explore the 19th-century novel: *Dracula*

Activity:

Read the extract from *Dracula* below, then complete the table by:

- listing the physical characteristics Bram Stoker describes Dracula as having
- giving an example of the language used
- considering the effect of the author's language choices on you as reader.

Try to be concise, selecting single words or short quotations.

His face was a strong—a very strong—aquiline, with high bridge of the thin nose and peculiarly arched nostrils; with lofty domed forehead, and hair growing scantily round the temples but profusely elsewhere. His eyebrows were very massive, almost meeting over the nose, and with bushy hair that seemed to curl in its own profusion. The mouth, so far as I could see it under the heavy moustache, was fixed and rather cruel-looking, with peculiarly sharp white teeth; these protruded over the lips, whose remarkable ruddiness showed astonishing vitality in a man of his years. For the rest, his ears were pale, and at the tops extremely pointed; the chin was broad and strong, and the cheeks firm though thin. The general effect was one of extraordinary pallor.

Hitherto I had noticed the backs of his hands as they lay on his knees in the firelight, and they had seemed rather white and fine; but seeing them now close to me, I could not but notice that they were rather coarse—broad, with squat fingers. Strange to say, there were hairs in the centre of the palm. The nails were long and fine, and cut to a sharp point.

Physical characteristics	Example of language used	Effect of language: how it adds interest; what it makes me think, feel or imagine
Dracula's ears	'His ears were pale, and at the tops extremely pointed'	The adjective 'pale' makes it seem as though his ears have no blood or life in them, and the fact that they are 'extremely pointed' creates an image of his ears as being like an animal's and totally unlike normal human ears.

'The Laboratory' (1844)

Now that I, tying thy glass mask tightly,

May gaze thro' these faint smokes curling whitely,

As thou pliest thy trade in this devil's-smithy—

Which is the poison to poison her, prithee?

He is with her; and they know that I know

Where they are, what they do: they believe my tears flow

While they laugh, laugh at me, at me fled to the drear

Empty church, to pray God in, for them! – I am here.

Grind away, moisten and mash up thy paste,

Pound at thy powder, – I am not in haste!

Better sit thus, and observe thy strange things,

Than go where men wait me and dance at the King's.

That in the mortar – you call it a gum?

Ah, the brave tree whence such gold oozings come!

And yonder soft phial, the exquisite blue,

Sure to taste sweetly, – is that poison too?

Had I but all of them, thee and thy treasures,

What a wild crowd of invisible pleasures!

To carry pure death in an earring, a casket,

A signet, a fan-mount, a filligree-basket!

Soon, at the King's, a mere lozenge to give

And Pauline should have just thirty minutes to live!

But to light a pastille, and Elise, with her head

And her breast and her arms and her hands, should drop dead!

Quick – is it finished? The colour's too grim!

Why not soft like the phial's, enticing and dim?

Let it brighten her drink, let her turn it and stir,

And try it and taste, ere she fix and prefer!

What a drop! She's not little, no minion like me—

That's why she ensnared him: this never will free

The soul from those masculine eyes, – say, 'no!'

To that pulse's magnificent come-and-go.

For only last night, as they whispered, I brought

My own eyes to bear on her so, that I thought

Could I keep them one half minute fixed, she would fall,

Shrivelled; she fell not; yet this does not all!

Not that I bid you spare her the pain!

Let death be felt and the proof remain;

Brand, burn up, bite into its grace—

He is sure to remember her dying face!

Is it done? Take my mask off! Nay, be not morose

It kills her, and this prevents seeing it close:

The delicate droplet, my whole fortune's fee—

If it hurts her, beside, can it ever hurt me?

Now, take all my jewels, gorge gold to your fill,

You may kiss me, old man, on my mouth if you will!

But brush this dust off me, lest horror it brings

Ere I know it – next moment I dance at the King's!

Robert Browning

Learning objectives:	Resources:
• To develop skills in reading and exploring language in 19th-century poetry • To explore the presentation of character in poetry	• Extract 9.1.2 • 9.1.2 Lesson 1 PowerPoint • 9.1.2 Lesson 1 Worksheet

Getting started

- Display **9.1.2 Lesson 1 PowerPoint slide 1** and introduce the learning objectives. Ask the students what they would expect to see in a poem and how it compares to prose; you could discuss rhyme and rhythm in a poem versus prose as one long text; poetry as shorter yet harder to decipher; prose tells a story so is usually easier to understand. Prompt the students to recall *Dracula* and use it to predict what they might find in a linked 19th-century poem (elements of the Gothic, supernatural or mystery).

- Display **PowerPoint slide 2** and ask the students to spend at least 1 minute just looking at the painting. They can then discuss what they see in pairs or as a group. You could use 'who, what and where' questions to prompt their discussion – for example: Who is in the painting? What is happening?

- Explain to the students that the painting is based on the poem they are going to study in this lesson, which is also called 'The Laboratory'. Ask what they think the poem is about based on the painting, encouraging consideration of both explicit and implicit meanings. Prompt them with questions such as: What can you infer about the woman and the man? What can you infer about their relationship? Take feedback, focusing in on their different ages; that the woman is younger than the man and looks wealthier; that she is leaning on the man and looking down at him, suggesting she has power over him.

- Hand out copies of **Extract 9.1.2** and read through the poem 'The Laboratory' at least twice.

- After a second reading, display **PowerPoint slide 3** and ask the students to work in pairs or as a class to unpack the poem, using the questions on the slide; they could make notes and annotations alongside the poem or in their notebooks. The purpose here is to consider at a basic level what is happening in each stanza; the students should recognise that the main character is having some poison made to kill the girlfriend of her love interest. The students will further unpack the poem throughout the lesson. Some groups may benefit from support to recognise the narrative and what is happening in each stanza.

Developing skills

- Hand out copies of **9.1.2 Lesson 1 Worksheet**. The students complete **Activity 1** working in pairs or independently. This activity should be fairly fast-paced; certainly no longer than 5 minutes. It is aimed at engaging the students with the main character before they explore her in greater depth. (Suggested answers: *1. A woman. 2. She's speaking to an 'old man', someone making a potion; the final stanza. 3. She's quite rude to him/bossy; this suggests she's of a higher status to him and is used to getting what she wants. 4. Harsh, bitter, angry or rude, demanding, unkind. 5. through her language; 'they believe my tears flow'; 'While they laugh, laugh at me'; 'pray God in, for them! – I am here'; 'Pound at thy powder'.*)

- Now display and read through **PowerPoint slide 4**. This would be a good point to ascertain the students' overall impressions of the poem and the character so far. Check that they recognise Maria's intentions and ask them to identify how she develops from stanza to stanza. Ask: How do you feel about her? Do your feelings for her change through the poem? Do you feel sorry for her at any point?

Trying it yourself

- The students now complete **Worksheet Activity 2** in pairs, noting down in the table each feeling or attitude they think Marie portrays and finding a quotation to support each idea. They might find it helpful to take on and then swap roles, for example, working as researcher or note-maker for each stanza.

- Display **PowerPoint slide 5** and introduce the students' independent work for this lesson: they imagine they are the 'old man' working in the laboratory, making Maria's poison, and write a letter to a friend describing their encounter with her. Encourage the students to creatively interpret the character of Maria while developing their thinking around the 'old man'. It may help them to refer back to the image on **PowerPoint slide 2**.

Introducing ways to explore 19th-century poetry: 'The Laboratory'

Activity 1:

Read the first three stanzas of 'The Laboratory' then answer the questions below.

1. Who is the voice in the poem? ....

2. Who is the speaker addressing? Where is this suggested? ....

    ....

3. How does she address him? What does this tell you about her? ....

    ....

4. What is her tone? ....

    ....

5. How is the tone created? Find a quotation to support your answer. ....

    ....

    ....

Activity 2:

Look closely at the way Browning reveals Maria's feelings and emotions throughout the poem.

For each feeling or attitude you think Marie portrays, find a quotation to support your idea. Record your ideas in the table below.

Maria's feeling or attitude	Quotation to support my idea

<table>
<tr><td>

Learning objective:

- To comment on the effect of choices of language and imagery

</td><td>

Resources:

- Extract 9.1.2
- 9.1.2 Lesson 2 PowerPoint
- 9.1.2 Lesson 1 PowerPoint
- 9.1.2 Lesson 2 Worksheet

</td></tr>
</table>

Getting started

- Display **9.1.2 Lesson 2 PowerPoint slide 1** and introduce the learning objective. Ask the students to recall what imagery is; establish that it is language or words used create an image in the reader's mind.

- Display **PowerPoint slide 2** and review the image of Maria from the poem 'The Laboratory'. Ask the students whether the painting on the slide is how they imagine Maria and discuss their responses. You could also display the painting *The Laboratory* by John Collier, on **9.1.2 Lesson 1 PowerPoint slide 2** and ask which paining the students feel is the best representation of her.

- Display **PowerPoint slide 3** and go through the text and questions on the slide. The students will need to refer to the copy of **Extract 9.1.2** they made notes on in the previous lesson.

- Re-read the poem twice, to remind the students of the content. When discussing the prompts on **PowerPoint slide 3**, they could make notes on their copy of the poem or in their notebooks.

Developing skills

- Display **PowerPoint slide 4** and read through the stanza from the poem. Then hand out copies of **9.1.2 Lesson 2 Worksheet**. Direct the students to complete **Activity 1**; they can do this working with a partner or independently.

- Take feedback. (Suggested answers: *1. Alliteration or list. 2. She appears almost evil; she wants to cause suffering or harm. 3. He wants us to feel horrified about her actions and behaviour; the reader imagines her as a bitter monster, almost like an animal, in the harm she wants to inflict.*) Highlight how Browning uses punctuation (dashes to represent a pause, and exclamation marks) to emphasise how little Maria cares about the people she wants to hurt.

- Now ask the students to complete the table for **Worksheet Activity 2** by focusing on Maria's actions, feelings and personality in the poem. This task will support them with writing IEC paragraphs later in the lesson. As with the previous lesson, the students could rotate the roles of investigating the poem and making notes. You could support them by discussing the example in the table first, so they're clear about what they need to do for this task.

- Take feedback. (Suggested answers: *Maria's actions: rhetorical question: 'Quick – is it finished?'; shows how impatient she is to get the potion and start killing people. Maria's feelings: repetition: 'While they laugh, laugh at me'; Maria feels humiliated that they are laughing at her; creates an image of her as a victim. Maria's personality: listing Elsie's positive attributes: 'But to light a pastille, and Elise, with her head, And her breast and her arms and her hands, should drop dead!'; this shows that Maria is jealous of Elise, and makes us wonder that perhaps Elise's crime is just being prettier than Maria.*)

Trying it yourself

- The students now complete the independent writing task (**Worksheet Activity 3**), writing two IEC (identify, exemplify, comment) paragraphs. To support them in this task, display **PowerPoint slide 5** and go over the modelled IEC response. Encourage the students to use the model to explain and explore the images created in their mind based on how the writer presents Maria. For the first IEC paragraph, they should use the sentence starters on the worksheet, drawing on textual references they have found and work done during the previous activities. Encourage the students to then write a second IEC paragraph without the prompts if possible.

- To round off the lesson, ask the students to peer-assess each other's responses. They should check whether they have managed to include all elements of the IEC response in their second paragraph.

Activity 1:

Read this stanza from 'The Laboratory' then answer the questions below.

> Not that I bid you spare her the pain!
>
> Let death be felt and the proof remain;
>
> Brand, burn up, bite into its grace—
>
> He is sure to remember her dying face!

1. Consider the language Browning uses here. What is the langue feature highlighted?

   ....

2. What impression do you have of Maria in this stanza? ....

   ....

3. What does Browning want us to think, feel or imagine about Maria? How do you know?

   ....

   ....

Activity 2:

Working with a partner, look back through the whole poem and select language (words or phrases) that you feel create a clear image in your mind of the following:

- Maria's actions
- Maria's feelings
- Maria's personality.

Add your choices to the table below. For each choice, explain the image created in your mind.

	Identify feature	Give example	The image this creates in my mind
Example	Alliteration	'Brand, burn up, bite'	Evil torturer who wants to see her victim suffer
Maria's actions			
Maria's feelings			
Maria's personality			

Activity 3: Independent work

How does Browning use language to present Maria in 'The Laboratory'?

Using your notes in the table you completed for Activity 2, write two IEC (identify, exemplify, comment) paragraphs in response to the question.

Use the sentence starters below to help you write your first IEC paragraph, then try and write a second IEC paragraph without the prompts.

Paragraph 1:

I: *Browning uses* ....

E: ....

....

C: *This creates an image of* ....

....

....

....

Paragraph 2:

....

....

....

....

....

....

....

....

....

....

....

9.1.3
Lessons 1 & 2

Introducing ways to enhance creative writing: Creating a mysterious character

Learning objectives:	Resources:
• To understand how the structure of a text is effective • To structure your work for effect • To develop your ideas and engage your reader	• 9.1.3 Lessons 1 & 2 PowerPoint • 9.1.3 Lessons 1 & 2 Worksheet

Lesson 1: Getting started

• Display **9.1.3 Lessons 1 & 2 PowerPoint slide 1** and introduce the learning objectives. Ask what the word 'structure' means. Explain that a good piece of writing should have a clear structure, and that most narratives follow a three-part structure: beginning, middle and end.

• Display **PowerPoint slide 2**. Discuss the idea of 'hooking' the reader in and why authors use hooks. Ask the students which books they have read that have 'hooked' them from the beginning.

Developing skills and Trying it yourself

• Display **PowerPoint slide 3**. The students can work individually, in pairs or as a whole group to consider the examples of narrative hooks; you might consider the first example together then move on to paired work. The students use the questions on the slide to explore their reaction to the opening lines and why they find them intriguing/want to know more. Ask which character interests them the most and why.

• Hand out copies of **9.1.3 Lessons 1 & 2 Worksheet** and ask the students to complete **Activity 1** in pairs or small groups; they match the opening lines to one of the potential approaches to narrative hooks. It could be argued that some of the approaches will fit under more than one type of hook, and the students should be encouraged to discuss and investigate this. (Answers: *1B, 2C, 3A.*)

• Display **PowerPoint slide 4** and introduce the writing task. Allow the students 1–2 minutes of thinking time to consider the story title, 'Human or Monster?' and then longer to write their opening line in their notebooks, ensuring it matches the style of one of the narrative hooks from the worksheet. Some of the students might benefit from guidance on the type of hook to use. The students then swap opening lines with a partner or present them to the class. The partner or group then guesses the type of hook and provides feedback using the model statements on the slide.

Lesson 2: Recap and review

• Revisit the learning objectives on **PowerPoint slide 1** and then display **PowerPoint slide 5**. Tell the students they will be planning a piece of creative writing for 10 minutes using the story title 'Human or Monster?' and their preferred method for planning (spider diagram, mind map, narrative arc, etc.); **Worksheet Activity 2** is provided to support this. Time the activity to prevent it creeping into other tasks.

Developing skills and Trying it yourself

• Now refer the students to **Worksheet Activity 3**, which focuses on an extract from *The Strange Case of Dr Jekyll and Mr Hyde*. The aim here is to get the students thinking about their own character, the image they want to create in their reader's mind and the language they will choose to achieve this. You could ask for comparisons between the character of Mr Hyde and Dracula (from Week 1). Ask: Why are both of these characters intriguing? The students don't need to analyse the extract, and the task should be a bridge and inspiration for their own writing rather than taking up too much lesson time.

• Go over the writing task on **PowerPoint slide 6**. The students should write at least one sentence in their notebook to introduce their main character, focusing on their language choices and structure to create a first impression. Thinking time should be given at the start so the students approach their writing with a clear idea of their character in mind. The students then swap sentences and/or read them out loud; peers can provide feedback using the question prompts on the slide.

• Display **PowerPoint slide 7**. The students now develop the approach they took in the last activity and write at least one paragraph developing their character. Whereas in the previous task they were writing to grab the reader's attention, now their focus should be on selecting language to create an image and have an effect on their reader. Encourage the students to share their writing and provide peer feedback using the prompts on the slide; they should incorporate any feedback so their writing shows progress.

Activity 1:

- Working with a partner, look through the opening lines below. Match each line (1–3) to the different approaches to introducing a character (narrative hooks A–C).
- Discuss why you think they match.
- Then answer the questions below.

Opening lines:

> **1:** It was a dark and cold November the day the Smiths torched their home.
>
> **2:** Not so long ago, there was a woman who woke up one day as a different person.
>
> **3:** If you're reading this assuming I'm a nice person, you're wrong!

Narrative hooks:

A: The reader is spoken to directly and feels involved from the start	**B:** There is lots of description to create a mood.	**C:** The writer appeals to the reader's sense of curiosity: who is she?

1. Do any of the opening lines fit under more than one hook?

....

....

....

2. Which is your favourite opening line and why?

....

....

....

....

Use the space below to complete a spider diagram or narrative arc for your story.

Activity 3:

Read the extract below. It is from *The Strange Case of Dr Jekyll and Mr Hyde* by Robert Louis Stevenson (1886). In this extract, the writer explores the character of Mr Hyde.

The lawyer stood awhile when Mr Hyde had left him, the picture of disquietude. Then he began slowly to mount the street, pausing every step or two and putting his hand to his brow like a man in mental perplexity. The problem he was thus debating as he walked was one of a class that is rarely solved. Mr Hyde was pale and dwarfish; he gave an impression of deformity without any nameable malformation, he had a displeasing smile, he had borne himself to the lawyer with a sort of murderous mixture of timidity and boldness, and he spoke with a husky whispering and somewhat broken voice, – all these were points against him; but not all of these together could explain the hitherto unknown disgust, loathing and fear with which Mr Utterson regarded him. 'There must be something else,' said the perplexed gentleman. 'There is something more, if I could find a name for it. God bless me, the man seems hardly human!'

1. Zoom in on the language used to present the character. What does it make you think, feel or imagine about Mr Hyde?

   ....

   ....

   ....

2. Working with a partner, underline examples of interesting language used to create an image of the character of Mr Hyde in your mind. What do you notice about the language or the image?

   ....

   ....

   ....

' "Spring Heeled Jack" in Darlington'

For some days the wildest rumours have been afloat in Darlington regarding some mysterious being who has been playing antics in the ghost line for nearly a week. First he was seen in Neasham-road, then he paid a visit to Eastbourne, and latterly he has honoured Rise Carr with his presence. It is said that he is on a visit to various towns in the North.

From a simple ghost he has developed into a kind of supernatural being. He can stride several yards at a time, leap hedges and walls like a greyhound, and one person actually declares that he has darted across the River Tees at Yarm!

At any rate, whatever he may be, the result is that in Darlington women and children scarcely dare to move out at night. Owing the nervous condition of several timid females in Darlington our representative there has been led to make some enquires concerning the 'Ghost,' and as the result we can assure all those who are in trepidation on the subject that the wild rumours now afloat have more existence in the imaginations of persons than in real life. The most difficult thing our representative had to do was to find any person who had really seen the ghost.

After about an hour's inquiry he at last found the man he sought. This was Thomas Nellis, a workman at the Bridge Yard, Neasham-road. Nellis informed him that on going down Neasham-road he distinctly saw a man in white standing near Mr Tree's gate. On Nellis saluting him he received no answer. Nellis at once walked up, and the ghost took to his heels. He thinks the white part of the performance is either produced by a light or white sheet. At any rate the moment Nellis approached the white disappeared, and he distinctly saw in the dusk a man about six feet high. He chased him down the field, but the ghost was very fleet of foot, and by the time they reached the bottom Nellis was forty yards behind. Nellis is of opinion that the man is assisted in running by some mechanical apparatus fixed to his boots, enabling him to take strides of immense length. One thing he is certain of – viz., that it is a man so that it is to be hoped that this announcement will dispel the fears of those persons who are in terror of a visit from the Eastbourne apparition.

The ghost is not yet in the Darlington Police cells, as currently reported, although it is expected he soon will be.

Daily Gazette for Middlesbrough, 28 January 1884

Learning objectives:	Resources:
• To make inferences from the text • To select relevant evidence to support viewpoint	• Extract 9.1.4 • 9.1.4 Lesson 1 PowerPoint • 9.1.4 Lesson 1 Worksheet

Getting started

- Display **9.1.4 Lesson 1 PowerPoint slide 2**. Ask the students to work in pairs and discuss the two images on the slide. Ask: What does each image show? Who might the people in the images be? Where are they? Encourage the students to be as imaginative as possible with this activity. Take time to share the students' ideas in small groups or across the class.

- Introduce 'Spring-Heeled Jack'. Explain that he was a well-known daemon who terrorised towns and cities across England in the 1800s, a 'devil-like creature' who could leap to extreme heights and lengths, jumping between rooftops and over bridges. Some people believed he was a man dressed up and others believed that he was a supernatural being. You might consider asking the students to make comparisons between Dracula and Spring-Heeled Jack. Prompt them to think about the subtle ways Dracula's monstrous and inhuman characteristics are presented in comparison to the more obvious fear in the account of Spring-Heeled Jack.

- Display **PowerPoint slide 1** and introduce the learning objectives. Ask the students to recall inference as using evidence to reach conclusions.

- Hand out copies of **Extract 9.1.4** and read the article through twice as a class. Ask the students for their initial opinions. Prompts for discussion include: What is your first reaction to the text? Might the article have been written to generate fear and excitement in the reader while also stating the facts? What are your thoughts on the subtle humour in the article?

Developing skills

- Display **PowerPoint slide 3** and introduce the partner task. Encourage the students to explore the whole text with a partner, then note down their ideas and responses to questions 1–3 in their notebooks.

- Take feedback. (Suggested answers: *1. The creature has become more extreme/fearsome; it seems like something to be more afraid of. 2. It has scared some people (mostly women and children); one eyewitness chased the 'being'. 3. Students' answers might include: they were very superstitious; they believed in the supernatural; they were easily scared and driven by rumours.*)

- Display **PowerPoint slide 4** and hand out **9.1.4 Lesson 1 Worksheet**. Ask the students to tell you what they remember about inference. The students can refer to the information on the slide while they complete the activity on the worksheet. Encourage them to spend a minute or two discussing and giving their own opinion on whether they believe in Spring-Heeled Jack. They then work through **Extract 9.1.4** in pairs, adding any relevant quotations they find to the table on the worksheet and explaining how the quotation proves the existence (or not) of Spring-Heeled Jack. The aim of the activity is to encourage exploration of the text alongside the selection of evidence and clear explanation.

- Take feedback. Answers will be the students' own but might include: *'Spring-Heeled Jack' is a real man based on the eyewitness account; he is not real; there is no evidence to prove his existence; the eyewitness account is unreliable; the journalist doesn't seem to believe in his existence.*

Trying it yourself

- Display **PowerPoint slide 5** and go over the instructions for the students' independent work: they imagine they live in a town close to where Spring-Heeled Jack was last seen and write a short letter to their local police station to give their opinion on what has happened and how best to deal with it. The students should be encouraged to write creatively, interpreting the text. They might approach this writing task in an informal way, using more colloquial language. This should be allowed if it supports them in reiterating the key points and showing a good understanding of the text.

- End the lesson by asking a selection of the students to read their letters aloud to the rest of the class.

Activity:

Do you believe 'Spring-Heeled Jack' is real?

Gather evidence from the text (quotations) to **prove** what you think.

I think Spring-Heeled Jack is ....

....

Quotation from the extract that proves my thinking	How the quotation proves my opinion (inference; what the quotation suggests)

Learning objectives:	**Resources:**
• To work towards a longer SQI response • To attempt critical evaluation and weighing up evidence	• Extract 9.1.4 • 9.1.4 Lesson 2 PowerPoint • 9.1.4 Lesson 2 Worksheet

Getting started

* Display **9.1.4 Lesson 2 PowerPoint slide 1** and introduce the learning objectives. Remind the students that SQI stands for statement + quotation + inference: making a statement, supporting it with a quotation from the text, and then using the evidence to infer and draw conclusions from the text.

* Display **PowerPoint slide 2** and introduce the task on the slide. The students re-read **Extract 9.1.4** as a group or independently. Allow time for them to share their knowledge of other monsters, daemons and mystical creatures; you could prompt them to think of examples such as the Loch Ness Monster and Big Foot. Ask the students to consider how people might regard them. Ask: Is such a creature real? Is it something to fear? Select some of the students to share their responses with the wider group. If it is okay to do so, introduce the idea of positive mythical creatures, such as the Tooth Fairy, Santa Claus, etc.

Developing skills

* Display **PowerPoint slide 3**. Ask the students to explain what you're doing when you *infer* from a text. Ensure they are clear that the skill of inference requires them to use the evidence in the text to come to conclusions/read between the lines/read what is not explicitly stated in the text. For example, they can infer that the journalist does not believe in Spring-Heeled Jack as a supernatural being from his statement about how difficult it was to find any evidence.

* Hand out copies of **9.1.4 Lesson 2 Worksheet** and introduce **Activity 1**. Encourage the students to highlight and annotate the model answer on the worksheet. Take feedback. (Suggested answer: *Statement: The text suggests Spring-Heeled Jack might be made up by the people in the town. Quotation: The author says the ghost has 'more existence in people's imaginations than in real life'. Inference: This suggests the people of Darlington have imagined the ghost and frightened each other with rumours rather than Spring-Heeled Jack actually existing.*)

* Now direct the students to complete **Worksheet Activity 2**; display **PowerPoint slide 4** to support your discussion and explanation of the task. Introduce the question statement (*A student reading the article said, 'It's clear the writer doesn't believe there's any Spring-Heeled Jack!' To what extent do you agree?*) then work as a whole group to ensure the students understand the focus of the question (i.e. the writer doesn't believe that Spring-Heeled Jack exists). The students then follow the steps on the worksheet: they start by reflecting on and considering the writer's point of view in order to decide whether they agree or disagree with the statement that Spring-Heeled Jack does not exist. Direct them to use the table on the worksheet to collate evidence that supports their response to the statement. Ensure sufficient time is left so that all the students have a go at explaining the evidence. If a student somewhat agrees, or wants to produce a more balanced response, you could encourage them to offer two examples of each (agree/disagree).

Trying it yourself

* Display **PowerPoint slide 5** and go over the task set as independent work. The students should use the table they completed for **Worksheet Activity 2** to write two or three SQI paragraphs in response to the same statement. The main aim of this activity is for the students to recognise the focus of a response from a statement, decode the writer's point of view and then respond to the statement using a clear structure. Some of the students might benefit from being directed to use the sentence starters from **Worksheet Activity 1** to get started, while you could challenge other students to fold or turn over the worksheet so that they are working entirely independently.

* To round off the lesson you could consider asking one or two of the students from each side to debate the existence (or not) of Spring-Heeled Jack, using evidence from the text and their own inferences to persuade the rest of the class to agree with their point of view.

Activity 1:

Review the model answer below, which was written in response to the question 'Do you believe that Spring-Heeled Jack is real?'

Highlight and label the statement, the quotation and the inference in the answer.

The text suggests that Spring-Heeled Jack might have been made up by the people in the town. The author says that the ghost has 'more existence in the imaginations of persons than in real life'. This suggests that the people of Darlington have imagined the ghost and frightened each other with rumours rather than Spring-Heeled Jack actually existing.

Activity 2:

A student reading the article said, 'It's clear the writer doesn't believe there's any Spring-Heeled Jack!' To what extent do you agree?

- Working with a partner, decide whether you agree, disagree or somewhat agree that the writer doesn't believe there's any Spring-Heeled Jack.
- Skim and scan the text for four pieces of evidence that back up the points you want to make.
- Add your evidence to the table below, along with an explanation of what it suggests.

Quotation to prove my thinking	Inference: What this suggests

'Seeing is believing' by Merrily Harpur

Sightings of mystery 'big cats' in Britain's countryside have snowballed since the 1980s, dividing opinion about their existence

Angus, a Warwickshire gamekeeper, went to feed his pheasants in a spinney one afternoon in November 2004 when he surprised an unusual poacher. He recalls: 'A black animal emerged with a hen pheasant in its mouth. It recoiled as it saw me and then took off, running down towards the brook. It was hardly more than 6ft away so I had a good look at it. It was definitely a big cat. A black panther – bigger than a Labrador, with a longer body. Its fur was scruffy and muddy. It had a long tail, and pointed ears like a cat – and as it ran the ears went back. I've lived in the country all my life and I've seen everything – foxes, deer, badgers. I know what should be there and what shouldn't.'

As it fled it left a footprint, 5in long and 4in wide, in the thick clay which, cast in plaster by the police, became one of many fragments of 'hard' evidence for the existence of big cats in the wild in Britain. But while sightings of anomalous big cats (ABCs) have snowballed since the 1980s, investigators are still searching for irrefutable proof: bodies, alive or dead, or unambiguous photos and films.

The absence of 'proof' is odd because of the huge scale of the phenomenon. It is estimated that up to 7,000 people a year see panther-like (black) animals, or puma-like (brown) animals at large in the UK, though only about a tenth of these come to light via police, newspapers or websites. In fact, it seems probable that more Britons have now seen a big cat than have ever seen a pig.

Eyewitnesses come from every walk of life and have one thing in common – their sighting was unexpected. Wiltshire landscape gardener Colin Booth was trimming a hedge when a black, panther-like animal, the size of his own Alsatian, emerged from it. They studied each other from a distance of 20ft before the animal turned and strolled off, leaving Booth stunned.

One theory claims such animals are the descendants of pets released into the countryside by their owners in 1976 when the Dangerous Wild Animals Act made it expensive to keep big cats; yet this is unlikely, for three reasons. First, only three people have ever claimed to have deliberately released big cats – it would have to be done on a vast scale for breeding populations to become established all over Britain, including the Isle of Mull. Second, there have been no bodies of big cats found alive or dead, despite intensive hunts over many decades. Third, while about a quarter of animals sighted have plain, sandy brown fur similar to a puma's, the others reported are jet black.

These mysteries divide those researching the nature and provenance of ABCs. The literalists speculate about hybridisation creating black pumas; the possibility of a relict population of native pre-ice age big cats lingering on unnoticed; and some suspect foul play – the captive breeding of big cats for criminal purposes, such as baiting or as 'frighteners'.

Above all, perhaps, it is the intensity of such experiences that invites deeper investigation. 'It was a beautiful creature, and it had a profound effect on me,' Booth says. 'I will remember it for the rest of my life.'

The Guardian, 22 March 2006

Learning objective:	Resources:
• To develop inference skills using a 21st-century text	• 9.1.5 Extract • 9.1.5 Lesson 1 PowerPoint • 9.1.5 Lesson 1 Worksheet

Getting started

• Display **9.1.5 Lesson 1 PowerPoint slide 2** and hand out copies of **Extract 9.1.5**. Encourage the students to look at the image on the slide and try to predict what the text will be about.

• Read twice through the extract 'Seeing is believing', about sightings of mystery 'big cats' in Britain's countryside. After the second reading, the students should work in pairs or as a whole group to discuss their impressions and what they believe or disbelieve. Ask them what links can be made between this text and the text on Spring-Heeled Jack from the previous lesson. Responses might include: *the writer also seems sceptical; there is also very little evidence of the big cats' existence; the big cats are described as real animals while Spring-Heeled Jack is a more superhuman or supernatural figure.*

• Display **PowerPoint slide 1** and introduce the learning objective. Remind student how, during the previous lesson, they worked through the text like detectives, looking for evidence that proved or disproved their opinion.

Developing skills

• Display **PowerPoint slide 3**. Ask the students to recall the SQI method: What does each letter of SQI stands for? (*statement, quotation, inference*) When and how might they use it? (*to infer information from a text*). Allow the students some thinking time to consider their responses to the task *How are the sightings presented?* During feedback establish that the sighting are presented as reasonable and realistic – for example, the witnesses seem calm, but each person who reports seeing a big cat was alone at the time, and this adds doubt as to whether their account is completely accurate. Encourage the students to make notes in their notebooks. Select some of the students to share their thinking with the class, or ask the students to share their ideas in pairs as the first step towards developing their opinion.

• Display **PowerPoint slide 4**. Encourage the students to work in pairs to complete the activity on the slide; they should note their responses directly onto their copy of the extract. Once they've finished, hand out copies of **9.1.5 Lesson 1 Worksheet**; the students can write up their findings using the frame there.

• Take feedback and discuss the students' responses. Clarify that there are more words or phrases that seem to prove the existence of the large cats, but the journalist writes with a tone that sounds sceptical – for example: *'The absence of "proof" is odd'; 'In fact, it seems probable that more Britons have now seen a big cat than have ever seen a pig.'*

Trying it yourself

• Display **PowerPoint slide 5** and introduce the final task. Direct the students to work independently to attempt to summarise the article. The purpose of this activity is to encourage the students to focus on the key information in the text in order to clearly and successfully summarise the content. They can complete this piece of extended writing in their notebooks.

• Answers will be the students' own, but might include references to the following: *A number of seemingly reliable sources have seen 'big cats' close to their homes or land. Some think the animal is a 'panther' while others think it's more like a 'puma', suggesting there's more than one type of animal. All sightings were 'unexpected' and people were taken by surprise. As yet, there is no 'proof' of the big cats' existence, no 'body' or 'unambiguous photos and film', implying that they might not exist at all. It has been argued that they came from wild cats that were dumped into the countryside, but this is seen as 'unlikely' because of the 'vast' numbers needed, which again questions the possibility of their existence.*

• To conclude the lesson, ask the students to compare the writer's response to the big cat sightings with the attitude of the writer of the article on Spring-Heeled Jack. For example, the students might consider the contrasting tones: the Spring-Heeled Jack article is more humorous, but both express cynicism.

Activity:

Working with your partner, go back through *The Guardian* article paragraph by paragraph.

- <u>Underline</u> words or phrases that seem to prove the existence of the big cats.

- (Circle) words and phrases that seem to disprove or question the existence of the big cats.

Use the writing frame below to bring together an overview of the presentation of the big cats in the article.

Reviewing the spread of circles and underline, I can deduce..

....

....

....

This suggests ....

....

....

....

I think the writer of the article thinks ....

....

....

....

A quotation to prove this is ....

....

....

....

Learning objectives:	Resources:
• To make a link between 19th-century and 21st-century non-fiction texts • To introduce a comparative response	• Extract 9.1.4 • Extract 9.1.5 • 9.1.5 Lesson 2 PowerPoint • 9.1.5 Lesson 2 Worksheet

Getting started

- Display **9.1.5 Lesson 2 PowerPoint slide 2**. Encourage the students to look at the images and recall the two texts. This could be done using hot-seating, hands-down questioning, or by cutting up and mixing the extracts and asking the students to sort them into the right order.

- Re-read **Extract 9.1.4** and **Extract 9.1.5** as a whole class or small group. This should be followed up with class feedback on whether the students remembered everything in the extracts.

- Display **PowerPoint slide 1** and introduce the learning objectives. Ask the students what they think 'linking' texts might mean; establish that this refers to linking the ideas in two or more different texts.

Developing skills

- Display **PowerPoint slide 3**. Introduce the two quotations on the slide, then work as a class to identify the link. You could encourage the students to discuss this together first and then share ideas as a class.

- Now hand out copies of **9.1.5 Lesson 2 Worksheet**. The students should work independently or in pairs to complete **Activity 1**. (Suggested answers: *1. In both texts the monster or beast disappears when approached. 2. It suggests that they're elusive or that people can't get real evidence of their existence.*)

- The students now move onto **Worksheet Activity 2**. You might find it useful to discuss a couple of quotations as a whole group first, or you might consider leaving the students to attempt the whole task independently.

- Take feedback. (Suggested answers: *Text 1: 'The most difficult thing our representative had to do was to find any person who had really seen the ghost'; Text 2: 'investigators are still searching for irrefutable proof'; Link and what this suggests: Both writers claim there's no proof of the existence of the creature, suggesting they might not be real. Text 1: 'Darlington women and children scarcely dare to move out at night'; Text 2: 'leaving Booth stunned'; Link and what this suggests: Both texts discuss the impact on people and suggest both creatures shock and scare people. Text 1: 'He can stride several yards at a time, leap hedges and walls like a greyhound.' Text 2: 'bigger than a Labrador, with a longer body. Its fur was scruffy and muddy. It had a long tail, and pointed ears like a cat – and as it ran the ears went back.' Link and what this suggests: Both texts describe the appearance of the creature as being like a mix of different animals or creatures, suggesting it's not clear what the creature is.*) The final part of this activity requires the students to identify the pair of quotes they feel have the strongest link. The purpose here is to encourage them to justify their thinking orally before writing a more developed response.

Trying it yourself

- Display **PowerPoint slide 4** and introduce the independent writing task, which the students can complete in their notebooks. Before the students begin writing, it is worth investing some time in a whole group conversation around the comparison of the two texts and the similarities between the two creatures, the way the journalists have written about them and the effect the sightings have had on people and communities. The students then work independently to respond to the question, using the model on the slide. (Note that text 1 in the model on the slide is the Spring-Heeled Jack article and text 2 is the big cats article, but some of the students might find it easier to swap the order and have the more modern text first.) The purpose of this activity is to encourage the students to develop their inferences and response, drawing from and linking two texts using a basic comparative model.

- To conclude the lesson, the students could peer-assess each other's answers, checking that all elements of the model are included and that their partner has managed to make a clear link between the texts. The students could then share their links and comparisons with the wider group.

Activity 1:

Discuss the following quotations with a partner then answer the questions below.

'The moment Nellis approached the white disappeared.' (From the article on Spring-Heeled Jack)

'...it saw me and then took off, running down towards the brook' (From *The Guardian* article)

---

1. Are there any similarities or differences in the texts? ....

    ....

    ....

2. What does this suggest about both 'beasts'? ....

    ....

    ....

Activity 2:

Read the quotations below.

- Discuss them with a partner then complete the table.
- After completing the table, highlight the pair of quotations that you feel have the strongest link.

From '"Spring-Heeled Jack" in Darlington':

'Darlington women and children scarcely dare to move out at night.'

'He can stride several yards at a time, leap hedges and walls like a greyhound'

'The most difficult thing our representative had to do was to find any person who had really seen the ghost.'

From 'Seeing is believing', *The Guardian*:

'investigators are still searching for irrefutable proof'

'leaving Booth stunned'

'bigger than a Labrador, with a longer body. Its fur was scruffy and muddy. It had a long tail, and pointed ears like a cat – and as it ran the ears went back.'

'Spring-Heeled Jack' quotation	'Seeing is believing' quotation	Link and what this suggests

Learning objectives:	Resources:
• To understand register and purpose in relation to a writing task • To complete part of a longer writing task	• 9.1.6 Lessons 1 & 2 PowerPoint • 9.1.6 Lessons 1 & 2 Worksheet

Lesson 1: Getting started

* Display **9.1.6 Lessons 1 & 2 PowerPoint slide 2**. Introduce the image of the girl with the 'fairies' and the fact that the sisters convinced people that fairies lived in their garden. Allow time for the students to discuss mythical creatures, and when and how they have believed in them. Question them about good and bad mythical creatures, what they still believe, and what it feels like to believe in mythical creatures.

* Display **PowerPoint slide 1** and introduce the learning objectives. Revisit the elements of the project and consolidate the students' understanding: they have looked at monsters and mythical creatures; language to present the strange and different; images created by monstrous characters and how we feel about them; how to hook your reader through openings, characters and setting; mythical creatures from the past and present, and how to make links between them. Explain that in this week's lessons they will plan and write a speech presenting their ideas and beliefs about mythical creatures.

Developing skills and Trying it yourself

* Display **PowerPoint slide 3**. Introduce the final task and emphasise its purpose (writing to argue). Encourage pair work or a whole group discussion around initial ideas, then hand out copies of **9.1.6 Lesson 1 Worksheet** and direct the students to complete **Activity 1** by mind-mapping their initial ideas.

* Display **PowerPoint slide 4** and discuss register. Ask the students when they might have used formal or informal language and prompt them for examples; it can be fun to highlight the difference by getting the students to say something in slang and then the same thing in Standard English.

* The students now complete **Worksheet Activity 2** working in pairs or small groups. Share responses. (Suggested answer: *Texts from most formal to most informal: 2, 3, 5, 8, 6, 7, 4, 1; the students may swap some round if they can justify it from personal experience.*)

* Display **PowerPoint slide 5** and go over the independent writing task. Before they begin their writing, the students should check that their plan (mind map) from **Worksheet Activity 1** shows a balanced point of view, adding any notes about what they will use at different points in the writing. They then move on to writing their opening line, using the skills they learned earlier in the project to hook the audience into their speech from the beginning. If time allows, share a selection of opening lines in groups or as a whole class and ask the students to offer each other feedback on how effective they found them.

Lesson 2: Developing skills and Trying it yourself

* Display **PowerPoint slide 6**. Encourage the students to recall the meaning of register and purpose. They will need to refer to their completed mind map from the previous lesson and the elements of the writing task, including spending 10 minutes revisiting their plan using the prompts on the slide.

* Display **PowerPoint slide 7** and read the information on the slide. Encourage pair work or a whole group discussion to support the students in thinking about a call to action. You could offer the following scenarios and ask what the final call to action might be: a speech in assembly about litter around school; a speech to your headteacher asking for a school trip to a funfair.

* The students then complete **Worksheet Activity 3**. Encourage them to share their call to action with a partner or within a small group.

* The students now write up all their notes onto the new plan provided on **Worksheet Activity 4**, ensuring they have something for each section. Allow around 10 minutes for writing up and sharing with a partner. Display the success criteria on **PowerPoint slide 8** while they write. This activity should be completed at pace so as not to seep into writing time. Most of the time in this session should be given over to writing.

* Display **PowerPoint slide 9**. Using their plans to support their writing, the students complete the writing task independently on a separate piece of paper. Allow the students time to check and edit their work against the success criteria on **PowerPoint slide 8**.

Activity 1:

Create a spider diagram below to note down all your ideas in relation to the task.

'Mythical creatures exist in our world,
not just in the imagination of children.'

Activity 2:

Use the sliding scale below to order the pieces of writing from the most formal to the most informal.

1. text to a friend

2. letter to your MP

3. speech at parents' evening

4. diary entry

5. article for the school newsletter

6. personal blog

7. Instagram post

8. this speech to your class.

Most formal .... *Most informal*

Activity 3:

Think about how you will conclude your speech. What do you want your audience to do or think after they listen to you? Write your call to action below.

....

....

....

Activity 4:

Use the writing grid below to complete your final plan for your speech.

Opening: Hook ....

....

....

Paragraph 1: My point of view ....

....

....

....

Paragraph 2: Others might think ....

....

....

....

Paragraph 3: My other point of view ....

....

....

....

Call to action: ....

....

....

From *Mary Barton* (1848)

There are some fields near Manchester, well known to the inhabitants as 'Green Heys Fields,' through which runs a public footpath to a little village about two miles distant. In spite of these fields being flat, and low, nay, in spite of the want of wood (the great and usual recommendation of level tracts of land), there is a charm about them which strikes even the inhabitant of a mountainous district, who sees and feels the effect of contrast in these commonplace but thoroughly rural fields, with the busy, bustling manufacturing town he left but half-an-hour ago.

Here and there an old black and white farmhouse, with its rambling outbuildings, speaks of other times and other occupations than those which now absorb the population of the neighbourhood. Here in their seasons may be seen the country business of haymaking, ploughing, etc., which are such pleasant mysteries for townspeople to watch: and here the artisan, deafened with noise of tongues and engines, may come to listen awhile to the delicious sounds of rural life: the lowing of cattle, the milkmaid's call, the clatter and cackle of poultry in the farmyards.

You cannot wonder, then, that these fields are popular places of resort at every holiday time; and you would not wonder, if you could see, or I properly describe, the charm of one particular stile, that it should be, on such occasions, a crowded halting place. Close by it is a deep, clear pond, reflecting in its dark green depths the shadowy trees that bend over it to exclude the sun. The only place where its banks are shelving is on the side next to a rambling farmyard, belonging to one of those old world, gabled, black and white houses I named above, overlooking the field through which the public footpath leads. The porch of this farmhouse is covered by a rose-tree; and the little garden surrounding it is crowded with a medley of old-fashioned herbs and flowers, planted long ago, when the garden was the only druggist's shop within reach, and allowed to grow in scrambling and wild luxuriance – roses, lavender, sage, balm (for tea), rosemary, pinks and wallflowers, onions and jessamine, in most republican and indiscriminate order. This farmhouse and garden are within a hundred yards of the stile of which I spoke, leading from the large pasture field into a smaller one, divided by a hedge of hawthorn and blackthorn; and near this stile, on the further side, there runs a tale that primroses may often be found, and occasionally the blue sweet violet on the grassy hedge bank.

I do not know whether it was on a holiday granted by the masters, or a holiday seized in right of Nature and her beautiful spring time by the workmen, but one afternoon (now ten or a dozen years ago) these fields were much thronged. Groups of merry and somewhat loud-talking girls, whose ages might range from twelve to twenty, came by with a buoyant step. They were most of them factory girls, and wore the usual out-of-doors dress of that particular class of maidens; namely, a shawl, which at midday or in fine weather was allowed to be merely a shawl, but towards evening, if the day was chilly, became a sort of Spanish mantilla or Scotch plaid, and was brought over the head and hung loosely down, or was pinned under the chin in no unpicturesque fashion. Their faces were not remarkable for beauty; indeed, they were below the average, with one or two exceptions; they had dark hair, neatly and classically arranged, dark eyes, but sallow complexions and irregular features. The only thing to strike a passer-by was an acuteness and intelligence of countenance, which has often been noticed in a manufacturing population.

Elizabeth Gaskell

<table>
<tr><td>

Learning objectives:

- To understand key contrasts in images of the city and the countryside
- To consider more developed inferences linked to contextual ideas

</td><td>

Resources:

- Extract 9.2.1
- 9.2.1 Lesson 1 PowerPoint
- 9.2.1 Lesson 1 Worksheet

</td></tr>
</table>

Getting started

- Display **9.2.1 Lesson 1 PowerPoint slide 1** and go over the learning objectives for the lesson. Explore how contextual ideas are linked to the situation out of which a text arises: the social backdrop from which it emerges and the issues of its time. If the students have worked on Projects 7.2 and 8.2, good examples here would be their work on *The Water Babies*, 'The Chimney Sweeper' and *Jane Eyre*.

- Hand out copies of **9.2.1 Lesson 1 Worksheet**. Read aloud the description of Coketown from the opening of Charles Dickens's *Hard Times*. The students work in pairs to complete **Activity 1**, identifying and commenting on all the references to colour and to industry in the extract.

- Discuss as a group what the students notice. Encourage them to pick up on the dark colours, noting that the 'black canal' and the 'purple river' suggest somewhere grim, perhaps from a horror story or apocalyptic scene. Ask the students what is worrying about the water being those colours. When they see the number of references to the chimneys, engines, etc., what are their first impressions? Do they think this a good place to live?

Developing skills

- Still working in pairs, allow the students 15 minutes to work on the remaining questions on the worksheet (**Activities 2**, **3** and **4**), making notes and annotations, before feeding back. Prompt them to think about how surreal the images seem and the grim atmosphere they evoke. Does the description appear like real life or a scene from a film? While taking feedback on **Activity 4**, encourage the students to consider how the structure of the complex sentence suggests how repetitive and endless the days might have been for the workers. Following feedback, explain to the students that in his novels Dickens tried to show how grim life was for workers in industry.

- Display **PowerPoint slide 2** then give out copies of **Extract 9.2.1**, from *Mary Barton*. Explain that it is from a novel about the Victorian working class, and is set in Manchester around 1840. Read the extract aloud as the class follows it. Allow the students a further 15 minutes to work in small groups to explore and discuss the questions on the slide, which focus on paragraphs 1, 2 and 3 of the extract.

- Display the image on **PowerPoint slide 3** from *The Illustrated London News*. Ask the students what impression they get of the workers and their environment from the illustration. What do they notice about their clothing and their ages? Is anything implied about family relationships? (*Whole families work in the mills.*) What do the the mills in the background suggest? (*They are the backdrop to their lives.*)

- Now display **PowerPoint slide 4** and ask the students to consider the quotation from the extract. Use the three questions to prompt whole-class discussion, and develop using the points the students have gathered in their group work. Encourage them to see the contrast between the city and the countryside, how it was a welcome relief from the grim atmosphere and pollution of the town, how everything seemed much nicer, simpler, more innocent and natural, with people enjoying fresh air, the natural world and each other's company. Explore how it might have been a rare occurrence for a 'holiday' to take place.

Trying it yourself

- The students look again at the final paragraph of **Extract 9.2.1** and the description of the factory girls. Use the illustration on **PowerPoint slide 3** to show what is meant by the description of the shawl. Then display **PowerPoint slide 5** and allow the students a few minutes working individually to jot down their thoughts about the selected quotations and to draw conclusions by looking back at the Coketown extract. Some may observe that the girls look unhealthy and plain; perceptive students may pick up on the fact that the girls could be bright and intelligent. Finish by asking the students to consider the number of intelligent young people, who, because they were poor, were condemned to the life of the factory worker.

Activity 1:

Read the following description of a fictional northern town – 'Coketown' – from the novel *Hard Times* by Charles Dickens, then answer the questions below.

It was a town of machinery and tall chimneys, out of which interminable serpents of smoke trailed themselves for ever and ever, and never got uncoiled.

It had a black canal in it, and a river that ran purple with ill-smelling dye, and vast piles of buildings full of windows where there was a rattling and a trembling all day long, and where the piston of the steam-engine worked monotonously up and down, like the head of an elephant in a state of melancholy madness. It contained several large streets all very like one another, and many small streets still more like one another, inhabited by people equally like one another, who all went in and out at the same hours, with the same sound upon the same pavements, to do the same work, and to whom every day was the same as yesterday and tomorrow, and every year the counterpart of the last and the next.

---

1. What do you notice about the colours used in the description?

   ....

   ....

   ....

2. How many references can you find to industry?

   ....

   ....

   ....

Activity 2:

What is the effect on you of the simile 'the piston of the steam-engine worked monotonously up and down, like the head of an elephant in a state of melancholy madness'?

What does this make you visualise or imagine?

....

....

....

....

Activity 3:

What is the effect of the metaphor: 'interminable serpents of smoke trailed themselves for ever and ever, and never got uncoiled'?

What does this make you think or feel?

....

....

....

....

Activity 4:

Read the following sentence from the extract above.

> It contained several large streets all very like one another, and many small streets still more like one another, inhabited by people equally like one another, who all went in and out at the same hours, with the same sound upon the same pavements, to do the same work, and to whom every day was the same as yesterday and tomorrow, and every year the counterpart of the last and the next.

1. What impression do you get of people's lives from this sentence?

....

....

....

....

....

2. Why do you think this is structured into one very long, complex sentence? Could this be deliberate? What does this structural technique make you feel about the place and the people?

....

....

....

....

<table>
<tr><td>

Learning objectives:

- To understand the presentation of the countryside and consider the writer's intentions
- To develop a mini essay-style response using familiar methods

</td><td>

Resources:

- Extract 9.2.1
- 9.2.1 Lesson 2 PowerPoint
- 9.2.1 Lesson 2 Worksheet
- sugar paper and marker pens

</td></tr>
</table>

Getting started

- Re-read and recap on **Extract 9.2.1** from *Mary Barton*, then display **9.2.1 Lesson 2 PowerPoint slide 1** and go over the learning objectives.

- Stimulate discussion and reflection of the extract using the questions on **PowerPoint slide 2**. Lead the students to see that before industrialisation the working classes may have had more of a rural existence and worked on the land or in small cottage industries, but the big mills put those livelihoods in jeopardy. Speculate whether Gaskell's piece is a little nostalgic and sad for the loss of the countryside. Ask the students to double check in the extract and note how far the walk was from the city of Manchester to Green Heys Fields (*the extract mentions two miles and half an hour's walk*).

- Now show the students the painting on **PowerPoint slide 3** and take their impressions. Ask: What is most shocking and surprising about the painting? How does the painting link to the description of Coketown that you read in the previous lesson? How does it reflect Gaskell's description of 'Green Heys Fields'? Most of the students will notice the contrast between the beautiful countryside in the foreground and the heavily polluted background that links to the description of Coketown. Note also the characters sitting and resting in the foreground.

- Ask the students to write down three sentences explaining what they think is: a) Dickens' view of industrialisation; b) Gaskell's view of industrialisation; c) the artist's view of industrialisation. Take feedback and establish that all three of them see industrialisation in a negative light: that it is damaging to people and the environment.

Developing skills

- Give out copies of **9.2.1 Lesson 2 Worksheet** and ask the students to complete the activity, which is connected to the imagery that Gaskell uses in the *Mary Barton* extract. If support is required, the students could work on this task in pairs or small groups, collating their thoughts on sugar paper.

- Take feedback. The students should be able to pick up on: the use of the natural world, particularly plants and flowers; the fact the countryside is made to seem pleasant, beautiful, old fashioned, idyllic, and like a paradise compared to the city. For question 3, encourage the students to think about the idea of a lost world or way of life. You could even encourage them to think about whether the same is true of our cities and countryside today. Answers and thoughts can be shared among the whole group to encourage wider responses to the final task.

Trying it yourself

- The final task encourages the students to begin to build a mini-essay-style response to a text using both their comprehension and analytical methods. Set up the task and give key reminders of the methods and advice using **PowerPoint slide 4**.

- Use **PowerPoint slide 5** as a model to remind the students of both the SQI (statement + quotation + inference) and IEC (identify, exemplify, comment) methods via the colour coding of each separate element. If any students need extra support, allow them to 'borrow' the model opening paragraph from the slide.

- In plenary, you could ask for volunteers to share paragraphs they are most proud of, or select three good examples to be read out that 'build' a complete collaborative model essay response.

Developing responses to the 19th-century novel: *Mary Barton*

Activity:

Look at the following words and phrases that Gaskell uses to describe the village in **Extract 9.2.1**, and then answer the questions below.

'a deep clear pond'	'old fashioned herbs and flowers'
'a rambling farmhouse'	'large pasture field'
'covered by a rose-tree'	'primroses may often be found'
'little garden'	'blue sweet violets'

1. What kind of imagery does Gaskell create with these words and phrases?

   ....

   ....

   ....

   ....

2. What picture is Gaskell trying to create of the countryside? Does she see the countryside as a positive or a negative place?

   ....

   ....

   ....

   ....

3. Why do you think Gaskell chose to begin her novel – which is about the working classes in a large city like the one Dickens describes – with this image of the countryside?

   ....

   ....

   ....

   ....

'Composed upon Westminster Bridge' (1802)

Earth has not anything to show more fair:

Dull would he be of soul who could pass by

A sight so touching in its majesty:

This City now doth, like a garment, wear

The beauty of the morning; silent, bare,

Ships, towers, domes, theatres, and temples lie

Open unto the fields, and to the sky;

All bright and glittering in the smokeless air.

Never did sun more beautifully steep

In his first splendour, valley, rock, or hill;

Ne'er saw I, never felt, a calm so deep!

The river glideth at his own sweet will:

Dear God! the very houses seem asleep;

And all that mighty heart is lying still!

William Wordsworth

'London', from *Songs of Experience* (1794)

I wander thro' each charter'd street,

Near where the charter'd Thames does flow.

And mark in every face I meet

Marks of weakness, marks of woe.

In every cry of every Man,

In every Infants cry of fear,

In every voice: in every ban,

The mind-forg'd manacles I hear

How the Chimney-sweepers cry

Every blackning Church appalls,

And the hapless Soldiers sigh

Runs in blood down Palace walls

But most thro' midnight streets I hear

How the youthful Harlots curse

Blasts the new-born Infants tear

And blights with plagues the Marriage hearse

William Blake

Developing responses to 18th- and 19th-century poetry: Structure and imagery in two contrasting poems

Learning objectives:	Resources:
• To understand the viewpoint of a poet in presenting London compared to other forms • To consider the imagery of a 19th-century poem compared to other forms	• Extract 9.2.2a • 9.2.2 Lesson 1 PowerPoint • 9.2.2 Lesson 1 Worksheet

Getting started

- Display **9.2.2 Lesson 1 PowerPoint slide 1** and go over the learning objectives for the lesson.

- Give out copies of **9.2.2 Lesson 1 Worksheet** and read aloud the diary entry. Ask the students to complete **Activity 1** on the worksheet in pairs, using the questions to investigate their initial impressions of the text and its writer. Take feedback.

- Display **PowerPoint slide 2**. Ask the students if they know where Westminster Bridge is (*London*). Point out that the painting is *View of Westminster Bridge and the Houses of Parliament with a hay barge* by James Francis Danby, painted in 1859. Tell them to note down the following: the three things in the painting capture their attention most; what they notice about the colours; what time of day they think the painting shows. Ask the students what is most interesting to them about this view of London and how it might compare with a similar view today.

- Now give out copies of **Extract 9.2.2a** and read the poem 'Composed upon Westminster Bridge' aloud. Reveal to the students that the writer of the poem, William Wordsworth, was the brother of the diary writer (Dorothy Wordsworth) from the worksheet. Ask: Do you think the poet looked at the same view as his sister? Were they in London and on the bridge at the same time? Does the diary share anything with the poem? Discuss with the students how the diary extract and poem share the same positive impression of London and appreciation of the sight as beautiful.

Developing skills

- The students now work through questions 1–7 on **PowerPoint slides 3**, **4** and **5**. They can work either as a whole class with the teacher leading or in small groups, with the students given time to work on each section of the poem. Groups should feed back ideas one slide at a time.

- Suggested responses might include some of the following ideas: *The poet's amazement at how beautiful the city looks in the early morning light; the idea of being royal, like a king. We can see all the achievements that humankind has made and all the things that can make life meaningful (for example, art, faith), but they are linked to nature. Here the city and everything in it looks as beautiful as anything in nature. People can make things that are lovely if we don't ruin them with pollution ('smokeless air'). The poem is celebrating what is good about humankind and makes Wordsworth/the persona feel calm and at peace, and he seems to be praising God for this. His view seems idealistic and therefore unrealistic, but this is a quiet time when the city is 'asleep' and 'lying still'. This, in turn, seems to make the poet/persona feel calm and at peace.* Answers here could also link back to the Mary Barton extract from Week 1 and the idea of a city ruined by pollution and industry.

Trying it yourself

- Refer the students back to **9.2.2 Lesson 1 Worksheet** and ask them to complete **Activity 2** individually now they have explored the poem fully. The students should make use of the ideas from their exploration on **PowerPoint slides 3**, **4** and **5**, and these ideas can form a useful checklist to ensure understanding as you assess. Allow the students to work in pairs if more support is required.

- Conclude the lesson by sharing responses to the six questions in **Worksheet Activity 2** and taking varied ideas. Ask the students in plenary which they prefer and why: the diary description, the poem or the painting.

Activity 1:

This is a diary entry from someone observing London early in the morning.

In pairs, investigate the extract and make notes in response to the questions below.

It was a beautiful morning. The city, St. Paul's, with the river, and a multitude of little boats, made a most beautiful sight as we crossed Westminster Bridge.

The houses were not overhung by their cloud of smoke, and they were spread out endlessly, yet the sun shone so brightly, with such a fierce light; that there was something like the purity of one of nature's own grand spectacles.

---

1. What items does the writer pick out? ....

   ....

2. Where and how do we see the writer's feelings? ....

   ....

   ....

3. When do you think the diary was written (i.e. how long ago)? ....

   ....

4. What ideas do you have about the writer – their age and gender? What makes you think this?

   ....

   ....

Activity 2:

The diary entry, the painting and the poet all present their view of London. Answer the following questions now you have had chance to explore all three.

1. What viewpoint does the diary entry share with the poem?

   ....

   ....

   ....

2. What does the painting have in common with the diary entry? Is there anything in the painting that seems similar to the viewpoint in the diary entry?

    ....

    ....

    ....

3. What does the painting have in common with the poem? Is there anything in the painting that seems to link closely with some of the imagery in the poem?

    ....

    ....

    ....

4. How does the poet seem to feel about London? How do you know?

    ....

    ....

    ....

    ....

    ....

5. What image of London does the poet present? What is your evidence?

    ....

    ....

    ....

    ....

    ....

6. What features of London does the poet highlight and why might this seem unusual to us today?

    ....

    ....

    ....

    ....

    ....

Learning objectives:
- To explore a contrasting view of London
- To explore the language, imagery and structure of two poems about London
- To write a comparative response to two classic poems

Resources:
- Extract 9.2.2a
- Extract 9.2.2b
- 9.2.2 Lesson 2 PowerPoint
- 9.2.2 Lesson 2 Worksheets a and b

Recap and reflect

- Ask the students about the previous lesson and what they remember of Wordsworth's view of London.

- Display **9.2.2 Lesson 2 PowerPoint slide 1** and consider the learning objectives, explaining that the previous work will now be developed and a second text explored in readiness for a longer task.

- Revisit **Extract 9.2.2a** and then hand out copies of **Extract 9.2.2b**, reading aloud Blake's poem 'London'. Ask for the students' first impressions of how this poet views London compared to Wordsworth. Ask: Which writer is more 'hard-hitting' in their view of industrialised cities? Does Blake's poem remind you of anything else you have read in this project? Revisit Dickens' description of Coketown in Week 1.

Developing skills

- Working as a whole class, use **PowerPoint slides 2, 3, 4 and 5** to guide the students step-by-step through this tricky text, using the questions on the slides to tease out their responses. Ask the students to annotate their copies of the poems with the key ideas. Allow 15–20 minutes for this task.

- Take feedback. Encourage the students to note the following in their responses: *1. The poet is moving aimlessly, in no particular direction. 2. The misery is visible to the poet everywhere; 'Weakness' and 'woe' (which you may need to define) suggest that people are both struggling and miserable. 3. The repetition suggests that no one is safe and that everyone, from the tiniest child to grown men, are victims of poverty and oppression. 4. We might ordinarily associate an infant with crying but 'every Man' suggests how vulnerable and upset adults are because of their situation. 5. The poet is suggesting that people are trapped or enslaved by the system. 6. Chimney sweepers were children (these are references to child labour). 7. Blake is suggesting that the Church (which was very wealthy) was not doing enough to help the poor. 8. The suggestion here is that those in power send young boys out to fight wars that they have started. 9. With no welfare system, young women in poverty, with no employment and with no husband or father to provide for them, had little choice but to turn to prostitution. 10. Wealthy upper- and middle-class men used poor women as prostitutes, spreading sexually transmitted disease and unwanted pregnancy, and creating more vulnerable infants.*

- In small groups or pairs, allow the students approximately 20 minutes to work with both poems and complete **9.2.2 Lesson 2 Worksheet a**, exploring the poems' contrasting vocabulary, imagery, patterns and tone, and collating their ideas in the table. If time allows, share ideas as a class. With a group working at a lower level, you may wish to end the lesson here and spend more time encouraging the sharing of ideas and completion of the table.

Trying it yourself

- The final task is an essay-type response that may be started in class, but which may also require homework time to complete. The students work through the instructions and information on **9.2.2 Lesson 2 Worksheet b**, highlighting how the structure of the essay mirrors the work completed in the group task table completed on **Worksheet a**. Use the model paragraph on the worksheet to give an example of a clear and simple comparative style for the students to follow. Also suggest they use different comparative words to add variety to their response.

- You could perhaps share opening paragraphs in class to check success before setting the remainder as homework or a follow-up lesson.

	'Composed upon Westminster Bridge' by William Wordsworth	'London' by William Blake
Vocabulary: What would you say are the three most important words or phrases in each poem, and what do they suggest or imply to you?		
What do you think is the most striking image in the poem what is its effect on you? What does it make you think, feel or imagine?		
What do you notice about the way the poem is put together and structured? Are there any patterns or a particular rhythm or pace? Do you think this could link to its meaning overall? If so, in what ways?		
What tone, mood or atmosphere is created in the poem? Describe it in three words.		
What message is the poet leaving us with here? What is the poet's intention?		

Final task:

Compare how the poets present their different impressions of London in 'Composed upon Westminster Bridge' and 'London'.

Use the notes and ideas from your group work and the table you completed on **Worksheet a**, and aim to write **five paragraphs** exploring:

- how the poets use different vocabulary to create their impression
- the different images the poets paint
- the different rhythms and patterns in each poem
- the different tone each poet creates
- what you think each poet's message about the capital city could be.

When you are writing about language, imagery and structure, remember to use the IEC method:

Identify, Exemplify, Comment on effect

Also remember to use **comparative words**: *however, whereas, contrastingly, in a different way.*

Model paragraph:

Wordsworth uses vocabulary like 'beautiful', 'bright' and 'glittering' to describe the city of London in the early morning. This makes me feel that the place is very special and an amazing sight as it is the capital city. However, Blake uses vocabulary such as 'weakness' and 'woe' to describe the expressions on the faces of the people who live and work there. This makes me think that although the city itself was wealthy and beautiful, there were many people who were very poor and oppressed in the capital city.

---

1. Can you see the IEC method?

2. Can you see how examples have been 'cherry picked' from each poem?

3. Can you see how the comment on effect focuses on think/feel/imagine?

4. Can you see how the comparative word has been used to link the ideas?

Learning objectives:	Resources:
• To develop an understanding of how contrasting images can be used in creative writing • To plan and write a creative piece using contrasting vocabulary, images and structural techniques	• 9.2.3 Lessons 1 & 2 PowerPoint • 9.2.3 Lessons 1 & 2 Worksheet

Lesson 1: Getting started

• Using **9.2.3 Lessons 1 & 2 PowerPoint slide 1**, introduce the lesson objectives. Emphasise the word 'contrasting' and linking back to the previous week's lessons, where contrasting images of London were created through the poetry.

• Display **PowerPoint slide 2**. Ask the students to look closely at the image and the read out the statement to them. Ask the students what they see in the picture at first glance and then what they see when they look closer. Ask them if they find anything startling or unusual then question them about the statement on the slide. How do they respond to the statistic: 'the world's richest 1 per cent has more than twice as much wealth as 6.9 billion people'? What does this imply about inequality in the world today? Explain to the students that they are going to use the image as part of a creative writing workshop leading to a final piece of independent writing.

Developing skills and Trying it yourself

• Introduce the first workshop task on **PowerPoint slide 3** and then move back to the image on **slide 2**. The students could work in pairs to generate more ideas. Allow 1 minute for the first word association task and then repeat for the second task describing the man. Take some feedback from pairs before using the tip to consolidate the point of the task.

• Now use **PowerPoint slides 4** and **5** to introduce and workshop ideas around creating imagery. Again working in pairs, allow the students a good 15 minutes to think about potential similes and metaphors using the prompts on **slide 5**. The students should note that the red plastic bag looks as though it may contain some of the man's belongings – perhaps *all* his belongings – while in the background the designer bag stands behind glass, almost like a museum display – something precious. You might even consider the cost of a high-end luxury bag compared to the man holding out his hat for loose change. Take feedback from the students to find their most creative ideas and possible similes and metaphors.

• Introduce the independent task using **PowerPoint slide 6** before displaying the photograph on **PowerPoint slide 7**. This is a powerful image. Allow the students a good few minutes to look at it and jot down their initial thoughts before opening up a discussion. Allow the students to guide the discussion based on what they see and feel when looking at the image. It is interesting to consider contrasting ideas about: crowding versus space; what the different materials the buildings on the two 'sides' are made of; the colours (where is the green and the blue?); the angle of the balconies on the luxury apartments.

• Close the lesson by handing out copies of **9.2.3 Lessons 1 & 2 Worksheet** so students can look at the choice of writing task. Explain that next lesson they will plan and write a response to one of those tasks so they should think about their choice. The challenge task allows them to independently read the Lawrence Ferlinghetti poem 'Two Scavengers in a Truck, Two Beautiful People in a Mercedes'.

Lesson 2: Developing skills and Final task

• Display and revisit the image on **PowerPoint slide 7**. Allow the students some time to select one of the tasks from the worksheet; you may wish to advise them that choices 3 and 4 are more challenging.

• Display **PowerPoint slide 8** and ask the students to consider how they might use the layout or structure of their piece of writing to great effect. You could refer them to a copy of the suggested poem for task 4 (Ferlinghetti's 'Two Scavengers in a Truck, Two Beautiful People in a Mercedes'), which is an extremely good exemplar text to illustrate how structure can be used to show the divide between rich and poor.

• Reiterate the guidance on the worksheet, then allow the students 10–15 minutes to plan and 30–35 minutes to write. Also 10 minutes to check and proofread with peers using the prompts on the worksheet in plenary. Share some of the successful pieces of writing together if time allows.

Final task:

Choose one of the tasks below.

For the task you have chosen:

- plan your ideas into five possible paragraphs
- use the five-point narrative arc structure to organise the sequence of your work
- think about the contrasting vocabulary you will need to use
- plan for some striking and interesting contrasting images
- aim to use some interesting structural techniques to show the contrasts between one side of this city (and possibly the characters you create) and the other.

1. Imagine you are a wealthy person living in the apartment block on the right of the image on **PowerPoint slide 6**. Describe your view and describe the moment when you recognise the gulf between you and your neighbours in poverty. What do you finally see? What does the realisation make you think and feel?

2. Imagine you are living in one of the crowded buildings on the left of the image on **PowerPoint slide 6**. Describe how you feel when you see the tall, impressive apartment block each morning with all its luxurious facilities and beautiful gardens. How might life there compare to yours? How do you feel about the wall that separates you?

3. Write a story about when a person who lives in one side of the city in the picture meets with a person from the other side of 'wall' and the 'wealth divide'. What would the outcome of their meeting be?

4. **Challenge task:** Read the Lawrence Ferlinghetti poem 'Two Scavengers in a Truck, Two Beautiful People in a Mercedes'. Write a story with the title 'As If Anything At All Were Possible'.

Peer proofreading:

✓ Is the work in paragraphs?

✓ Can you read the piece of work right through from beginning to end without stumbling?

✓ If not, where does your partner need to add extra punctuation to help it make sense?

✓ Can you see evidence of contrasting adjectives?

✓ Can you see some contrasting images?

✓ Are there any areas where extra information is needed?

✓ Are there any better words you can suggest?

✓ Does your partner try out any interesting structural techniques?

✓ If not, can you suggest an area that would benefit from this?

From *Passages in the Life of a Radical*

Part 1: Having crossed Piccadilly [in Manchester], we went down Mosely Street, then almost entirely inhabited by wealthy families. We took the left side of St. Peter's Church; and at this angle, we wheeled quickly and steadily into Peter Street, and soon approached a wide unbuilt space occupied by an immense multitude, which opened and received us with loud cheers. We walked into that chasm of human beings, and took our station from the hustings across the causeway of Peter Street and so remained, undistinguishable from without, but still forming an almost unbroken line, with our **colours** in the centre. My wife I had not seen for some time; but when last I caught a glimpse of her, she was with some decent married females; and thinking the party quite safe in their own discretion, I felt not much uneasiness on their account, and so had greater liberty in attending to the business of the meeting. 'The soldiers are here,' I said, 'We must go back and see what this means.' 'Oh,' someone made reply, 'they are only come to be ready if there should be any disturbance in the meeting.' 'Well, let us go back,' I said, and we forced our way towards the colours.

Part 2: On the cavalry drawing up, they were received with a shout of goodwill, as I understood it. They shouted again, waving their **sabres** over their heads; and then, slackening rein and striking spur into their steeds, they dashed forward, and began cutting the people. 'Stand fast,' I said, 'they are riding upon us, stand fast.' And there was a general cry in our quarter of 'Stand fast.' The cavalry were in confusion: they evidently could not, with the weight of man and horse, penetrate that compact mass of human beings; and their sabres were plied to hew a way through naked held up hands, and defenceless heads, and then chopped limbs, and wound gaping skulls were seen; and groans and cries were mingled with the din of that horrid confusion. 'Ah! ah! 'for shame! for shame' was shouted. Then, 'Break! break! they are killing in front and they cannot get away!' and there was a general cry of 'break! break!' For a moment, the crowd held back as in a pause; then was a rush, heavy and resistless as a headlong sea; and a sound like low thunder, with screams, prayers, and imprecations from the crowd moiled and sabre-doomed, who could not escape...

Part 3: On the breaking of the crowd, the yeomanry wheeled; and dashing wherever there was an opening, they followed, pressing and wounding. Many females appeared as the crowd opened; and **striplings** or mere youths were also found. Their cries were piteous and heart-rending, and would, one might have supposed, have disarmed any human resentment: but here, their appeals were vain. Women – white vested maids, and tender youths, were indiscriminately sabred or trampled; and we have reason for believing, that few were the instances in which that forbearance was vouchsafed, which they so earnestly implored. In ten minutes from the commencement of the havoc, the field was an open and almost deserted space. The sun looked down through a sultry and motionless air.

Samuel Bamford

colours: flags

sabres: a type of sword

striplings: young men, perhaps in their early teens

9.2.4 Lesson 1

Developing an understanding of 19th-century non-fiction: *Passages in the Life of a Radical*

Learning objectives:	Resources:
• To understand key ideas and events in an eyewitness account • To draw inferences from those ideas and interpret with increased empathy	• Extract 9.2.4 • 9.2.4 Lesson 1 PowerPoint • 9.2.4 Lesson 1 Worksheet

Getting started

• Display and go over the lesson objectives on **9.2.4 Lesson 1 PowerPoint slide 1**. Recap the idea of 'empathy' as shared feelings and responding in a way that helps us to appreciate another person's view.

• Display the cartoon on **PowerPoint slide 2**: *Massacre at St Peter's, or 'Britons Strike Home'!!!* by George Cruikshank (1819). Prompt the students by asking: What seems to be happening here? Who do you imagine the people in blue coats to be? What are they doing? Is this your expectation of soldiers? What is most shocking and horrifying about the scene? What do you notice about the people being trampled? Take initial ideas and thoughts.

• Hand out copies of **9.2.4 Lesson 1 Worksheet** and read through the fact file with the class (**Activity 1**). For each fact, ask the students how it adds to our understanding of the image on **PowerPoint slide 2** and the event it portrays (the Peterloo Massacre). The students should consider the word 'massacre' and then look at the words the soldier is saying in the speech bubble; explore what they reveal about attitudes to the poor asking for more of a share. Question students as to whether they think the poor were being treated with any 'empathy' at all.

Developing skills

• Hand out copies of **Extract 9.2.4**. Explain that the extract is taken from an account of the Peterloo Massacre: the attack by government soldiers on a peaceful protest rally of factory and mill workers in Manchester on 16 August 1819. The protestors were hoping for the right to vote, and the author, Samuel Bamford, was due to speak at the rally.

• Organise the class into small groups and allow each group 5–10 minutes to work on the tasks on **PowerPoint slide 3** before taking feedback. The students should be encouraged to pick up on the following: *1. The leaders of the rally move through an area where 'wealthy families' live, who presumably have comfortable lives, maybe even owning some of the mills where workers were employed. 2. We know that an 'immense multitude' is in attendance, which shows how many people want to protest for their rights. 3. Bamford sees that his wife is with 'decent married females', so she is safe; we see that there are respectable people at the rally and not troublemakers. 4. Bamford's instinct is that the soldiers are not there for a good reason and he immediately makes his way to find out what's going on.*

• Repeat the exercise for 5–10 more minutes using **Extract 9.2.4 Part 2** and the questions on **PowerPoint slide 4**. Encourage students to identify the following: *1. The people greet the soldiers initially as though they are on the side of the workers. 2. This changes when the soldiers wave their sabres (swords) and make their horses ready to ride into the crowd. 3. The crowd is packed so tightly that the soldiers can't get through to separate the people; they begin to use their sabres to fight their way through.*

• Repeat for a third time for 5–10 more minutes, using **Part 3** of the extract and the questions on **PowerPoint slide 5**. Students should note the following: *1. The soldiers seem to lose control and actively use violence against the crowd; they are not just breaking up the crowd but ride in and ignore people's cries for help and mercy. 2. We learn that there are young women in white gowns and young boys ('striplings') who are cut and trampled. 3. The feeling here from Bamford is disbelief, sorrow, incredulity (take any sensible suggestions).*

Trying it yourself

• Introduce the final task (**Worksheet Activity 2**), which builds on the in-depth group work. The students can use the remainder of the lesson time, and perhaps homework time, to complete this work in their notebooks. Encourage them to use the full range of their ideas from the discussion to complete the two more developed inferential reading tasks. Give a brief reminder of the SQI comprehension method and allow 20–25 minutes for the work to be completed in depth.

Developing an understanding of 19th-century non-fiction

Activity 1:

Read through the fact file below. For each fact, consider:

- how it might link to the image on **PowerPoint slide 2**
- how it adds to our understanding of the image and the event it portrays.

Fact file: The Peterloo Massacre

1. On 16 August 1819, up to 60,000 working-class people came from the towns and villages around the city of Manchester to a rally in St Peter's Field, to protest about the fact they did not have the right to vote and so were not represented in parliament.

2. Oxford and Cambridge Universities had their own MP in parliament, but Manchester and Salford, with a population of 150,000, did not. It was thought that only those with wealth and influence should be able to vote.

3. Many of the women who worked in the mills and factories came in their Sunday best white dresses to hear the speakers at the rally on the sunny afternoon.

4. Working people had very few rights and low wages. Many struggled for work as more machines took away jobs in the cotton industry.

5. The powerful local magistrates ordered soldiers, paid for by rich locals, to break up the crowd with sabres. Some suspect the soldiers were given large amounts of alcohol before they rode to the meeting.

6. More than 650 people were badly injured in the chaotic charge on the meeting, and it is estimated that 18 people died.

Activity 2: Final task

- Answer the following questions using the SQI (statement + quotation + inference) method.
- Include two or three ideas in each of your answers, drawing on all the ideas from your exploration of the text.
- Complete the task in your notebook.

1. What do we learn about the thoughts and feelings of Samuel Bamford from the extract?

2. What do you understand about the presence and actions of the soldiers at the rally?

Learning objectives:	**Resources:**
• To explore the effect of the language choices in an eyewitness account • To consider the effect of the structure of the account	• Extract 9.2.4 • 9.2.4 Lesson 2 PowerPoint • 9.2.4 Lesson 2 Worksheet a • 9.2.4 Lesson 2 Worksheet b

Recap and reflection

* Ask the students what they remember of Samuel Bamford's account of the Peterloo Massacre from the previous lesson. Gauge some initial empathetic responses to the following questions: How do you feel about the workers having no vote and no say? Were the workers right to organise the meeting and the protest rally? How might the wealthy families have been feeling in their large houses, seeing the crowds of workers gather in such big numbers? Were they right to call in the soldiers?

* Re-read the whole of **Extract 9.2.4** and then organise the class into pairs or small groups.

Developing skills

* Display the learning objectives on **9.2.4 Lesson 2 PowerPoint slide 1**. Explain to the students that in this lesson, they are going to focus on exploring the language and structure of the extract.

* Display **PowerPoint slide 2**. Encourage the students to recognise that, even though this is a non-fiction account by an eyewitness, Bamford uses a number of language features that are often found in creative writing. Explain how these help bring the scene to life and make it more vivid and shocking.

* Leaving **PowerPoint slide 2** displayed as support, hand out copies of **9.2.4 Lesson 2 Worksheet a** for the students to work on in pairs or small groups. They complete the chart for the activity by identifying the techniques used from the list on the slide and by considering with their partner/within their group the effect or impact of those choices for each quotation on the worksheet. To support the students in commenting on effect, prompt them to write down what the language makes them think, feel or imagine, and how they respond to it. Allow 10–15 minutes for this task and take feedback if time allows.

* Now ask the students about the way the events unfold in Bamford's account. Ask: What is Bamford's mood at the start of the rally? Is he hopeful? Is he delighted to see such a large number of people there? At what point do his feelings change to concern? (*Perhaps when feeling the need to check his wife is safe in the crowd and then spotting the soldiers.*) Is there a moment where the mood or feeling changes significantly? (*Consider the opening of part 2 and the last haunting line.*)

* Display **PowerPoint slide 3** and explain to students that when they look at how a text is put together, it is useful to ask the kinds of questions on the slide.

* Now hand out **9.2.4 Lesson 2 Worksheet b**. Direct the students to complete the activity, working in pairs for support; reinforce the instructions in the bullet points. A 'terminology toolbox' is provided on the worksheet to allow the students to 'match' the examples with the correct definition and gently introduce those terms, some of which they may be already familiar with. Leave **PowerPoint slide 3** displayed for additional support. Allow 10–15 minutes for this task and take feedback if time allows.

Trying it yourself

* Use the remainder of the lesson time and/or homework time for the students to complete the final task on **PowerPoint slide 4**. Ask them to draw on the ideas they have collated in the two group tasks. Remind them that in analytical work we use the IEC method: identify (the feature or technique), exemplify (give an example), comment on the effect (say what the technique makes them think, feel or imagine and how they respond to it). Display **PowerPoint slide 5** to remind the students of the IEC method and the key things to consider for language and structure when writing.

* As the students write, display the modelling on **PowerPoint slide 6** to remind them how to apply the IEC method to writing about structure, and also to show how you can develop a comment on effect to include more than one point.

* **PowerPoint slide 5** could be revisited in plenary as a checklist for overall success with peers.

Developing an understanding of 19th-century non-fiction

Activity:

Use the table below to explore the imagery and language techniques used by Samuel Bamford.

Imagery	Language technique(s)	What this makes us think, feel or imagine; how we respond
'We walked into that chasm of human beings...'		
'and then, slackening rein and striking spur into their steeds, they dashed forward, and began cutting the people'		
'then was a rush, heavy and resistless as a headlong sea; and a sound like low thunder...'		
'Their cries were piteous and heart-rending...'		
'The sun looked down through a sultry and motionless air...'		

Activity:

Explore the structure of Samuel Bamford's account of the Peterloo Massacre in pairs.

Look at the following six extracts from the text. For each one:

- highlight the example on your copy of the extract; label it with the technique chosen from the toolbox below
- think about what this structural choice actually does to change things in the text; annotate the example with those ideas
- think about the effect it has on you as reader; annotate the example with those ideas.

1: 'We took the left side of St. Peter's Church; and at this angle, we wheeled quickly and steadily into Peter Street...'

2: 'The soldiers are here,' I said, 'We must go back and see what this means.' 'Oh,' someone made reply, 'they are only come to be ready if there should be any disturbance in the meeting.'

3: 'waving their sabres', 'cutting the people', 'dashing', 'pressing and wounding'

4: 'and then, slackening rein...', 'For a moment, the crowd held back as in a pause...'

5: 'Stand fast,', 'Ah! ah! 'for shame!,', 'Break! break!'

6: 'The cavalry were in confusion: they evidently could not, with the weight of man and horse, penetrate that compact mass of human beings; and their sabres were plied to hew a way through naked held up hands, and defenceless heads, and then chopped limbs, and wound gaping skulls were seen; and groans and cries were mingled with the din of that horrid confusion.'

Terminology toolbox:

- **Complex sentence:** a sentence that takes one main idea (or clause) and adds more and more detail (subordinate clauses) separated by commas and semicolons.
- **First-person perspective:** when a person within the events or action tells a story or account using 'I'.
- **Dynamic verbs:** a verb that shows continued action.
- **Time references:** references that indicate time passing or moving on, or references to specific times or dates in the past or present.
- **Dialogue:** spoken words that a person or character actually says; direct speech.
- **Minor sentence:** a sentence using only one or two words and which does not make complete grammatical sense on its own.

'Cotton production linked to images of the dried up Aral Sea basin' by Tansy Hoskins

What do the catwalks of Paris have to do with 25,000 miles of exposed seabed thousands of miles to the east? While all eyes have been fixed on designer collections and members of the front row, the true cost of the fashion industry has been revealed in a shock announcement by NASA that the Aral Sea in Central Asia has now completely dried up.

The Aral Sea was once the world's fourth largest lake, home to 24 species of fish and surrounded by fishing communities, lush forests and wetlands. While the lake was saltwater, the rivers that fed it were fresh water. In the 1950s the Soviet Union began using the rivers to irrigate the surrounding agricultural area…

The exposure of the bottom of the lake has released salts and pesticides into the atmosphere poisoning both farm land and people alike. Carcinogenic dust is blown into villages causing throat cancers and respiratory diseases.

The fashion industry is linked to this horror of […] environmental devastation by the fact that the crop being grown with the river water is cotton – 1.47m hectares of cotton. A hugely water intensive crop, one shirt can use up to 2,700 litres.

"Conventional cotton (as opposed to organic cotton) has got to be one of the most unsustainable fibres in the world," says fashion designer and environmentalist Katharine Hamnett. "Conventional cotton uses a huge amount of water and also huge amounts of pesticides which cause 350,000 farmer deaths a year and a million hospitalisations."

Reflecting on the loss of the Aral Sea, Hamnett states: "This is not just climate change this is an extinction issue. […] The fashion industry is one of the most polluting industries in the world, causing human misery, enormous cost of life and gigantic environmental devastation."

[…] The harvest itself is also a horror story, on top of the environmental devastation, this is cotton picked using forced labour. Every year hundreds of thousands of people are systematically sent to work in the fields by the government.

Under pressure from campaigners, in 2012, Uzbek authorities banned the use of child labour in the cotton harvest, but it is a ban that is routinely flouted. In 2013 there were 11 deaths during the harvest, including a six-year-old child […] who accompanied his mother to the fields and suffocated after falling asleep on a cotton truck.

Campaigners have also managed to get 153 fashion brands to sign a pledge to never knowingly use Uzbek cotton. Anti-Slavery International have worked on this fashion campaign but acknowledge that despite successes there is still a long way to go.

The Guardian, 1 October 2014

Learning objectives:	Resources:
• To explore ideas around fast fashion • To understand the issues raised in a broadsheet newspaper article about cotton production	• Extract 9.2.5 • 9.2.5 Lesson 1 PowerPoint • 9.2.5 Lesson 1 Worksheet

Getting started

* Hand out copies of **9.2.5 Lesson 1 Worksheet** and give students 5–10 minutes to complete **Activity 1**, the survey questions, in pairs, allowing some time for feedback of the answers as a whole class. Use questions 5 and 6 of the survey to lead the students into thinking about the different ways our clothes might impact on the environment/sustainability. Some of the students may think about shops and delivery; others might have ideas about where clothes are made and low wages in developing countries.

* Now introduce the learning objectives on **9.2.5 Lesson 1 PowerPoint slide 1**.

* Display **PowerPoint slide 2** and develop ideas from the survey by asking the students to reflect on the speed at which fashions change, the amount of clothes shops on most high streets or in shopping malls, and the amount of clothing within them. Take their personal ideas on where they think unsold clothing goes, before sharing the facts on **PowerPoint slide 3**. Introduce the term 'fast fashion' and explain that this describes the speed at which the fashion industry produces clothes and keeps changing.

Developing skills

* Go over the five key statements about fast fashion on **PowerPoint slide 3**, which are sourced from Greenpeace. Share in class and ask the students: Which do you find most shocking? Which is most surprising? Which one is most worrying in its impact? To add to the shocking statistics, you may also want to refer the students to the BBC documentary *Confronting High Street Shoppers with a Shocking Truth: Stacey Dooley Investigates* (available on YouTube at the time of publication).

* Hand out copies of **Extract 9.2.5**. Explain that this article from *The Guardian* explores the environmental and human cost of cotton production for the fashion industry in the 21st century. Read it aloud to the class, pausing to deal with any vocabulary issues the text may introduce; for example, words such as irrigate, carcinogenic and respiratory may require explanation. Pause also to gauge reactions to some of the statistics in the article: can the students visualise, for example, 2,700 litres of water and cotton, and then relate that to their own school shirt?

Trying it yourself

* Direct students to complete **Worksheet Activity 2**, pointing out that they should answer the retrieval questions (1 and 2) in short, clear statement sentences and the comprehension tasks (3, 4 and 5) using the SQI (statement + quotation + inference) method. Feedback could be done in class with peer assessment, accepting different ideas from the students for the inferences of the comprehension tasks based on the earlier discussion and the five fashion facts on **PowerPoint slide 3**.

* When taking feedback for questions 1 and 2, ask students if they can visualise what the loss of the sea might look like: what do they imagine? Then display **PowerPoint slide 4**, which shows images of the shrinking Aral Sea in Central Asia taken by NASA satellites in August 2000 (left) and August 2014.

* As you lead into responses for question 5, remind the students of the cotton workers they encountered in *Mary Barton* and Samuel Bamford's account. How do they feel about the way workers are being treated in the cotton industry today? Ask the students if any other workers might have been affected by the loss of the sea, then display **PowerPoint slide 5**, which shows the desert and rusting fishing boats.

Final task

* Keep **PowerPoint slide 5** on display and direct the students **Worksheet Activity 3**. This task, which the students should complete in their notebooks, aims to bring together some of the thoughts and inferences surrounding the issues raised by the article, the fast-fashion facts and the images of the Aral Sea. It also encourages the students to use empathy in their final response.

Activity 1:

Complete the following survey in pairs.

1. How many items of new clothing have you bought in the past month? ....

2. How many t-shirts do you own? ....

3. How many pairs of jeans do you own? ....

4. Do you buy any clothing that is vintage? Why? Why not? ....

    ....

5. How important is it to you on a scale of 1 to 5 (where 1 = not important and 5 = very important) that the clothing you buy is sustainable/good for the environment?

    ....

6. In what ways do you think the fashion industry might have an impact on the environment?

    ....

    ....

Activity 2:

*   Answer questions 1 and 2 (retrieval questions) in short statement sentences.
*   Answer questions 3, 4 and 5 (comprehension questions) using the SQI (statement + quotation + inference) method.

1. What announcement did NASA make about the Aral Sea?

    ....

    ....

2. List four different facts you learn about the Aral Sea from the second paragraph.

    ....

    ....

    ....

    ....

3. What things have been poisoned by the loss of the sea and how have they been affected?

....

....

....

....

....

4. Why is the fashion industry a big part of the problem with the loss of the sea?

....

....

....

....

....

5. What do you learn about the people who harvest the cotton?

....

....

....

....

....

Activity 3: Final task

Look at the image of the fishing boats on **PowerPoint slide 5**.

*   Imagine you are a journalist interviewing the fisherman whose family owned these boats and fished on the Aral Sea for generations. Write five questions in your notebook that you would like to ask him about his home, his livelihood and his feelings about the loss of the sea.

*   Swap your questions with a partner.

*   Now imagine you are the fisherman and write answers to your partner's questions, trying all the time to empathise with the situation members of the fishing community in this area have found themselves in. Think carefully about the impact of the loss of the sea on his life.

Learning objectives:	**Resources:**
• To develop empathy and understanding with the ideas and issues raised in the newspaper article • To present a more detailed inferential response to those ideas and issues	• Extract 9.2.5 • 9.2.5 Lesson 2 PowerPoint • 9.2.5 Lesson 1 PowerPoint

Recap and reflection

- Remind the students of the previous lesson and the article on the disappearance of the Aral Sea before displaying and considering the learning objectives on **9.2.5 Lesson 2 PowerPoint slide 1**.

- Re-read **Extract 9.2.5** up to the end of the second paragraph, and then display **PowerPoint slide 2**. Ask the students to comment on how the sea looks in this older, black-and-white photograph, thinking about the volume of water, how beautiful it looks, the amount of fresh fish coming from the water.

- Read through paragraphs 3 and 4 of the extract before displaying **PowerPoint slide 3**. Ask the students to comment on what is most bizarre about this image (*the fact that the boats are in the middle of dry land rusting away and are surrounded by cattle grazing*). Ask the students what kind of place we would normally associate with such a barren landscape before reflecting on their final task from the previous lesson. If time allows, share some of the questions and responses from the final task empathising with the fisherman.

Developing skills

- Explain to the students that they are going to develop their ideas on the issue of fast fashion by looking at it from different points of view through a forum theatre exercise.

- Option 1 is to organise the class into teams of three. Each person in the team takes on one of the characters on **PowerPoint slide 4**. Allow the students 10–15 minutes to debate the issue from the point of view of their character. Move around each of the teams giving prompts and ideas for development. You could create a scenario such as a TV or radio interview involving the three characters, allowing each character one minute at a time to speak or share their viewpoint.

- Option 2 with a smaller class is to have three small teams with a spokesperson taking a character on **PowerPoint slide 4**. This is more supportive for less confident students and more fun for whole classes. You can act as facilitator and give each spokesperson 1 minute to prepare what they would like to say with their teams. Teams can only speak through their spokesperson. Character A may begin, Character B responds, etc. Each time a spokesperson becomes stuck for the next point or counter-argument, they may say 'time out'and confer with their team for 1 minute. Run the forum for 10–15 minutes, or for as long as the debate is meaningful.

Trying it yourself

- Display **PowerPoint slide 5** and set the two final 'mini essay' tasks, allowing less confident students to choose one option only for their more developed inferential response. Explain to the students that they should make clear points supported with evidence from the article or from the fast-fashion facts from Lesson 1 (**9.2.5 Lesson 1 PowerPoint slide 3**). In essence, the students use the SQI (statement + quotation + inference) method, drawing on a number of ideas and points from the two lessons and developing their inferences based on their more creative exploration and forum theatre drama exercise. Ask the students to make three strong, developed SQI constructs for each question if they can. Allow 30 minutes for the completion of these tasks to encourage more developed writing and responses.

- If time allows, share some of the written responses and viewpoints, and reflect on whether the students' views on 'fast fashion' have changed as a result of the study.

Learning objectives:

- To develop an understanding of the connected ideas and issues of the project
- To develop skills in planning a blog post on a key related issue
- To write a blog post and evaluate those of your peers

Resources:

- 9.2.6 Lessons 1 & 2 PowerPoint
- 9.2.6 Lessons 1 & 2 Worksheet

Lesson 1: Recap and reflection

- Display and discuss the lesson objectives on **9.2.6 Lessons 1 & 2 PowerPoint slide 1**.

- Distribute copies of **9.2.6 Lessons 1 & 2 Worksheet** and ask the students to complete **Activity 1** by reflecting on the texts and images they have worked with as part of this project. Working in pairs, the students match the texts to the main themes or ideas in the table. It's possible that the students may be able to justify more than one choice for each theme.

- Take feedback. (Suggested answers: *1: Gaskell, Wordsworth. 2. Gaskell, Dickens, Aral Sea article and images. 3. Gaskell, Blake, modern images of inequality, Bamford's account. 4. Gaskell possibly, Blake, modern images of inequality possibly, Bamford's account of Peterloo Massacre, Aral Sea article and images. 5. Gaskell, Blake, modern images of inequality, Bamford's account of Peterloo Massacre, Aral Sea article and images.*)

- Now ask the students to consider the five main themes, ideas and issues from the table alongside **PowerPoint slide 2**. Explore other contemporary links, for example pollution/loss of the rainforest (theme 2) or zero hours contracts (theme 5), depending on the breadth of the students' knowledge.

- Now direct the students to complete **Worksheet Activity 2**; they decide which of these issues are most relevant or important to them today, and which they feel most passionate about and why.

- Display **PowerPoint slide 3** and introduce the final task the students will work towards. Ask them to recap on what they learned in Week 5 that makes the five key issues from the table relevant to this task.

Developing skills

- Use **PowerPoint slide 4** and the writing frame provided for **Worksheet Activity 3** to explore what a blog is and in what ways it is different to an article. Explain to the students that their blog post can focus on the issue they feel most strongly about – for example, that fast fashion is highly destructive to the environment, or that fast fashion can exploit workers in less economically developed countries.

- Use **PowerPoint slide 5** to recap on the planning structure for discursive or persuasive writing. Allow time for the students to gather their ideas in the writing frame on the worksheet, explaining that the topic sentence operates as a mini summary of the paragraph, and that ideas and viewpoints develop from this.

- Now use **PowerPoint slide 6** to recap on some of the structural techniques the students can use, and to emphasise the importance of the headline to the post. Allow time for this to be considered and added to the plan. If time allows, encourage the students to research their angle further, perhaps as homework. There are a number of interesting blogs available online about the issue of fast/sustainable fashion.

Lesson 2: Recap and reflection and Trying it yourself

- Display **PowerPoint slide 7** to recap on some of the key devices for persuasion the students have learned through previous projects. Use the checklist reminders on **Worksheet Activity 3** to provide additional support and reminders. Revisit the task on **PowerPoint slide 3** and allow most of the lesson for the students to complete the 'Big Write' of the draft of their blog post.

- As a final task, the students redraft and polish their blog post, adding in visuals and presenting it with the stylistic elements in place, including a comments box, as shown in the examples on **PowerPoint slides 8** and **9**.

- Allow the students time to read each other's completed blog posts and complete peer evaluation by using the 'Comments' box. They should consider how persuasive, engaging and powerful a read each blog is, and how successfully it presents the writer's personal views.

Activity 1: Recap and reflect

Think back over the different texts you have studied in this project and complete the table below.

- Decide which of the texts relates to the main themes, ideas and issues in the first column. Record the name of the text or texts in the second column.

- You could also add to the table any images from the project that you think are relevant.

Texts studied: Charles Dickens: 'Coketown' from *Hard Times*; Elizabeth Gaskell: 'Green Heys Fields' from *Mary Barton*; William Wordsworth: 'Composed upon Westminster Bridge'; William Blake: 'London'; Samuel Bamford's account of the Peterloo Massacre; *The Guardian* article on the impact of fast fashion.

Main themes, ideas and issues	Which text(s)
1. The loss of the countryside to or growth of the big city	
2. Pollution of the environment/natural world	
3. The gap between the rich and the poor	
4. Bad decisions made by those in charge	
5. Poor treatment of workers/ordinary people	

Activity 2:

Answer the questions below. Your answers will help you decide what to write your blog post on.

1. Which of the issues and ideas dealt with in the texts above do you think is the most important in today's society?

   ....

   ....

2. Which **one** issue do you feel most strongly about and why?

   ....

   ....

   ....

Activity 3: Blog post planning

Use the planning frame below to gather your ideas for your blog post.

Blog post title: ....

Call to action: ....

....

Main topic / outline: ....

....

....

....

....

....

....

Progress checklist:

- Decide on outline plan.
- Research.
- Draft post.
- Create and add images.
- Test it.
- Proofing and editing.
- Edit post.

Key points / paragraph plan: ....

....

....

....

....

....

....

Content checklist:

- Keywords in headline/title.
- At least 40 characters in title.
- Word count > 350 words.
- Key words in first paragraph.
- Grammar/spell check.
- Images are strong and appropriate to content.
- Add a 'Comments box' for readers.

....

....

....

Photographs and graphics: ....

....

....

....

From *Oliver Twist* (1838)

He sat down on a stone bench opposite the door, which served for seat and bedstead; and casting his blood-shot eyes upon the ground, tried to collect his thoughts. After awhile, he began to remember a few disjointed fragments of what the judge had said: though it had seemed to him, at the time, that he could not hear a word. These gradually fell into their proper places, and by degrees suggested more: so that in a little time he had the whole, almost as it was delivered. To be hanged by the neck, till he was dead—that was the end. To be hanged by the neck till he was dead.

As it came on very dark, he began to think of all the men he had known who had died upon the scaffold; some of them through his means. They rose up, in such quick succession, that he could hardly count them. He had seen some of them die,—and had joked too, because they died with prayers upon their lips. With what a rattling noise the drop went down; and how suddenly they changed, from strong and vigorous men to dangling heaps of clothes!

Some of them might have inhabited that very cell—sat upon that very spot. It was very dark; why didn't they bring a light? The cell had been built for many years. Scores of men must have passed their last hours there. It was like sitting in a vault strewn with dead bodies—the cap, the noose, the pinioned arms, the faces that he knew, even beneath that hideous veil.—Light, light!

At length, when his hands were raw with beating against the heavy door and walls, two men appeared: one bearing a candle, which he thrust into an iron candlestick fixed against the wall: the other dragging in a mattress on which to pass the night; for the prisoner was to be left alone no more.

Then came the night—dark, dismal, silent night. Other watchers are glad to hear this church-clock strike, for they tell of life and coming day. To him they brought despair. The boom of every iron bell came laden with the one, deep, hollow sound—Death. What availed the noise and bustle of cheerful morning, which penetrated even there, to him? It was another form of knell, with mockery added to the warning.

The day passed off. Day? There was no day; it was gone as soon as come—and night came on again; night so long, and yet so short; long in its dreadful silence, and short in its fleeting hours. At one time he raved and blasphemed; and at another howled and tore his hair. Venerable men of his own persuasion had come to pray beside him, but he had driven them away with curses. They renewed their charitable efforts, and he beat them off.

Saturday night. He had only one night more to live. And as he thought of this, the day broke—Sunday.

Charles Dickens

Learning objectives:	Resources:
• To read and understand 19th-century fiction • To explore how a writer presents a character's thoughts and feelings	• Extract 9.3.1 • 9.3.1 Lesson 1 PowerPoint • 9.3.1 Lesson 1 Worksheet

Getting started

• Display **9.3.1 Lesson 1 PowerPoint slide 2** and use the image of the gallows and the question prompts to generate class discussion about public hangings. Establish that the image is of a gallows outside a castle, and that gallows were used to hang criminals when public execution was legal in the UK. Clarify that hanging was used as punishment for crimes including murder, treason and theft; you might share with the students that the last public hanging in England was in 1867. Further questions to prompt discussion could include: Why were hangings public? (*to act as a deterrent and so they could be officially witnessed*) Why did large crowds of people attend? (*they provided a gruesome spectacle/macabre form of 'entertainment'; people would jeer at the condemned person and throw rotten fruit*)

• Now display **PowerPoint slide 1** and discuss the learning objectives. Recap on inference as a method a writer uses to suggest how a character is feeling without stating it explicitly.

Developing skills

• Hand out copies of **9.3.1 Lesson 1 Worksheet** and ask the students to complete **Activity 1** by matching each language device to its definition. (Answers: *1d; 2e; 3f; 4b; 5c; 6a.*)

• Then hand out copies of **Extract 9.3.1** and read it thought together as a class. Explain that the extract focuses on the character Fagin as he sits in his prison cell having had a death sentence passed on him for his life of crime. Contextualise the character of Fagin as an old Jewish man in London, who teaches homeless children to pickpocket. His crimes include selling stolen goods, keeping Oliver in a criminal life and misinforming Sykes that he's been betrayed, leading to the murder of Nancy. Discuss whether the students think Fagin's crimes deserve the death penalty.

• Display **PowerPoint slide 3** and go over the annotated opening sentence from the extract, which explains how we can deduce Fagin's feelings from the phrases 'blood-shot eyes' and 'tried to collect his thoughts'. Ask the students to copy the annotations from the slide onto their copy of **Extract 9.3.1**.

• Now continue to work as a class through the rest of the first paragraph of the extract, annotating Fagin's thoughts and feelings. Ensure the students annotate 'hanged by the neck, till he was dead', suggesting Fagin's shock and despair. Focus on the finality of 'that was the end', emphasising both Fagin's death and how there is to be no reprieve, further discussion or negotiation.

• The students now work in pairs, annotating the rest of the extract in the same way. Support them with further demonstration and by providing key feelings for them to look for, such as regret, loneliness, fear, despair and denial.

Trying it yourself

• The students now build on their close review of the extract by completing **Worksheet Activity 2**. Support them by referring back to the completed Activity 1 and their annotations. You can remove or add paragraph references according to ability. (Suggested answers: *Onomatopoeia: 'rattling', 'boom', 'howled'; all suggest Fagin's desperation, pain and anger, as well as his fear in the darkness of his cell. Metaphor: 'dangling heaps of clothes'; emphasises the inhumane conditions and the futility of Fagin's situation. Rhetorical question: 'Day?'; shows Fagin's confusion and anxiety, suggests the prison darkness and his sense of hopelessness. Simile: 'like sitting in a vault strewn with dead bodies'; suggests Fagin's fear, disgust, hopelessness and misery. Alliteration: 'dark, dismal'; suggests Fagin's hardship, anguish and distress.*)

• Conclude by displaying the discussion points on **PowerPoint slide 4**, which ask the students to consider Dickens' intentions. Encourage them to reflect on the extract as a form of social criticism, and that Dickens' purpose here may have been to highlight inhumane prison conditions and punishments.

Activity 1:

Read the lists of language devices and definitions below.

Match each language device to its definition by drawing a line between them.

Language devices	Definitions
1. Repetition	**a.** Words beginning with the same letter sound
2. Onomatopoeia	**b.** A comparison stating one thing is another
3. Rhetorical question	**c.** A comparison using 'like' or 'as'
4. Metaphor	**d.** A repeated phrase or word
5. Simile	**e.** Words creating the sound they describe
6. Alliteration	**f.** A question where no answer is expected

Activity 2:

Complete the table below to show the methods Dickens uses in **Extract 9.3.1** to present Fagin's thoughts and feelings.

The first method has been completed as an example.

Method	Evidence from the extract	What this suggests about Fagin's thoughts and feelings
Repetition	'to be hanged by the neck till he was dead'	Suggests Fagin's shock and despair
Onomatopoeia (paragraphs 2, 5 and 6)		
Metaphor (paragraph 2)		
Rhetorical question		
Simile		
Alliteration		

<table>
<tr><td>

Learning objectives:
- To read and explore a 19th-century text
- To develop critical evaluation of a text using familiar methods

</td><td>

Resources:
- Extract 9.3.1
- 9.3.1 Lesson 2 PowerPoint
- 9.3.1 Lesson 2 Worksheet
- a dictionary per pair of students

</td></tr>
</table>

Recap and reflection

- Display the learning objectives on **9.3.1 Lesson 2 PowerPoint slide 1**. Recap on the 'familiar methods' of SQI (statement + quotation + inference; identifying and selecting information to explain *what* is happening in a text) and IEC (identify, exemplify, comment; using terminology to analyse *how* writers use language and structure to deliver meaning).

- Display **PowerPoint slide 2** and discuss as a class the different visual presentations of the character of Fagin. The students may compare Fagin's attempts to dress as a gentleman and the depiction of pickpocket tutoring in the left image, to the more abject, lonely and distressed depiction in the right image. Consider Dickens' intention in the extract to highlight social injustice and the inhumanity of punishments. Discuss the artists' attempts to portray Fagin negatively in both images.

Developing skills

- Re-read **Extract 9.3.1** and then ask pairs of students to complete **9.3.1 Lesson 2 Worksheet Activity 1**, which develops the students' understanding of the extract. Each pair of students will need access to a dictionary for this task. Take feedback and discuss the meanings of the words. Establish that Victorians would have disapproved greatly of Fagin's blasphemy and may have viewed him as ungrateful, disrespectful and offensive.

- Now display and go through the table content on **PowerPoint slide 3**. Ask the students to annotate their copy of the extract in response to the structural questions in the table.

- Take feedback. Answers could include: *1. Viewpoint: third-person omniscient/all-seeing narrator allows us into Fagin's thoughts and feelings. 2. Time: chronological but deliberately vague about nights/days to show the continual darkness and Fagin's loss of bearings; the quick move to Sunday at the end is dramatic and anticipates Fagin's death. 3. Where: clues (stone bench, darkness) foreshadow the 'cell' (paragraph 3); 'hanged', 'scaffold' reveal the century; 4. Who: 'he' denotes Fagin but not naming him dehumanises him; other men are mentioned briefly but not introduced as characters – this emphasises Fagin's loneliness and lack of real friendship. 5. What: the repetition of Fagin's death sentence at the start of the extract emphasises its finality; the motif of bells among other sounds presents his despair; the list in paragraph 3 makes his thoughts more vivid and haunting.*

Trying it yourself

- Display **PowerPoint slide 4** and introduce the final task, which requires the students to develop critical evaluation of the text. Use the slide to remind the students of the familiar SQI and IEC methods. Clarify that they are to write three paragraphs using both techniques, and must add a comment at the end of each paragraph to show consideration of the writer's aims and intentions.

- As preparation for this final task, the students now complete **Worksheet Activity 2**. Encourage them to select three quotations from the extract that they can write a lot about.

- Display **PowerPoint slide 5** to model the writing. Go through where the SQI and IEC methods can be seen in the response. Draw attention to the final line, which comments on the writer's intentions, and suggest the students try to do this to extend their answers.

The students then work independently on their three paragraphs, writing in their notebooks. They should refer to their completed work from this and the previous lesson. Support them by further modelling, by providing a selection of quotations and through paired writing of their first paragraph. Challenge the students by extending the number of paragraphs they should write and by asking them to include context about why the death penalty was used but later abolished and how Dickens may have felt about this.

Activity 1:

Working with a partner, answer the questions below.

Use a dictionary to find the meaning of the words in *italics*.

1. What was the purpose of the *scaffold* at a hanging?

....

....

....

2. How many of something does a *score* refer to?

....

....

....

3. What was an underground *vault* used for?

....

....

....

4. When is a *knell* usually sounded?

....

....

....

5. Religion was important to most Victorians, so how would Fagin's *blasphemy* towards the *venerable* men have been viewed?

....

....

....

Quotation 1: ....

....

Write down at least two thoughts or feelings that are revealed by this quotation:

....

....

Identify the methods Dickens has used in this quotation: ....

....

Quotation 2: ....

....

Write down at least two thoughts or feelings that are revealed by this quotation:

....

....

Identify the methods Dickens has used in this quotation: ....

....

Quotation 3: ....

....

Write down at least two thoughts or feelings that are revealed by this quotation:

....

....

Identify the methods Dickens has used in this quotation: ....

....

From 'The Ballad of Reading Gaol', Part 1 (1898)

I never saw a man who looked
With such a wistful eye
Upon that little tent of blue
Which prisoners call the sky,
And at every drifting cloud that went
With sails of silver by.

I walked, with other souls in pain,
Within another ring,
And was wondering if the man had done
A great or little thing,
When a voice behind me whispered low,
'That fellow's got to swing.'

Dear Christ! the very prison walls
Suddenly seemed to reel,
And the sky above my head became
Like a casque of scorching steel;
And, though I was a soul in pain,
My pain I could not feel.

I only knew what hunted thought
Quickened his step, and why
He looked upon the garish day
With such a wistful eye;
The man had killed the thing he loved,
And so he had to die.

Yet each man kills the thing he loves,
By each let this be heard,
Some do it with a bitter look,
Some with a flattering word,
The coward does it with a kiss,
The brave man with a sword!

Some kill their love when they are young,
And some when they are old;
Some strangle with the hands of Lust,
Some with the hands of Gold:
The kindest use a knife, because
The dead so soon grow cold.

Some love too little, some too long,
Some sell, and others buy;
Some do the deed with many tears
And some without a sigh:
For each man kills the thing he loves,
Yet each man does not die.

He does not die a death of shame
On a day of dark disgrace,
Nor have a noose about his neck,
Nor a cloth upon his face,
Nor drop feet foremost through the floor
Into an empty space.

Oscar Wilde

Learning objectives:	Resources:
• To secure skills in understanding 19th-century poetry • To secure use of the IEC method when exploring the poet's use of structure	• Extract 9.3.2 • 9.3.2 Lesson 1 PowerPoint • 9.3.2 Lesson 1 Worksheet • highlighter pens

Getting started

* Display **9.3.2 Lesson 1 PowerPoint slide 2** and discuss the questions. Then ask: What might a prisoner have done to pass the day in the 19th century? What is meant by 'hard labour'? Discuss the 19th-century penal practices of prisoners 'picking oakum' (pulling old rope apart), breaking stones and walking the treadmill (to mill corn, pump water or just as punishment) and compare these with modern prison work, conditions and punishments (sewing, metalwork, watching TV, isolation, loss of privileges, etc.). Consider modern human rights in relation to Victorian punishments such as hard labour, whipping and transportation. Discuss the effectiveness and morality of punishments like stoning and hanging.

* Display **PowerPoint slide 1** and go over the lesson objectives with the class. Recap on the IEC (identify, exemplify, comment) method, which the students used in their final task in the previous lesson.

Developing skills

* Hand out copies of **Extract 9.3.2** and read the poem together as a class. Explain that the extract is from a longer poem reflecting Oscar Wilde's sympathetic view of Charles Thomas Woolridge, a fellow prisoner at Reading Gaol, who was sentenced to death for killing his wife. Contextualise this by explaining that Wilde was imprisoned in 1895 for two years for homosexuality, which was illegal at the time.

* Display **PowerPoint slide 3**. The students use the questions to explore the extract in pairs; they can note down their thoughts on their copy of the extract or in their notebooks. Use the last question to draw out the students' interpretations of Wilde's message, and why he felt he should write about prison.

* Display **PowerPoint slide 4**. Ask the students to read the information then answer the questions independently or in pairs for support. During feedback, focus on how the themes of love and death are suggested by words such as 'killing', 'cold', 'the deed', 'love', 'lust', 'die', 'dead', 'knife', 'sword' and 'noose'. Establish that this ballad, like a song, use rhyme, repetition ('some') and a refrain ('Yet each man kills the thing he loves') and, like a story, provides a third-person narration of Woolridge's sentence.

* The students complete **9.3.2 Lesson 1 Worksheet Activity 1** in pairs. During feedback, focus on the refrain, 'Each man kills the thing he loves'; ask if any of the statements can be used to work out Wilde's meaning here.

* Now use **PowerPoint Slide 5** to analyse the metaphor 'Each man kills the thing he loves'. Support the students by reflecting on passions in their own life that have died, such as a close friendship that ended. Consider how Wilde uses the metaphor to try to create sympathy for Woolridge by suggesting humanity's inherent self-destructiveness and the hypocrisy of killing a killer.

Trying it yourself

* The students complete **Worksheet Activity 2** working independently. Support them by modelling the rhythm and rhyme scheme on a different verse from the poem. Begin with counting syllables and words. Look to draw out the ABCBDB rhyme scheme, and the repetition of 'some' and 'each' to show individuality and the variety of human love. Track how the rhythm creates a plodding, repetitive feel, suggesting the slow pace and repetitiveness of a 19th-century prison sentence. Link this to prisoners on the treadmill and the rhythm of their walking/grinding. The students then complete **Worksheet Activity 3** by producing an IEC paragraph on why Wilde chooses such a slow rhythm in the poem.

* The students now write three IEC paragraphs in response to the question *How does Wilde use the ballad form to present a story?* Display **PowerPoint slide 6** to introduce the task and to provide the students with a checklist for their response; use **PowerPoint slide 7** to remind them of the IEC method. Where appropriate, challenge those students working at a higher level to identify and use terminology to explain the poet's use of three (trimeter) and four (tetrameter) metrical feet to emphasise key words.

Securing ways to explore 19th-century poetry

Activity 1:

'The Ballad of Reading Gaol' explores ideas about love and death.

- Working with your partner, read the statements in the table below. Which of these statements does the poem present evidence to support?
- Complete the chart with evidence from the ballad.

Statement	Evidence from the poem to support the statement
Love never runs smoothly.	
Love is easy to kill.	
Love can never die.	
Love means different things to different people.	

'The Ballad of Reading Gaol' has a specific rhyme scheme and rhythm.

One metric foot in poetry is a combination of **unstressed syllables** and **stressed syllables**. For example, 'Yet each' in the first line below, is one metric foot as 'yet' is the unstressed syllable and 'each' is the stressed syllable.

Yet each man kills the thing he loves,

By each let this be heard,

Some do it with a bitter look,

Some with a flattering word,

The coward does it with a kiss,

The brave man with a sword!

Activity 2:

Focusing on the verse from the poem above:

- Work out which syllables are stressed and which are unstressed by reading the verse aloud. The stressed syllables will be said louder and with an emphasis, while the unstressed syllables will be softer and without emphasis. Underline all the stressed syllables.

Then label the verse:

- Use a different letter of the alphabet (A, B, C, D) for each line for the rhyme scheme. Where a line rhymes with an earlier line, use the same letter as earlier.
- Label any repetition.
- Highlight any stressed words that you think the poet specifically wants to emphasise.
- Think about what makes your favourite songs memorable, such as the chorus. Label any of those features you can see in the poem.

Activity 3:

Answer the question below using the IEC (identify, exemplify, comment) method. Use your notes from Activity 2 to organise your response.

Why do you think Wilde chooses such a slow rhythm in 'The Ballad of Reading Gaol'?

....

....

....

....

....

....

....

....

....

....

....

....

Learning objectives:

- To explore and evaluate how a poet presents their point of view
- To identify and analyse language and structure

Resources:

- Extract 9.3.2
- 9.3.2 Lesson 2 PowerPoint
- 9.3.2 Lesson 2 Worksheet
- 9.3.2 Lesson 1 Worksheet
- highlighter pens

Recap and reflection

- Re-read Oscar Wilde's poem 'The Ballad of Reading Gaol' (**Extract 9.3.2**), then display **9.3.2 Lesson 2 PowerPoint slide 2**. The students look for evidence of key themes in the poem; this can be done in pairs or as a whole class. (Suggested answers: *Suffering: verse 2 line 1; verse 5 line 1. Death: verse 4 lines 5–6; verse 6 line 6; verse 7 lines 3 and 5–6; verse 8 line 3. Freedom: verse 1. Guilt: verse 7 lines 3–4. Conflict: verse 6.*)

- Display **PowerPoint slide 1** and discuss the lesson objectives. Recap on the work from the previous lesson on rhyme, rhythm and the ballad form in 'The Ballad of Reading Gaol', as well as Wilde's messages about man destroying what he loves and the hypocrisy of capital punishment.

Developing skills

- Hand out copies of **9.3.2 Lesson 2 Worksheet** and ask the students to work in pairs to complete **Activity 1**. Support them with alternatives for the word 'some', which appears 10 times. Possible alternative words include: men, women, lovers, killers, the guilty, the impassioned, the innocent, the young, the old, or superlatives like meanest and craziest.

- The students complete **Worksheet Activity 2**. Support them by first defining injustice (a lack of fairness), morality (a sense of right and wrong) and hypocrisy (claiming to have higher standards than you practise); ask for examples of each. Try to cover a wide spectrum, from the hypocrisy of arguing against zoos but keeping a caged pet, to killing a murderer. The students could stand on a continuum line from 'most agree' at the front of the class to 'least agree' at the back. then discuss their choices.

Trying it yourself

- Display **PowerPoint slide 3** and go over the definitions on the slide. The students label their copy of **Extract 9.3.2** with examples of metaphor, anaphora, plosives and foreshadowing, and consider their effect. (Suggested answers: *1. Metaphor: 'Yet each man kills the thing he loves'; could suggest betrayal, loss, abandonment, rejection or actual murder. 2. Anaphora: 'some': Wilde compares Woolridge and himself to other prisoners to justify the crimes and humanise the prisoner, and to suggest the hypocrisy that many cruel killers are not executed. 3. Plosives: 'b', 't' in verse 5 and 'd' in verse 8; suggest prison conditions and prisoner treatment is dehumanising; prison is meant to reform but can destroy; Wilde is moved by Woolridge's acceptance of his impending execution, yet Wilde and other prisoners suffer. 4. Foreshadowing: verse 8 and refrain 'each man kills': everyone faces death and judgement of sins.*)

- Display **PowerPoint slide 4** and introduce the final task. Go over the modelled IEC paragraph on the slide and discuss as a class how the 'Comment' section could be completed. Support the students by reminding them that Wilde knew of Woolridge's death sentence for a crime of passion: he killed his wife during an argument. Ask the students to consider whether this murder was planned and think about Wilde's observation that not all killers were executed. This could lead to a number of interpretations, such as Wilde is commenting on the hypocrisy of killing a killer or the injustice of punishments that can vary for the same crime.

- The students now complete the final task independently on a separate piece of paper; they should aim to write three IEC paragraphs. Display the checklist on **PowerPoint slide 5** and refer the students back to their work in this and the previous lesson, as well as their annotated copies of the extract. Further support can be provided by suggesting sentence starters and topic sentences, or a short list of points to include, such as the contrast of the last verse with the rest of the poem, the metaphorical interpretation of 'kills', the repetition of 'some', and the plodding, repetitive rhythm.

1. On your copy of the extract, underline each time the poet used the word 'some'. How many times does the poet use this word in the poem?

   ....

2. With a partner, substitute the word 'some' with alternative words by writing them above the word 'some' on your copy of the extract. Record your replacement word choices below.

   ....

   ....

3. How does changing the word 'some' in this way change the meaning of the poem?

   ....

   ....

In the last verse of 'The Ballad of Reading Gaol', Wilde presents the hypocrisy of killing a person because they have killed someone else.

Statement	Order (1–4)	Counter-argument/opposite point of view
Execution is 'a death of shame' because it is a dishonourable way to die.		
Execution is hypocritical because it is just legalised murder.		
Execution is a fair punishment.		
The Bible and the Qu'ran state 'an eye for an eye', so it is fair and moral to punish all murder by execution.		

Learning objectives:	Resources:
• To understand the conventions of crime and detective fiction • To structure, plan and write a piece of crime fiction using those conventions	• 9.3.3 Lessons 1 & 2 PowerPoint • 9.3.3 Lesson 1 Worksheet

Lesson 1: Getting started

• Display **9.3.3 Lessons 1 & 2 PowerPoint slide 2** and invite responses to the questions. Many of the students will recognise the character Sherlock Holmes, and some may identify the author as Arthur Conan Doyle. Ask if the students know when the character became popular (in the latter part of the 19th century) and give some background – for example, Conan Doyle enjoyed the work of Edgar Allan Poe, who created a fictional detective (Auguste Dupin) in the 1840s. If time allows, you could read some extracts from Conan Doyle or Poe to add more cultural capital to the lesson. Explain how these writers created a kind of formula or set of conventions for crime or 'detective' fiction that we still see today.

• Display the lesson objectives on **PowerPoint slide 1** and explain that, in this week's lessons, the students will learn about the conventions of crime and detective fiction, and try them out for themselves.

Developing skills

• Hand out copies of **9.3.3 Lesson 1 Worksheet** and ask the students to work in pairs to complete **Activity 1** by compiling a mind map of any crime, mystery or detective texts they are familiar with. You could get them started by thinking about Sherlock Holmes as a character in the original stories but also on TV, and modern fictional equivalents like the *Skulduggery Pleasant* series by Derek Landy. The students might also consider texts where children or young people solve crimes – these range from the Famous Five to Scooby Doo, but all follow some of the conventions of the genre. Feed back ideas.

• Now invite the students to complete **Worksheet Activity 2** by thinking in their pairs of what these texts, films and TV programmes have in common in terms of the key features of the genre. The most obvious starting point is that they all have a crime or a mystery to solve. Allow the students time to think and share ideas before taking feedback, then consolidate by displaying **PowerPoint slide 3**. You might consider how these conventions work or are adapted in the texts the students have listed; for example, Sherlock Holmes is very intelligent, while his assistant Dr Watson is more down to earth.

• Display **PowerPoint slide 4** to show the key elements needed to write a piece of crime fiction. Explore each one using the development on the slide, to encourage examples or suggestions. For example, for setting you could explain that Agatha Christie's famous story *Murder on the Orient Express* was set on a train so the suspects could not easily get away. Ask: Where else would be a good setting?

• Now allow the students 20–25 minutes to plan their piece of crime fiction using the planning grid (**Worksheet Activity 3**). Introduce the task using **PowerPoint slide 5** and use the story prompts on **PowerPoint slide 6** to help the students get started or to develop their own ideas.

Lesson 2: Trying it yourself

• Begin the lesson by displaying **PowerPoint slide 5** to recap on the task set. Invite the students to share some of their ideas from their plans for their own crime fiction piece.

• Now display **PowerPoint slide 7**. Remind the students that a five-point narrative structure is generally used to create a complete short story, but that in crime fiction a three-part element is often followed. This is because the climax or high point often comes towards the end of the story and there is a much slower pace of rising action, as motives and clues become apparent. The students should bear this structure in mind as they draft their stories. Continue to display the slide as a reminder.

• Allow most of the remainder of the lesson time for drafting. The stories could be continued for homework if desired and if developed work is emerging. If time allows (or next lesson if more suitable), encourage the students to read out some of their crime stories up to part two of the three-part structure. You could ask the remaining students to predict the outcome as a valuable plenary exercise in close listening and inference.

Securing creative writing: Crime fiction

Activity 1:

Create a mind map of all the crime and mystery-solving texts that you are familiar with. Include fictional stories, novels, TV shows and films.

Activity 2:

What features do they have in common? List the stereotypical features you might expect to find in this genre.

....

....

....

....

....

....

Activity 3:

Use the planning grid below to plan your piece of crime fiction.

Setting	
Crime (and possibly victim)	
Suspects and their motives	
Key clues and ideas for a twist	
Resolution: who is responsible and why?	

'The murderer hanged on the Sussex Downs'

At last we came to the yard. In the right-hand corner as we looked upon them rose a couple of thick black posts, with a huge cross piece, from which dangled a staple and a long, thick rope; in the other, about 10 yards distance, an open grave.

As we filed into the yard, I noticed that we were being one by one saluted by a somewhat diminutive man clothed in brown cloth and bearing in his arms a quantity of leather straps. William Marwood it was who thus bade us welcome, and the straps on his arms were nothing less than his 'tackle'.

I confess to a shudder as I looked upon the girdle and arm pieces that had done duty on so many a struggling wretch, and half expected that the man who carried them would have attempted to hide them. But no such thing! To him they were implements of high merit, and together with the gallows formed what he now confidentially informed his hearers was 'an excellent arrangement'. It was evident that in the gallows and the tackle too he had more than a little pride. He was even ready to explain with much volubility the awful instruments of his craft.

'That rope that you see there,' quoth he, as he gazed admiringly at the crossbar of black wood, 'is two and a half inches round. I've hung nine with it, and it's the same I used yesterday.'

The hangman was already busily at work, passing the leather belt round his body, fastening his elbows and wrists, and baring his neck. The bell was tolling, and nine o'clock had nearly come. It was time to be moving. The clergyman, in his white surplice, was ready; two warders had taken their places, one on either side of the condemned; Marwood, with one strap yet unused in his left hand, and his right hand firmly fixed on the leather belt that confined his victim, was prepared to move.

It was not far, only a few score yards in all, but the march to the grave, or rather to the scaffold, seemed terribly painful; all the bravado that was witnessed in the dock at Maidstone had gone; the terrors of death were in full force upon the hapless culprit. As he approached the scaffold this was particularly noticeable; he could scarcely take the step which was to place him where he had never stood before and from whence he would never step again.

I do not suppose for a moment that Marwood intended to be rough; he was possibly excited, and anxious to do everything as expeditiously as possible. But it certainly appeared to me that in attempting to fix the cap on Lefroy's head, and in pulling it down over his face, he hurt the prisoner somewhat unnecessarily. The worst of this was, however, yet to come. The long rope dangling about Lefroy had now to be adjusted, and the thimble through which the noose ran to be placed beneath his neck. I did not time it; it may have lasted only a few seconds; but to me it seemed appallingly long, while the swaying of Lefroy's body showed the agony he was enduring.

Daily Telegraph, 30 November 1881

From the diary of Francis Place, describing 'the pillory' (1829)

The time for standing, or rather walking round, on and in the Pillory, was one hour usually, from 12 to 1 o'clock at noon, the common dining hour of all sorts of persons who earn their livings by the labour of their hands, and consequently the time when the streets were crowded by such people.

Charing Cross was the most usual place for "Pillorying" those who were sentenced to this punishment for offences committed in the metropolis on the north of the Thames, and without the City of London. As it was always well known that such an exhibition was to take place at a certain time, a large mob always assembled, a considerable portion of which consisted of the lowest vagabonds, men and women, girls and boys. Some of these people brought with them on donkeys, and in baskets, rotten eggs, which they procured from the egg warehouses, decayed cabbages, etc., etc. the refuse of Covent Garden Market. The "fun" commenced by throwing mud and eggs from behind the constables who permitted a number of women to pass between them, into the open space round the pillory. These women were supplied with the materials for offence from the baskets of those who brought them, the bystanders giving them money, for their "wares". Near the pillory were two stands for Hackney coaches, under these there was a quantity of hay, dung and urine trampled into a the mud in the kennels and this handed to the women to pelt the men in the pillory, each of whom with their hands full of this stuff waited till one of the miserable wretches came close to her as she stood at the edge of the platform, to discharge the offensive matter at his face, and as the number of these vile women was considerable there was no intermission, the poor creatures hands were so confined as to be useless to him, and the adhesive mass stuck to the pillory, and his face, and stuck on his head until the quantity thus accumulated entirely obscured his visage, and either fell off in a mass by its own weight or suffocated the victim.

Francis Place

Learning objectives:	Resources:
• To secure exploration of ideas and attitudes in 19th-century non-fiction texts • To consider how those ideas and attitudes are presented	• Extract 9.3.4a • 9.3.4 Lesson 1 PowerPoint • 9.3.4 Lesson 1 Worksheet

Getting started

• Display **9.3.4 Lesson 1 PowerPoint slide 1** and go over the lesson objectives.

• Then display **PowerPoint slide 2** and introduce the concept of crime and punishment. Use the questions to discuss the death penalty and the risk of executing an innocent person. Ask whether some crimes are so serious that the death penalty is justified, or whether all such methods of execution are inhumane and barbaric. Ask: How might a writer feel about the death penalty and the treatment of criminals? Recap and consider Dickens' and Wilde's fictional responses to the death penalty from Weeks 1 and 2. Then ask the students to consider how a writer's views about the death penalty might manifest in a non-fiction account of an execution. Ask the students to try to recall the techniques the writers used to communicate viewpoint and to persuade in non-fiction accounts the students explored in previous projects.

Developing skills

• Hand out copies of **Extract 9.3.4a** and read it together as a class. Explain that executions in the 19th century were often carried out in public; be aware that this is an eyewitness account of a hanging so should be used with sensitivity.

• Now display **PowerPoint slide 3** and ask the students to discuss the questions in pairs. During feedback, establish that we experience the hanging from the viewpoints of a hangman, a journalist and a criminal. The tone is serious yet the hangman appears enthusiastic about his work; the criminal is terrified and the journalist is deeply affected by what he witnesses. Those watching include a clergyman and two warders. The witnesses don't seem involved in what is happening. The hangman's energetic approach lacks compassion and he hurts the prisoner 'unnecessarily'.

• Hand out **9.3.4 Lesson 1 Worksheet**. Refer back to the class discussion to ensure that the students understand what irony is, then ask them to complete **Activity 1**. Support them by highlighting unexpected points, such as comments made by the hangman. (Suggested answers: *'he had more than a little pride'*; *'what he now confidentially informed his hearers was "an excellent arrangement"'*; *irony highlights the gap between the reader's expectations of an executioner and his behaviour.*)

• The students now complete **Worksheet Activity 2**. Support them by discussing what happens to the prisoner and how he is treated. Take feedback about the writer's criticisms of the actual punishment, the prisoner's humiliation, the way the execution is carried out and the keenness of the executioner. Consider how the account is written and discuss how this reveals the writer's attitude.

• Ask the students to define emotive language (the language a writer uses to provoke a particular reaction in the reader). The students then work in pairs to annotate each paragraph of the extract to show examples of emotive language. Take feedback and discuss. (Suggested examples from the extract: *'hapless culprit'*; *'on the leather belt that confined his victim'*; *'whence he would never step again'*.)

• The students complete **Worksheet Activity 3** by identifying emotive language and commenting on its effect. Support them by reminding them that the effects may be implicit or explicit. (Suggested examples from the extract: *'I confess to a shudder'*; *'march seemed terribly painful'*; *'he hurt the prisoner somewhat unnecessarily'*; *'it seemed appallingly long'*).

Trying it yourself

• Display **PowerPoint slide 4** and introduce the final task. Encourage the students to demonstrate that they know which method to use for each type of question: for 'what' questions they should use the SQI (statement + quotation + inference) method; for 'how' questions they should use the IEC (identify, exemplify, comment) method. You can support the students with sentence starters, highlighted quotations, pair work or by modelling the first statement sentence.

Activity 1:

Give an example of irony from the extract and suggest why it may have been used at this point.

Example of irony: ....

....

Reason irony used here: ....

....

....

Activity 2:

Complete the chart below with examples of the writer's viewpoint in the extract.

In what ways is he critical of the punishment the criminal is receiving?

Criticism	Example from the extract

Activity 3:

Complete the chart below with examples of emotive language in the extract and their effect on the reader.

Emotive language	Effect on the reader

<table>
<tr><td>

Learning objectives:

- To secure exploration of ideas in 19th-century non-fiction texts
- To secure comprehension skills by synthesising those ideas

</td><td>

Resources:

- Extract 9.3.4a
- Extract 9.3.4b
- 9.3.4 Lesson 2 PowerPoint
- 9.3.4 Lesson 2 Worksheet
- 9.3.4 Lesson 1 Worksheet

</td></tr>
</table>

Recap and reflection

- In pairs, ask the students to recall **Extract 9.3.4a** from the last lesson – an eyewitness account of an execution – and to suggest a) an example of emotive language, b) an example of irony, c) the writer's attitude to the way the execution is carried out.

- Display **9.3.4 Lesson 2 PowerPoint slide 1** and go over the learning objectives. Ask the students the meaning of the word 'synthesise' (*to summarise information and ideas*) and explain that their final task this week will draw on two extracts on the treatment of criminals in the 19th century.

Developing skills

- Display **PowerPoint slide 2**. Use the questions on the slide to guide discussion. Explain what a pillory is (a wooden framework with holes for the offender's head and hands, imprisoning them and exposing them to public abuse; a common punishment in most towns during the 19th century).

- Move on to discuss the questions on **PowerPoint slide 3**. Establish that the pillory was intended to punish a person through public humiliation – the criminal would be shamed; the crowd enjoyed throwing rubbish and old food, and seeing someone humiliated. The atmosphere was like a carnival for the crowd and not so pleasant for the criminal. Some of the students may know that Covent Garden is a famous fruit and vegetable market in London. Discuss with the students why the majority of people today would not be happy with public humiliation as a punishment. Extend by asking: Are modern laws stricter? Would our laws prevent this type of punishment? Why? How? Guide the students towards recognition of human-rights laws and the right to human dignity and protection from harm.

- Hand out copies of **Extract 9.3.4b** and read through the diary of Francis Place describing 'the pillory' together as a class. Ask the students to focus on the tone of the account and the writer's attitude to the crowd and the criminal.

- Display **PowerPoint slide 4** and introduce the task: *What do you learn from the extract about how criminals were treated in the pillory in the 19th century?* The students should answer the question using the SQI (statement + quotation + inference) method to consolidate their understanding and exploration of Extract 9.3.4b, before bringing their study of both texts together.

Trying it yourself

- Introduce the final task: *Both texts deal with the topic of punishing criminals. What are the similarities between the way criminals are treated and punished in the two extracts?* The students prepare for the task using the grid on **9.3.4 Lesson 2 Worksheet**, gathering initial ideas and evidence.

- Display **PowerPoint slide 5** and explain that this six-point technique provides a framework for answering the final synthesis question.

- Then display and discuss the modelled example on **PowerPoint slide 6**, which matches the framework on **PowerPoint slide 5**. Stress the importance of the final step, which synthesises the similarities in the two writers' attitudes.

- To complete the final writing task, the students use their completed planning grids from the worksheet to help them to write about three similarities between the texts, drawing out the inferences and adding the final synthesising overview statement.

Activity:

Both texts deal with the topic of punishing criminals. What are the similarities between the way criminals are treated and punished in the two extracts?

- In preparation for this answering this synthesis question, complete the planning grid below.
- You will be writing about **three similarities** between the texts.

In Extract a, the punishment of criminals is...	Evidence from the text

In Extract b, the punishment of criminals is...	Evidence from the text

'Secret Teacher: teaching in prisons is where I can make a real difference'

No bell marks the start of our day. Instead, a slow drip-feed of men in grey tracksuits amble their way into classes. Sometimes 10 sit in front of me, aged 21 up to 60 or 70. They are the disaffected and the despicable. They are the proud, the defensive and the downright disagreeable; funnelled into education during their first days inside, where they complete assessments in literacy and numeracy. Their scores determine their placement into a classroom, and their subsequent opportunities for work. [...]

The most challenging part of working with offenders is the disparity between students in the classroom – the range of ages, their level of literacy and their attitude to learning. Often their only common ground is their criminality. Some learners arrive spoiling for a fight, desperate to avoid the torture of school all over again, determined to prove themselves. Behaviour is an issue, with many refusing to work. Challenging inappropriate language is a constant battle when, for some, the f-word is used in every sentence.

These men require sensitive handling. Custody issues, homelessness, bullying, debt, addiction, poverty, loneliness, alcoholism, abuse, self-harm – a smorgasbord of issues make up these complex, challenging and often frustrated learners. [...] Many people will say that all prisoners are bad people but the reality is that they are just like everyone else. They are the grown-up manifestations of frightened, abused, lonely and unloved boys. It's no wonder they're disaffected: many have the behaviour of teenagers and the reading levels to match.

The biggest rewards [...] come when someone makes you rethink your first impressions of them, when someone proves you wrong. A learner once came to my class, asked what subject it was, reeled off a load of expletives and refused to stay. He was a London lad, a football hooligan. Three weeks later, he returned, calmer, and took his seat. Three months later, I nominated him for an adult learner award because of his success in literacy. I saw him change from this thuggish brute with a bad attitude to one of the most dedicated learners I have had – he even went on to support a young man who was struggling. It's so satisfying as a tutor when, despite initial reluctance, your pupils relax, and begin to trust you and your teaching. They begin to realise that if they attend, and they listen, and they try, they can actually do this.

Another memorable student was a man in his 50s with very low literacy and numeracy levels. We worked together one-to-one, and his resilience and effort were outstanding. His fear of exams was his big downfall: he would clam up and be unable even to write. He never used a calculator, and instead would perform long multiplications on scraps of paper.

After several weeks, I told him we were doing a practice exam. When he passed, I revealed that he had taken his entry level 2 maths and he cried with relief.

You know that difficult, unruly lad in bottom set maths? You know that boy who's been suspended countless times? You know that one they talk about in the staffroom, who throws chairs and spits and swears and tests everyone paid to care for him to the point of tears? Recent figures show he stands a high chance of entering the criminal justice system, and even more so if he gets expelled (with pupils thrown out aged 12 four times more likely to go to jail). If he does, if he's lucky, and brave, and determined, we'll pick him up, dust him down and carry on where he left off. And maybe second, third or 20th time around, he'll succeed.

From *The Guardian*, 3 May 2014

Securing skills with connected modern non-fiction: Comparing viewpoints from two texts

Learning objectives:	Resources:
• To understand a writer's viewpoint and methods in a piece of journalism • To present and support a response analysing viewpoint and method	• Extract 9.3.5 • 9.3.5 Lesson 1 PowerPoint • 9.3.5 Lesson 1 Worksheet

Getting started

- This is the final set of lessons in the final project dealing with reading skills. Explain to the students using the learning objectives on **9.3.5 Lesson 1 PowerPoint slide 1** that this lesson will consolidate their skills and present and support a response to a text more independently, in preparation for GCSE study.

- Display the task on **PowerPoint slide 2**, which is a simplified version of a GCSE task covering writer's viewpoints. This lesson will deal with one text as a stepping-stone into comparison in the next lesson. Give the students the opportunity to demonstrate that they know which method, taught throughout the projects, they should use for which assessment objective. Explain that comprehension skill at GCSE is AO1 (and so requires the SQI method) and exploring language and structure with its effect is AO2 (and requires the IEC method).

- Give out copies of **Extract 9.3.5** and read the 'Secret Teacher' article from *The Guardian* aloud. Ask: What is the text about? What job does the writer do? Take the students' first thoughts and impressions of what they think that point of view is. Ask: Does the writer's point of view change through the piece? Establish that at first the view of the prisoners seems very negative, but the writer goes on to show the benefits and rewards of teaching in a prison.

Developing skills

- Use **PowerPoint slide 3** to illustrate the method the students should use for exploring and annotating the extract in preparation for the task.

- Then use **PowerPoint slide 4** to model this approach. Explain that the students need to work with a selected section of the text – not just a few words or a brief quotation – and use that section to gather inferences for the 'what' aspect of the task. They then identify the writer's methods and thoughts/feelings for the 'how' aspect of the task.

Trying it yourself

- Give out copies of **9.3.5 Lesson 1 Worksheet** and ask the students to complete **Activity 1**. Explain that this time, sections of the text have been pre-selected for them to work with, to help them get started. Ask the students to work with a partner to annotate their individual ideas and choices regarding the methods, as per the instructions on the sheet. Leave **PowerPoint slide 4** displayed to remind the students of the kinds of annotations they should be making.

- Take feedback. There are numerous possibilities for both inferences and methods for each given section, so allow time for pairs to share some of the different ways they have responded to the text and the viewpoint of the writer, as well as the different aspects of language and structure they may have discovered. This is a good opportunity for you to monitor and assess how confident the students are with terminology, and whether they recognise with confidence some of the key features of discursive texts taught throughout the sequence of projects prior to GCSE study.

- Now display **PowerPoint slide 5**, which models an opening paragraph to the task. As a whole class, ask the students to identify where they can see the statement, the supporting quotation, the inference, the identified features, the examples and the comment on effect.

- Explain that the students will now complete the essay-style response from the modelled opening on **PowerPoint slide 5** using two of their annotated sections from **Worksheet Activity 1**. The model paragraph ensures that the students will then have a complete response, demonstrating all of their skills. **Worksheet Activity 2** provides a copy of the modelled paragraph along with the activity instructions. This task could be completed within the lesson or as a homework task should more time be required.

Activity 1:

Annotate each of these extracts from the article with a partner.

- On the left side, add annotations to explore the 'what' part of the task: what is suggested or implied; what can be inferred about the writer's views on education in prison.

- On the right side, add annotations identifying the methods the writer uses and your notes on the effect of those choices: what they make you think, feel or imagine.

Many people will say that all prisoners are bad people but the reality is that they are just like everyone else. They are the grown-up manifestations of frightened, abused, lonely and unloved boys. It's no wonder they're disaffected: many have the behaviour of teenagers and the reading levels to match.

I saw him change from this thuggish brute with a bad attitude to one of the most dedicated learners I have had – he even went on to support a young man who was struggling. It's so satisfying as a tutor when, despite initial reluctance, your pupils relax, and begin to trust you and your teaching. They begin to realise that if they attend, and they listen, and they try, they can actually do this.

You know that difficult, unruly lad in bottom set maths? You know that boy who's been suspended countless times? You know that one they talk about in the staffroom, who throws chairs and spits and swears and tests everyone paid to care for him to the point of tears? Recent figures show he stands a high chance of entering the criminal justice system, and even more so if he gets expelled (with pupils thrown out aged 12 four times more likely to go to jail). If he does, if he's lucky, and brave, and determined, we'll pick him up, dust him down and carry on where he left off. And maybe second, third or 20th time around, he'll succeed.

This writer has a very strong viewpoint about education in prisons. Explore:

- *what you learn about this viewpoint.*
- *how the writer presents their viewpoint.*

Complete the essay-style response from the modelled opening below.

Choose **two** of your annotated sections from **Activity 1** to use in your answer.

At first the writer's viewpoint seems quite negative towards education in prison, as he tells us his students are the 'disaffected and the disagreeable', which suggests that his classes are made up of men who are very challenging and don't want to be there learning. This is emphasised by the writer's choice of the verb 'amble' to describe their slow movement into class and the adjectives 'disaffected', 'defensive' and 'disagreeable', which makes me think that the men are not only reluctant to be there, but may also be putting up barriers because they are a little afraid of being back in class.

....

....

....

....

....

....

....

....

....

....

....

....

....

....

....

9.3.5 Lesson 2

Securing skills with connected modern non-fiction: Comparing viewpoints from two texts

<table>
<tr><td>

Learning objectives:

- To make comparisons between 19th-century and modern viewpoints and how they are presented
- To write a comparative response

</td><td>

Resources:

- Extract 9.3.4a
- Extract 9.3.5
- 9.3.5 Lesson 2 PowerPoint
- 9.3.5 Lesson 2 Worksheet

</td></tr>
</table>

Getting started

- Display **9.3.5 Lesson 2 PowerPoint slide 1** and go over the learning objectives. Explain how this lesson will build on the skills from the previous lesson by using two texts together to plan and write a comparative response, using the same skills and sequencing of methods developed in Lesson 1.

- Display the simplified GCSE-style task on **PowerPoint slide 2** and focus in on the key words and things that students need to bear in mind for a task such as this. First focus on 'the writer': explain that this task is not about the content of the text but about making inferences about the writer themselves – their thoughts, feelings, perspectives, viewpoints and attitudes. These must be deduced or inferred from the text. Then focus in on 'compare': explain that in a task like this, the students are looking for ways in which the two different writers might have similar viewpoints or attitudes, or in what ways their viewpoints differ. Explore how this may be subtle and in some cases the view may change within a text (for example, from positive to negative). 'What' and 'How' should by now be very firmly embedded, but remind the students of the key SQI and IEC methods and how they link to AO1 and AO2 at GCSE.

Developing skills

- Give the students fresh copies of **Extract 9.3.4a** and **Extract 9.3.5** and punctuate the reading of both texts using **PowerPoint slide 3**. Ask the students to consider the questions on the slide as you read the second text.

- Take feedback and ideas as you read. Ideas that may arise might include: the writer of the older text seems to feel real concern for the prisoner right from the start, whereas initially we are left wondering if the writer has a negative viewpoint in *The Guardian* article. As the texts progress, the writer of the older text becomes increasingly sympathetic with the prisoner's plight and the fate that awaits him. However, the writer of the modern text becomes more optimistic and shows the benefits and rewards of working closely with prisoners. Both writers show concern and care.

- Now hand out copies of **9.3.5 Lesson 2 Worksheet**. Explain that the students are going to work in pairs to select and annotate material from each text to work with, and that this is a step up from the previous lesson where material was pre-selected. The first section has been pre-selected to get them started. Allow the students time to select material from the extracts (they can glue it to their worksheet scrapbook-style if they prefer), before allowing the students at least 20 minutes to annotate their four selected sections and the two pre-selected sections. Constantly monitor to check depth of ideas and use of terminology. If time allows, take feedback on ideas gathered from the exploratory work.

- Now use **PowerPoint slide 4** to recap on the variety of linking words the students can use in their responses to make points of comparison where similarities occur and differences.

- Display **PowerPoint slide 5** to remind the students of the sequencing of the method and how to link the second text. Recap now on the final task using **PowerPoint slide 2**.

Trying it yourself

- This is the final reading task in the final project. It allows for the reading of two complex texts, the use of both the SQI and IEC methods in harness, and the use of comparative skills. It could be completed as homework, to allow the students plenty of time to show all of those skills. Alternatively it could be used in a double lesson as a final assessment task to allow you to assess the students' overall individual progress and confidence in a range of core skills prior to GCSE study.

Securing skills with connected modern non-fiction

Activity: Select sections from your text extracts and add them to the spaces below. The first sections have been selected for you to get you started.

With a partner, annotate each section. Use the left side to add annotations to explore what is suggested or implied and can be inferred. Use the right side to add annotations identifying the methods each writer uses and your notes on the effect of those choices.

What	21st century text	How
	They are the disaffected and the despicable. They are the proud, the defensive and the downright disagreeable; funnelled into education during their first days inside, where they complete assessments in literacy and numeracy.	

What	19th-century text	How
	I confess to a shudder as I looked upon the girdle and arm pieces that had done duty on so many a struggling wretch, and half expected that the man who carried them would have attempted to hide them. But no such thing!	

<table>
<tr><td>

Learning objectives:

- To secure the conventions of arguing a case
- To present speeches for the prosecution and the defence in a mock trial

</td><td>

Resources:

- 9.3.6 Lessons 1 & 2 PowerPoint
- 9.3.6 Lessons 1 & 2 Worksheet

</td></tr>
</table>

Lesson 1: Getting started

- Introduce the learning objectives for the lesson on **9.3.6 Lessons 1 & 2 PowerPoint slide 1**. Then display **PowerPoint slide 2** and explore the focus of the lesson more closely. Ask the students to recap on the texts they have studied in this unit and decide which one they found most vivid/memorable. Many of the texts – especially those from the 19th century – deal with the impact of harsh punishments, including capital punishment. Spend some moments with the students exploring how serious a responsibility it must have been to order that punishment. Do they have strong views on the death penalty: can it ever be morally right? Perhaps they have a religious view to share. Take ideas sensitively before leading into the task for the lesson using the final bullet point on **PowerPoint slide 2**.

- Hand out copies of **9.3.6 Lessons 1 & 2 Worksheet** and use **Activity 1** to remind the students of the extract from *Oliver Twist* they read in Week 1. You may even like to recap and re-read this extract (**Extract 9.3.1**) or read a little more of *Oliver Twist* to create a feeling for the character of Fagin. (he is introduced in Chapter 8 of the novel, and Chapter 9 is his first interaction with Oliver, where he teaches him to pickpocket.) Present and read aloud the 'Fagin fact file' on the worksheet. Draw out some inferences to increase speculation among the students. There are no right or wrong answers here, but the speculation itself may lead to richer writing later. Why might Fagin operate under an assumed name or a different identity? If this is not his first trial, what does that imply about his life? Are his crimes petty or serious? How do the students feel about homeless children being trained as thieves?

- At this point, organise the group into two teams: defence and prosecution.

Developing skills

- The students now use the planning sheet (**Worksheet Activity 2**) to record whether they are acting for the defence or prosecution. Explain that at the start of a case, a lawyer always makes an opening statement in a highly formal way. Use **PowerPoint slides 3 and 4** to model two exemplar openings and then allow 5 minutes for the students to write a draft opening statement on their planning sheet.

- Now use **PowerPoint slide 5** to support the students with creating ideas for their case. Allow some planning and thinking time before inviting them to write up their speeches in the remainder of the lesson. At this point in their studies – the final writing task of all the projects – the students should feel very confident in using and applying persuasive language features, but a 'toolkit' of reminders is provided on the worksheet. Explain to the students that this is a chance for them to demonstrate their secure expertise in writing persuasively. The writing up of the speeches could be completed for homework.

Lesson 2: Trying it yourself

- Invite the students to place their finished speeches in front of them, along with their completed planning sheet from **Worksheet Activity 2**. If time allows, pair up students from the defence team to read each other's speeches and suggest improvements; likewise with the prosecution team. Display **PowerPoint slide 6** and establish the structure that the mock trial of Fagin will take.

- Now introduce the idea of the closing statements using **PowerPoint slide 7**. This is an additional challenge, as the students will have to listen carefully to the preceding speech given by the opposing team in order to respond to it. Explain that they should make notes on their planning sheet as they listen, and refer to it in their closing statement. Emphasise how powerful it can be to end a speech like this with a highly charged rhetorical question ('Can this be justice?') or emotive language ('Ladies and gentleman of the jury, do not send this frail old man, in the twilight of his years, to the gallows.')

- After hearing the speeches from both teams, the students could peer-assess who has presented the strongest argument in each team before you present the real verdict using **PowerPoint slide 8** and the extract from *Oliver Twist*.

**9.3.6
Lessons 1 & 2
Worksheet**

**Securing persuasive writing:
Presenting different sides to an
argument**

Activity 1:

Read the following fact file about the character of Fagin from *Oliver Twist*.

Fact file: Fagin

1. An older gentleman has been arrested who goes by the name of Fagin, though this may not be his real name or identity.

2. The accused was arrested for a number of offences, and this is not his first arrest or trial.

3. The accused is on trial for receiving stolen goods, including silk pocket handkerchiefs, wallets, jewellery and watches from pickpocketing, as well as silverware and jewellery from burglary and house-breaking.

4. The accused is additionally on trial for running a gang of thieves, including children of a young age, who he has allegedly trained in the art of pickpocketing.

5. Additionally, the accused is on trial for being an accomplice in the abduction of a young boy, one Oliver Twist, from his rightful home, and in the murder of a young woman, known as Nancy (a member of his gang) who was brutally killed by her partner Bill Sykes for sharing information that may have led to the arrest of the accused.

Activity 2:

Use the planning grid below to plan your speech for Fagin's trial.

Refer to the techniques toolkit to help you.

Planning a speech for the .... of Fagin.

Opening statement: ....

....

....

....

....

....

....

Key points to argue for the defence/prosecution:

Argument 1: ....

....

....

....

....

Argument 2: ....

....

....

....

Argument 3: ....

....

....

....

Notes for my closing statement: ....

....

....

....

Techniques toolkit:

- ✓ statements of fact
- ✓ direct address
- ✓ rhetorical questions
- ✓ expert quotations
- ✓ listing or lists of three

- ✓ imperatives or commands
- ✓ inclusive pronouns
- ✓ emotive language
- ✓ use of abstracts (e.g. *justice, fairness*)

Acknowledgements

Every effort has been made to trace copyright holders and to obtain their permission for the use of copyright materials. The publishers will gladly receive any information enabling them to rectify any error or omission at the first opportunity.

Texts

We are grateful to the following for permission to reproduce copyright material:

An extract on p.22, from "Sir David Attenborough and a macabre murder mystery in Lyme Regis" by Sarah Marshall, *The Telegraph*, 07/01/2018, © Telegraph Media Group Limited, 2018; An extract on p.52, from "Child Labour 'rampant' in Bangladesh factories" by Michael Safi, *The Guardian*, 07/12/2016, copyright © Guardian News & Media Ltd 2020; Extracts on p.59 and PPT 7.2.6, Lesson 1, slide 3, 'Protect a child from slavery' copyright © 2020 Anti-Slavery International, https://www.antislavery.org/protect-child-slavery. Reproduced with permission; An extract on p.81, from *Mud, Sweat and Tears* by Bear Grylls, published by Channel 4 Books, 2012. Reprinted by permission of The Random House Group Limited and Peters, Fraser & Dunlop (www.petersfraserdunlop.com) on behalf of Bear Grylls; Extracts on pp.110, 112, 115, from "Tim Peake: I orbited the earth 2,720 times" by Joanne O'Connor, *The Guardian*, 25/11/2017, copyright © Guardian News & Media Ltd 2020; Extracts on pp.138, 141-142, from "Professor Green: I've spent time in Britain's food banks – the destitution these people are facing is appalling" by Professor Green, *The Independent*, 09/11/2019, copyright © The Independent, 2019, www.independent.co.uk; An extract on p.164, from "'You did not act in time': Greta Thunberg's full speech to MPs" by Greta Thunberg, *The Guardian*, 23/04/2019, copyright © Guardian News & Media Ltd 2020; Extracts on pp.191, 195 and PPT 9.1.5, Lesson 2, slide 3, from "Seeing is believing Sightings of mystery 'big cats' in Britain's countryside have snowballed since the 1980s, dividing opinion about their existence" by Merrily Harpur, *The Guardian*, 22/03/2006. Reproduced by permission of the author; A statistic on p.215 and PPT 9.2.3, Lessons 1&2, slide 2, from "5 shocking facts about extreme global inequality and how to even it up", Oxfam https://www.oxfam.org/en/5-shocking-facts-about-extreme-global-inequality-and-how-even-it, copyright © Oxfam. Reproduced with permission; An extract on p.222, from "Cotton production linked to images of the dried up Aral Sea basin" by Tansy Hoskins, *The Guardian*, 01/10/2014, copyright © Guardian News & Media Ltd 2020; A statistic on PPT 9.2.5, Lesson 1, slide 3, from 'Fast fashion facts' https://www.greenpeace.org.uk/news/9-reasons-to-quit-fast-fashion-this-black-friday/, copyright © Greenpeace. Reproduced with permission; and an extract on p.251 from "Secret Teacher: teaching in prisons is where I can make a real difference" *The Guardian*, 03/05/2014, copyright © Guardian News & Media Ltd 2020.

Images

We are grateful to the following for permission to reproduce their images:

7.1.1, Lesson 1 PPT Slide 2: Peter Barritt/Alamy Stock Photo; 7.1.1, Lesson 2 PPT Slide 2: Peter Barritt/Alamy Stock Photo; 7.1.3, Lessons 1&2 Worksheet page 1: Sudowoodo/Shutterstock; 7.1.3, Lessons 1&2 Worksheet page 1: AlexHliv/Shutterstock; 7.1.3, Lessons 1&2 Worksheet page 1: johavel/Shutterstock; 7.1.5, Lesson 1 PPT Slide 2: Adam Seward/Alamy Stock Photo; 7.1.6, Lessons 1&2 PPT Slide 2: Yana Tomashova/Shutterstock; 7.2.1, Lesson 1 PPT Slide 2: Chronicle/Alamy Stock Photo; 7.2.1, Lesson 2 PPT Slide 6: Chronicle/Alamy Stock Photo; 7.2.2, Lesson 1 PPT Slide 2: Chronicle/Alamy Stock Photo; 7.2.2, Lesson 2 PPT Slide 2: Chronicle/Alamy Stock Photo; 7.2.3, Lessons 1&2 PPT Slide 2: nsf/Alamy Stock Photo; 7.2.3, Lessons 1&2 PPT Slide 3: nsf/Alamy Stock Photo; 7.2.4, Lesson 1 PPT Slide 4: Ian Dagnall Commercial Collection/Alamy Stock Photo; 7.2.4, Lesson 1 PPT Slide 5: Geoff Marshall/Alamy Stock Photo; 7.2.4, Lesson 1 Worksheet Page 1: Ian Dagnall Commercial Collection / Alamy Stock Photo; 7.2.4, Lesson 1 Worksheet Page 1: Geoff Marshall/Alamy Stock Photo; 7.2.4, Lesson 2 PPT Slide 3: Pictorial Press Ltd/Alamy Stock Photo; 7.2.5, Lesson 1 PPT Slide 3: clicksabhi/Shutterstock; 7.2.5, Lesson 1 PPT Slide 3: Tinnakorn jorruang/Shutterstock; 7.2.5, Lesson 1 PPT Slide 4: paul prescott/Shutterstock; 7.2.5, Lesson 1 PPT Slide 4: paul prescott/Shutterstock; 7.2.5, Lesson 1 PPT Slide 5: Imagine Rural/Shutterstock; 7.2.5, Lesson 1 PPT Slide 5: Alchemist from India/Shutterstock; 7.2.5, Lesson 1 Worksheet Page 1: clicksabhi/Shutterstock; 7.2.5, Lesson 1 Worksheet Page 1: Tinnakorn jorruang/Shutterstock; 7.2.5, Lesson 1 Worksheet Page 1: paul prescott/Shutterstock; 7.2.5, Lesson 1 Worksheet Page 1: paul prescott/Shutterstock; 7.2.5, Lesson 1 Worksheet Page 1: Imagine Rural/Shutterstock; 7.2.5, Lesson 1 Worksheet Page 1: Alchemist from India/Shutterstock; 7.2.5, Lesson 2 PPT Slide 2: paul prescott/Shutterstock; 7.3.1, Lesson 1 PPT Slide 2: Rudra Narayan Mitra/Shutterstock; 7.3.1, Lesson 2 PPT Slide 2: beibaoke/Shutterstock; 7.3.2, Lesson 1 PPT Slide 2: beibaoke/Shutterstock; 7.3.3, Lesson 1 PPT Slide 2: chingyunsong/Shutterstock; 7.3.4, Lesson 1 Worksheet page 1: Granger Historical Picture Archive/Alamy Stock Photo; 7.3.4, Lesson 1 PPT Slide 2: Shujaa_777/Shutterstock; 7.3.4, Lesson 2 PPT Slide 2: Peppy Graphics/Shutterstock; 7.3.5, Lesson 1 PPT Slide 2: WENN Rights Ltd/Alamy

Stock Photo; 7.3.5, Lesson 2 PPT Slide 2: Quayside/Shutterstock; 7.3.6, Lessons 1 & 2 PPT Slide 3: Dave Head/Shutterstock; 7.3.6, Lessons 1 & 2 PPT Slide 4: shutterupeire/Shutterstock; 7.3.6, Lessons 1 & 2 PPT Slide 5: stemack/Shutterstock; 7.3.6, Lessons 1 & 2 PPT Slide 6: Elena11/Shutterstock; 8.1.1, Lesson 2 PowerPoint slide 2: Pictorial Press Ltd/Alamy Stock Photo; 8.1.1, Lesson 2 PowerPoint slide 2: Pictorial Press Ltd/Alamy Stock Photo; 8.1.2, Lesson 1 Worksheet page 1: Patrick Frilet/Shutterstock; 8.1.2, Lesson 1 PowerPoint slide 2: Patrick Frilet/Shutterstock; 8.1.2, Lesson 1 PowerPoint slide 4: Patrick Frilet/Shutterstock; 8.1.3, Lessons 1 & 2 PowerPoint slide 2: Christos Georghiou/Shutterstock; 8.1.3, Lessons 1 & 2 PowerPoint slide 5: Juergen Faelchle/Shutterstock; 8.1.4, Lesson 1 PowerPoint slide 4: ssuaphotos/Shutterstock; 8.1.4, Lesson 1 PowerPoint slide 4: Thanyapat Wanitchanon/Shutterstock; 8.1.4, Lesson 1 PowerPoint slide 4: Smit/Shutterstock; 8.1.4, Lesson 2 PowerPoint slide 2: Jasper Chamber/Alamy Stock Photo; 8.1.4, Lesson 2 PowerPoint slide 5: Jasper Chamber/Alamy Stock Photo; 8.1.5, Lesson 1 PowerPoint slide 2: Volodymyr Burdiak/Shutterstock; 8.1.5, Lesson 1 PowerPoint slide 3: NASA Archive/Alamy Stock Photo; 8.1.5, Lesson 2 PowerPoint slide 2: NASA Archive/Alamy Stock Photo; 8.1.6, Lessons 1 & 2 PowerPoint slide 4: Jurgen Ziewe/Shutterstock; 8.2.2, Lesson 1 PowerPoint slide 4 (left): ayelet-keshet/Shutterstock; 8.2.2, Lesson 1 PowerPoint slide 4 (right): muskocabas/Shutterstock; 8.2.2, Lesson 2 PowerPoint slide 4 (left): Everett Historical/Shutterstock; 8.2.2, Lesson 2 PowerPoint slide 4 (right): Juanmonino / Getty Images; 8.2.3, Lessons 1 & 2 PowerPoint slide 6: ZtoAlphabet/Shutterstock; 8.3.1, Lesson 1 PowerPoint slide 2: Eladora/Shutterstock; 8.3.1, Lesson 1 PowerPoint slide 4: Eladora/Shutterstock; 8.3.1, Lesson 1 PowerPoint slide 1: Eladora/Shutterstock; 8.3.2, Lesson 1 PowerPoint slide 2: MNStudio/Shutterstock; 8.3.2, Lesson 1 Worksheet page 1: mimomy/Shutterstock; 8.3.3, Lessons 1 & 2 PowerPoint slide 2 (top): Lightspring/Shutterstock; 8.3.3, Lessons 1 & 2 PowerPoint slide 2 (bottom): pathdoc/Shutterstock; 8.3.4, Lesson 1 PowerPoint slide 3: Hulton Archive/Stringer/Getty images; 8.3.4, Lesson 2 PowerPoint slide 3: Hulton Archive/Stringer/Getty images; 8.3.5, Lesson 1 PowerPoint slide 3: Jasper Chamber/Alamy Stock Photo; 8.3.6, Lessons 1 & 2 PowerPoint slide 2: Memo Angeles/Shutterstock; 9.1.1, Lesson 1 PowerPoint slide 2 (top): Moviestore Collection Ltd/Alamy Stock Photo; 9.1.2, Lesson 1 PowerPoint slide 2: Art Collection 2/Alamy Stock Photo; 9.1.2, Lesson 2 PowerPoint slide 2: History and Art Collection/Alamy Stock Photo; 9.1.3, Lessons 1 & 2 PowerPoint slide 2: maglyvi/Shutterstock; 9.1.4, Lesson 1 PowerPoint slide 2 (left): Chronicle/Alamy Stock Photo; 9.1.4, Lesson 1 PowerPoint slide 2 (right): FLHC15/Alamy Stock Photo; 9.1.5, Lesson 1 PowerPoint slide 2 (right): David Beauchamp/Shutterstock; 9.1.5, Lesson 2 PowerPoint slide 2: Chronicle/Alamy Stock Photo; 9.1.5, Lesson 2 PowerPoint slide 2: David Beauchamp/Shutterstock; 9.1.6, Lessons 1 & 2 PowerPoint slide 2: Granger/Shutterstock; 9.2.1, Lesson 1 PowerPoint slide 3: Artokoloro/Alamy Stock Photo; 9.2.1, Lesson 2 PowerPoint slide 3: The Print Collector/Alamy Stock Photo; 9.2.2, Lesson 1 PowerPoint slide 2: Photo © Christie's Images/Bridgeman Images; 9.2.3, Lessons 1&2 PowerPoint slide 2: © Eleanor Farmer: Oxfam; 9.2.3, Lessons 1&2 PowerPoint slide 7: Tuca Vieira; 9.2.4, Lesson 1 PowerPoint slide 2: Niday Picture Library/Alamy Stock Photo; 9.2.5, Lesson 1 PowerPoint slide 2 (left): THINK A/Shutterstock; 9.2.5, Lesson 1 PowerPoint slide 2 (right): Sorbis/Shutterstock; 9.2.5, Lesson 1 PowerPoint slide 4: Planet Observer/UIG/Shutterstock; 9.2.5, Lesson 1 PowerPoint slide 5: Moehring/Shutterstock; 9.2.5, Lesson 2 PowerPoint slide 2 (top left): SPUTNIK/Alamy Stock Photo; 9.2.5, Lesson 2 PowerPoint slide 3: Matyas Rehak/Shutterstock; 9.3.1, Lesson 1 PowerPoint slide 2: Taqadiny/Shutterstock; 9.3.1, Lesson 2 PowerPoint slide 2 (left): Design Pics Inc/Shutterstock; 9.3.1, Lesson 2 PowerPoint slide 2 (right): Design Pics Inc/Shutterstock; 9.3.2, Lesson 1 PowerPoint slide 2: Mr.Bu/Shutterstock; 9.3.2, Lesson 2 PowerPoint slide 2: nobeastsofierce/Shutterstock; 9.3.3, Lessons 1 & 2 PowerPoint slide 2 (right): OSTILL is Franck Camhi/Shutterstock; 9.3.3, Lessons 1 & 2 PowerPoint slide 5 (right): Jelena990/Shutterstock; 9.3.4, Lesson 1 PowerPoint slide 2: Fer Gregory/Shutterstock; 9.3.4, Lesson 1 PowerPoint slide 3: Alexander_P/Shutterstock; 9.3.4, Lesson 2 PowerPoint slide 2: Mike H/Shutterstock; 9.3.6, Lessons 1 & 2 PowerPoint slide 7: Design Pics Inc/Shutterstock; 9.3.6, Lessons 1 & 2 Worksheet page 1: Design Pics Inc/Shutterstock.